THE
GOLDEN
FLEECE

THE
GOLDEN
FLEECE

SELLING THE GOOD LIFE TO AMERICANS

Joseph J. Seldin

The Macmillan Company, New York
Collier - Macmillan Ltd., London

© Joseph J. Seldin 1963

First Printing

The Macmillan Company, New York
Collier-Macmillan Canada Ltd., Galt, Ontario
DIVISIONS OF THE CROWELL-COLLIER PUBLISHING COMPANY

Printed in the United States of America

Library of Congress catalog card number: 63-12137

Designed by Christian Ohser

To Rose,
Peter, Scott, Clem

Contents

THE
GOLDEN
FLEECE

The Madison Avenue Symbol

If it is true that the values expressed in advertising at the same time express the values of society, then a study of contemporary advertising may help us to a more perceptive understanding of the American way of life since 1945. Many magazine articles have been written on the techniques employed by Madison Avenue, and several books, a few of which have achieved eminence as long-term best-sellers. But relatively little has been written on the burden of the advertising itself, and the values it holds for society today.

Before we begin an examination of these advertising values, however, it may prove worthwhile to examine the symbol that Madison Avenue evokes for the public at large and for the admen themselves. As industries in the U.S. go, advertising is tiny —the 2,800 advertising agencies listed in the published directories employ only about 25,000. About 50,000 additional advertising workers are now employed by advertisers, media, and suppliers.

Yet this small group spent an estimated $11.9 billion in 1961 to influence both the shopping habits and social thinking of 185 million Americans, adults and children alike. Truly, never have so few influenced so many so much.

In today's big business world no marketing decision of any consequence is ever made without the fullest participation of the admen. They sit in with top management from the first preliminary discussions to the eventual launching of a new product, providing their experience and counsel at every step of the way. In packaging, advertising, research, and sales promotion, in every phase of the merchandising process, they offer promotional guidance and often are the deciding voice in multi-million-dollar marketing decisions. In many instances it can truly be said that they wield influence equal or superior to that of any member of the Board of Directors. They rise with the success of a decision, fall with its failure. Often, as a result, failure of a promotional venture means dismissal by the company, for the admen provide convenient whipping boys for corporate mistakes. Almost daily, the Madison Avenue trade press notes the switching of corporate clients from one advertising agency to another, implying loss of confidence and the hope that the new agency will do better. Sooner or later most big advertising agencies get a crack at most big accounts. In 1961, some 260 major accounts switched their agency connections. Rather than lend stability to the advertising industry, it makes of Madison Avenue a rumor mill in which the real or rumored arrival and departure of choice accounts is discussed daily over luncheon tables.

Despite the integration of the admen in the corporate directorate that guides the business destiny of practically every fair-sized corporate enterprise in the U.S., they have yet to earn the respect that is automatically accorded to persons holding important policy-making posts. That has become one of the chief complaints along Madison Avenue. Perhaps because of their antecedents as medicine men years ago—a tradition that persists in today's radio and TV pitchmen—their social status is not on a par with their business status. They are looked on with suspicion by the masters they serve. In survey after survey of business opinion, the admen are rated pretty far down the ladder of social esteem. An opinion survey of Philadelphia businessmen, for example, described the advertising industry as being more devoid of plain ordinary honesty than any of the seven professions surveyed.

Nor are community leaders as a group any more kindly disposed toward the advertising industry than the businessmen. If anything, their reaction is harsher. When Edward L. Bernays, a well known public relations consultant, polled community leaders on their reaction to TV commercials, the consensus was that most commercials were in bad taste, lacked dignity, and dealt with unesthetic subject matter. The adjectives with which they characterized the commercials included demoralizing, insulting, juvenile, antisocial, monotonous, obtrusive, trite, and repulsive. For example, Grayson Kirk, president of Columbia University, was disturbed by TV commercials that cast a "withering blight over the early development of an important communications medium." Dr. David W. Barry, of the National Council of the Churches of Christ in the U.S.A., felt that nine out of ten commercials did nothing more than act as irritants. Norman Draper, of the American Meat Institute, confined his attack to the advertising of products that have to do with health: "Every thinking person knows that the bulk of these are pure phonies and [he resents] them." Alfred H. Barr, Jr., of the Museum of Modern Art, found TV commercials the quintessence of "inexpressible boredom." Dr. Frank L. Eversull, of the First Presbyterian Church of Belleville, Illinois, described the flow of commercials as "juvenile, puerile, and [continued] ad nauseam." Dr. Edward

T. Sandrow, rabbi at Temple Beth El, Cedarhurst, was "repelled" by the pitchman and felt a deep "distrust of the salesman and his product."

Distressed at the public disapproval of the advertising business turned up by the independent opinion surveys, many advertising trade journals conducted their own surveys, but came up with no different results. *Printers' Ink*, for example, was told by Henry M. Wriston, former president of Brown University, that he found it difficult to believe that every cigarette is milder, every pain-killer is faster, and he scolded admen for "extravagance, appeals to lower tastes, and slippery slogans." Erwin D. Canham, editor of the *Christian Science Monitor*, weighed the "undeniable and enormous advantages of advertising" against its "high price in bad taste and extravagance." Henry C. Fleisher, spokesman for the CIO, hit at "spurious exaggerations, false claims, tasteless repetition." Professor Henry Steele Commager, Columbia University, condemned advertising for fostering the snob instinct, vulgarizing the American taste, wide appeals to fear and self-indulgence, and a general all-around misreading of the American character.

The public image of the advertising business is handled just as roughly, or more so, by working-class and lower-middle-class people who constitute the bulk of the TV viewing audience. Another Bernays opinion survey turned up their earthy expressions of distaste. A Cincinnati butcher got "so confounded mad at all the commercials during the Blank program I could throw the set out of the house." A barkeeper in the same city was angered by high-pressure commercials that cut into every program. A New York barber called the TV pitchmen "fakers and liars." A Boston beautician laughed outright at sales talks for beauty products: "They're a farce." A Chicago barkeeper snorted at "borax and bunk." A New York barber fumed: "There ought to be a law against big-mouthed, low, cheap commercials."

Naturally the advertising trade journals reflected daily agitation at the adman's poor public image, and the Minneapolis Advertising Club set out to see for itself what the typical adman was really like. It found that the typical adman lives in a modest $19,600 home in the suburbs where nightly he works for an hour or two on office problems, and on an occasional weekend. He reads two newspapers a day, likes general magazine reading, watches TV for 7½ hours each week (his preference being news, drama, and Westerns, in that order), listens to the radio for 4½ hours each week (favoring news, classical music, and disk jockey offerings), drinks quite sparingly, is a gregarious joiner of all kinds of community clubs and social organizations, and loves to get away to hunt, fish, and golf. The portrait of the real adman turned up by the Minneapolis Advertising Club was that of a churchgoing, community-minded, suburbanite Republican, 37½ years old, who plays with 2.8 kids, owns 1.3 cars, 1.5 TV sets, and earns upwards of $10,000 a year. "The chances are," the study concluded, that this portrait "is pretty typical of his associates from New York to San Francisco despite the folklore propounded by movies and novels."

Admen are generally inclined to blame novelists for their unflattering public image. Since the war there has been a spate of novels commencing with Frederic Wakeman's *The Hucksters* in 1946, each of which has painted the advertising world in terms of immoral wheeling and dealing, fleshpots, and mayhem. Wakeman spelled out the kind of morality that governs the advertising business, and established the genre for subsequent novels about Madison Avenue, in these words: "A man cooks up some fat and presses it into a bar of soap. He perfumes it. Wraps it up fancy. Then he needs a barker to sell this miraculous combination of herbs, roots and berries. So he calls me in to bark for him." Other novelists have developed the point. John G. Schneider in *The Golden Kazoo* related the promotional antics of an ad agency president and his secretary-associate concubine to get Henry Clay Adams elected President of the U.S. in 1960.

Herman Wouk in *Aurora Dawn* described the attempts to bring "Father Stanfield and his Fold of the Faithful Shepherd on a nation-wide radio program to make the fastest selling soap in America sell even faster." George Panetta in *Viva Madison Avenue!* wrote of two Italian-American admen who got themselves into no end of scrapes, leaving the impression that what goes on in the advertising world is nothing short of a big goofy party. In Samm Baker's mystery books the protagonist moved around his ad agency in pugnacious Mike Hammer style, all the time consuming vast numbers of Martinis. It is quite possible that William H. Whyte, Jr., was thinking of the schizophrenic effect of the advertising business on its admen practitioners when he wrote in *The Organization Man:* "The usual hero of the postwar rash of 'New York' novels, for example, is overwhelmingly spiritual on this score [materialism]. After making his spurious choice between good and evil, the hero heads for the country where, presumably, he is to find real meaning in life." Vance Packard's *The Hidden Persuaders* added a menacing "Big Brother" dimension to Madison Avenue's already unsavory reputation, by describing the motivation research techniques developed by marketers in an attempt at secret coercion of people to buy against their free will.

Hollywood has added to the disreputable public image of the advertising business by movies such as *Will Success Spoil Rock Hunter?* which portrayed a Madison Avenue flunky reaching the heights of lunacy, and must have impressed on millions of moviegoers the silly, useless character of advertising. *A Face in the Crowd* featured a guitar strummer who conned his way up to the Cabinet post of Secretary for National Morale. *The Great Man* dealt with a power-mad radio personality who, although not an adman, undoubtedly was accepted in the public mind as a Madison Avenue symbol.

Summing up the sorry state of the adman's public image, the trade publication, *Advertising Age,* wrote: "The fictionalized adman is essentially a mercenary character. He would double-cross his grandmother for an account. He has the morals of an alley cat. He is a first-rate conniver. He also has a hollow leg, judging by his capacity for martinis." And he has a fitting companion in the fictionalized adwoman, generally a bewitchingly beautiful blonde. "She has no compunctions about using her body to advance her career. She tends to be hard-boiled. As a conniver, she is the match for any adman." Another trade publication, *Tide*, traced the links that together made up the unsavory image of the adman in the public mind: "Advertising men are (1) fast living, (2) big spending, (3) women chasing, (4) con men, (5) wear nothing but gray flannel, (6) sell nothing but soap, (7) and do it all through the most unscientific means, e.g., hunches and 'off the top of the head' decisions."

In an attempt to redeem its image in the public mind, the advertising industry in recent years has stepped up support of public service campaigns through its public service arm, the Advertising Council. In 1958–1959 the Council spent an estimated $170 million of advertising space and time, most of it on sixteen major public service campaigns. Among the campaigns was the promotional drive before the 1958 election which urged citizens to "register, vote and contribute." The Council takes some credit in the result: more Americans went to the polls than in any previous bielection, and an estimated $12 million was collected in small gifts by the major parties and candidates. Other major campaigns were the 1958 antirecession campaign aimed at boosting public confidence, a "pursuit of excellence" campaign to increase the prestige of learning, and a drive to win greater public cooperation with the Census Bureau. In the years since then, the Council has stepped up its spending, reaching a record $226 million in 1961. The value of these campaigns was appraised by *Printers' Ink* as "a valuable public relations job not only for advertising, but also for the whole system of private enterprise." What could be more fitting, another trade publication mused, than that the advertising phalanx which has made the automobile so attractive and saleable by a compelling description of its chrome, dashboard gadgets, and dual headlights, or the bar of ordinary soap so desirable in its gold-foil wrapping, should also help make good citizenship more fashionable in the U.S.

But admen are not naïve enough to believe that their shady reputation is exclusively the derivative of novelists, writing with an eye on book clubs, reprint houses, film companies, and television packagers. Among the advertising promotions cooked up by Madison Avenue many deliberately contain sizable elements of deception mixed into the selling froth. In soaps, dentifrices, cigarettes, and proprietaries the art of public deception is well developed. The clever copywriter who can write an advertisement that deftly deceives the listening or viewing public into buying, yet sidesteps for the advertiser any legal onus for the deception when called to task for it by the federal agencies or other watchdogs of the nation's advertising, is in demand and can pretty much write his own salary figure. The need for deception is an outgrowth of the fierce sales competition by giant companies in these and other fields, and its rationale is the protection of millions of promotional dollars that each company stakes on its product.

Often as not, at the annual conference of the American Association of Advertising Agencies, when the troublesome problem of the adman's public image is raised, a speaker or two will demand an industry housecleaning, particularly of pitchmen. Radio and TV pitchmen are belabored for giving all advertising a black eye, and the broadcasting industry is asked that they be driven from the living rooms of the nation. At one conference Fairfax M. Cone, president of Foote, Cone & Belding, called for their excommunication before an assemblage of several hundred admen: "We have hucksters in our own Association and we should throw them out." His denunciation was front-paged in *Advertising Age*, which editorialized on the marvelously simple expedient of showing the hucksters the Association's door. "The problem is really that simple. If the advertising business doesn't want hucksters, all it has to do is throw them out—and there is nothing inherently difficult about that. By the very nature of the business, everyone in it operates right out in the open. It takes relatively little effort to determine who the hucksters are, and to establish effective curbs on their operation." But later in the editorial *Advertising Age* began to speculate on how the inquisition could get started, knowing from experience that no adman ever was willing to step forward and confess his guilt— it was always the other fellow who consorted with witches. Yet practically everybody in the business occasionally played around with the witches. "The will to do something about the situation," concluded *Advertising Age,* "is far weaker than one might gather from all the conversation which is devoted to the subject. Like the weather, everyone talks about it and no one does anything."

Nevertheless admen are hopeful that their seat on the public frying pan is temporary. They often express the conviction that just as Wall Street was a term of opprobrium in the depressed thirties, now it is their turn. "Medicine went through the same stage," recalls Charles H. Brower, president of Batten, Barton, Durstine & Osborn, "where doctors were widely considered to be quacks. So did the law, where many lawyers were referred to as shysters. And it's only natural that some derogatory name like 'hucksters' be attached to us." David Ogilvy, the creator of the man-with-the-beard and man-with-the-eyepatch ads, also takes comfort from history: "The pioneers in any industry tend to be buccaneers. Oil, banking, railroads had their men who said 'let the public be damned.' It has worked the same way in advertising." The common, if hopeful, belief is that tomorrow it probably will be the turn of the automation or guided missile boys.

After all, the trade press points out, advertising is of vital importance in today's world. It is the giant spark plug of the American economic machine, bringing comfort, luxury, and ease to millions for the first time in their lives. As a result of advertising, the first Gem razor, a stroplike affair which sold for $2, now is vastly superior and sells for about one dollar. The same goes for the 60-watt lamp which, unadvertised, sold in 1905 for $1.75, and now sells for about a quarter. Jello-O was sold at 12 cents a package when General Foods took it over; now, heavily advertised, the price is down to about 9 cents. Advertising is credited with bringing to most families in the U.S. electric and gas ranges, refrigerators, washing machines, electric clocks, automobiles, toasters, electric irons. A substantial number of families enjoy vacuum cleaners, water heaters, coffee makers, phonographs, waffle irons, heating pads. On a grander scale, touching every family in the U.S., advertising pays the nation's entire bill for radio and TV entertainment, pays about 70 percent of the cost of turning out metropolitan newspapers, about 60 percent of the cost of magazines and farm papers. Of course the financing of the press and entertainment world has as its purpose the selling of something or other, but the end result is clearly and patently for the public good.

Admen are occasionally reminded of Winston Churchill's toast to advertising at the International Advertising Conference in London in 1924. "Advertising nourishes the consuming power of men. It creates wants for a better standard of living. It sets up before a man the goal of a better home, better clothing, better food for himself and his family. It spurs individual exertion and greater production." Churchill acclaimed advertising as a "true world tonic for better times" and admen for playing an "indispensable part toward the material well-being of the millions." In the same spirit, Franklin D. Roosevelt told the Advertising Federation of America, when he was New York Governor in 1931: "If I were starting life over again . . . I would go into the advertising business in preference to almost any other." He too lauded advertising for "raising of standards of modern civilization."

The trade press offers evidence that a few influential writer-thinkers are beginning to accept the important role of advertising in the modern world. It points to such signpost books as Paul Mazur's *The Standards We Raise* and David M. Potter's *People of Plenty* in which advertising is hailed for the first time as a force for public good. These authors welcome advertising as the means of distributing the huge wealth of goods and services turned out by the galloping U.S. economy. As additional evidence, the trade press applauds Martin Mayer's *Madison Avenue, U.S.A.*, a sober study of advertising as a business, and Shepherd Mead's *The Admen*, a companion piece in the fiction world.

But in spite of the handful of scholarly voices raised in their behalf, the warm gentlemanly acknowledgments by world-famous figures, and the innumerable case histories showing how advertising helps reduce prices and spread the economy's goods to the impoverished millions, the somewhat schizophrenic character of the advertising business remains solidly entrenched. In general, admen remain unconvinced of their worth, dubious of their commercial mission, fearful of their professional status. Evidence of the anxieties that gnaw away at the practitioners appears in the handbook given to new employees on the first day they report for work at Young & Rubicam. It reads in part: "If you think every adman or woman is 'suspect' and the business is a dress parade of economic waste, don't get involved in it. It is hard to be happy and successful when you think you are not completely proud of your association." It turns up in opinion surveys such as Gallup-Robinson's "Mirror of America," disclosing what admen think other people think of them and their occupation. In this survey, 100 housewives were asked their opinion on how respectable, honest, hard-working, neurotic, and heavy-drinking admen were, and a similar number of admen were asked how they thought the housewives would rate them on each item. The result: the housewives held a considerably more favorable opinion of the admen than the admen thought they would. Forty-three housewives labeled the admen respectable, only nine admen thought they would. Twenty housewives called the admen honest, only four admen figured they would. Three housewives thought the admen neurotic, 28 admen thought they would.

Why do admen hold themselves in such low esteem? Why do they insist on measuring themselves against the huckster image portrayed in popular novels and Hollywood movies, instead of as professional persuaders so vital to the economy as depicted in the trade press and by trade associations?

For an answer, *Sponsor*, a trade magazine, went to an eminent New York psychiatrist who numbers many admen among his patients, and a psychiatric explanation of their woes was spread in the magazine. The good doctor perceived many moth-like drives in admen. First, advertising men tend to live higher than other occupational groups drawing equal paychecks. Perhaps because so much of their day is occupied with convincing wealthy corporate clients to spend more advertising money, they are subject to intense guilt "if they don't spend at the same or a faster rate." A typical case was that of an adman who earned $12,000 but spent $15,000 yearly on the theory that by an external display of success he would drive himself harder in order to catch up with his appearance. At first the theory seemed to work, for in less than a year he was promoted to Associate Media Director at $15,000, so he stepped up his spending rate to $18,000. But the unrelenting mental strain of digging an ever-deeper hole of debt finally was too much for him. His work suffered and he was soon pounding the Madison Avenue pavement looking for another job. When he landed one months later as a timekeeper at $8,000, he chucked his theory after psychiatric help, cut his spending to $7,500 and now feels more at ease with himself.

Second, admen are torn daily by a tug-of-war between their

creative efforts and a sense of meaninglessness of these efforts. As they watch a TV program which they have had a hand at creating, they are overblown with pride, but assailed by misgivings at the meaninglessness of the program when it is over. No matter how often they are told that their creative work has a salutary effect on the economy, they feel deep down that theirs is no real contribution to society. Their egos are thus daily pumped and deflated like a bellows. And, as a result, their repressed conflicts often are vented in passionate outbursts against the client (when he is not around), referring to him in mock veneration as the "Great White Father." In short, the psychiatrist said, the advertising business attracts restless, ambitious men and women who thrive on excitement and day-to-day uncertainty because they are "more frightened and anxiety-ridden than any other professionals."

Charles Lehman, senior analyst at Daniel Starch & Staff, offered his own nonpsychiatric explanation. Caught between the product-selling desires of the manufacturers and the product-buying desires of the public—desires which usually are in some degree of conflict—admen can serve only as the buffer, the punching bag for both.

2 Admen in the Seventeenth to Nineteenth Centuries

Unfortunately, nothing in the history of advertising seems to justify the optimism of today's admen that their public image is due for a refurbishing in the future. From its earliest beginnings in seventeenth century English coffeehouses, advertising has drawn criticism from the more literate sections of society. But as the spokesman for the rising merchant middle class, advertising could no more be criticized out of existence than the middle class could be held down by the feudal remnants of the upper-class nobility. It was a time in history when the middle class was taking over the center of the stage and the upper-class nobility was being shunted into the wings, albeit unwillingly. As a result, although the excesses of advertising were roundly condemned, particularly by the literati, the trade of advertising flourished as did the middle class itself. It is hard, if not impossible, to find any history of advertising written by the literati which has more than a few kind words for advertis-

14

ing and its practitioners. In Henry Sampson's classic *History of Advertising*, E. J. Turner's *The Shocking History of Advertising*, and in articles that appeared sporadically in the last century in the English and U.S. press and magazines, advertising assumes more the role of a new societal demon. But no amount of criticism could exorcise the demon, and advertising continued to con the gullible public into buying worthless products on the strength of unconscionable promises of benefits.

Advertising daily brought "miraculous newes" to readers of seventeenth century newspapers. There was a dentifrice in 1660 that guaranteed to its users a lifetime of freedom from toothaches. Not only did it clean the teeth "white as ivory" but it fastened loose teeth, sweetened the breath, and preserved the gums and mouth from "Cankers and Impostumes." Lozenges were hawked as a remedy for a variety of ills ranging from simple hoarseness and colds to consumption, lung diseases, catarrhs, and asthma. Coffee was prescribed for eyesores, headache, dropsy, gout, scurvy, King's evil, and "to prevent mis-carryings in child-bearing women." During the terrible year of the plague, 1665, the newspapers were crowded with ads promising protection by the use of charms, exorcisms, incantations, and amulets. The situation was described by a shocked Daniel Defoe in his *Journal of the Plague Year*—how the frightened populace was gulled by advertisers into swallowing "multitudes of Pills, Potions and Preservatives." The best-selling brands were Anti-Pestilential Pills, Incomparable Drink Against the Plague, The Only-True Plague-Water, The Royal Antidote Against All Kinds of Infection, Infallible Preventive Pills against the Plague, Never-Failing Preservatives against the Infection, and Sovereign Cordials Against the Corruption of the Air. But despite dosing of themselves with an imposing array of magic pills, thousands died from the pestilence. The same fate caught up with many advertisers who were reluctant to leave the stricken cities while they were doing such a brisk pill business. For their unconscionable actions they were bitterly denounced by the literati. The lowly esteem in which the adman was held by the seventeenth century intellectuals is epitomized in Ben Jonson's *Every Man in His Humour*, in which one of the characters, Shift, is a good-for-nothing adman.

In the eighteenth century the ads that filled to overflowing the pages of the *Spectator* and other newspapers marked the arrival of what has been termed the "century of magnificent quacks." The middle class was rising in power and the ads of these merchant robbers traded even more boldly on the ignorance of the general populace. It was a time of ascendancy for a small portion of the community that looked on the larger portion as its oyster. No matter how mysterious the bodily ailment, a specific cure was made available by the merchants. There were elixirs that promised to stimulate clarity of thought, judgment, reason, and memory; nerve powders that put an end to bad dreams, memory lapses, and "horrors"; magic drops that went to work on the tough-to-get-rid-of "humours" that inhabited the human body and were the true and deep cause of "melancholly, direful views, and black reflections." There was a "True Royal Chymical Washball" that rid the skin permanently of ringworm, sunburn, scurf, pimples, and facial deformities. There was a tincture that restored the sense of smell to people who had lost it "for many years"; a facial balm that protected against "horrid thoughts"; a "chymical liquor" that restored gums to healthy condition even after they were "almost eaten away"; a confection that cured children and grown-ups of stuttering and stammering; a vegetable balm that quickly rid the sufferer of asthma. Coffee was still in everybody's medical armory as a tried and true remedy for consumption, gout, dropsy, and scurvy. And there were even advertisers who announced themselves as specially blessed by God with the ability to cure "Luniticks or Mad People," requiring no more than three months to complete the job even for "the Maddest Person."

The number of benefits attributed to smoking "cephalick

and opthalmick tobacco" easily awards that weed first place as the most impressive cure-all of the eighteenth century. It worked marvels for the "Head, Eyes, Stomach, Lungs, Rheumatism, Gout, Thickness of Hearing, Head-Ach, Tooth-Ach, or Vapours." For the old it restored sight, for the young it preserved the eyes. "So that by using this Tobacco Persons may never come to wear Spectacles; and if they have already used them may leave them off, by its so Strengthening and Clearing the Sight." Smoking was also the one tried and true way to get rid of "Phlegm, and Foul Humour from the Breast, Stomach and Lungs, and such terrible wheezings that Persons can hardly fetch their breath." Apparently only the dead were beyond help from smoking.

Eighteenth century ads also hawked to aging gallants at a stiff price a special brew of aphrodisiacs which was guaranteed "to make old age presume to feele new Lust and Youthful Flames Again." The concoction stepped up the "Animal Spirits" and presumably kept the old gents going for the rest of their lives. It was vaingloriously advertised as "the most noble and grand Preparation in the whole Materia Medica." Preoccupation with sex was, in fact, a notable characteristic of eighteenth century ads. The newspapers were filled with countless Personals in which impoverished ladies offered to exchange their womanly charms for a monetary consideration. Typical was the "most lively lady" who asked for a "loan" and suggested that the security for the loan would undoubtedly be "very agreeable to a Single Gentleman of Spirit." E. J. Turner offers the comment that a reading of the Personals in the newspapers of the time would make a hardened member of today's vice squad blush. One ad apparently was addressed to jaded voluptuaries and described the extra physical joys that awaited the couple who spent one night together in a contraption called the "Celestial Bed." The inventor was a Dr. Graham who attributed the ability of his invention to deliver new heights of sensuality to the "most springy hair . . .

from the tails of English stallions" in the mattress, powerful magnets that infused the bed with mysterious rays, and irresistible Oriental perfumes that wafted around the bedchamber. All these forces acted in grand concert to communicate the "celestial fire to the bed-chamber."

A leading eighteenth century denunciator of these advertisements was Dr. Samuel Johnson. He announced in the *Idler* that he was fed up with advertisements. He rebuked advertisers for playing "too wantonly with our passions" and held up for particular scorn the advertiser of an anodyne necklace who "warned every mother that she would never forgive herself if her infant should perish without the necklace." Dr. Johnson noted that "promise, large promise, is the soul of an Advertisement." Another denunciator was Joseph Addison, who chided advertisers in the *Tatler* for indulging the hypochondriacal tendencies in people by peddling nostrums for any and every fancied bodily ill—for "Pain in his Head, Cholic in his Bowels, or Spots on his Cloathes." Addison characterized ads as "instruments of ambition" and derided the advertiser's invariable claim that his product was held in "universal esteem" when, as a matter of fact, the product had "never been heard of before."

The pace of commerce quickened in the nineteenth century and many unscrupulous advertisers piled up huge personal fortunes. Everywhere the gullible public was victimized. The newspapers of the time made initial feeble efforts to protect their readers from "the wily arts of the insidious advertiser," as one newspaper noted editorially. During this period newspaper solvency was more dependent on readers than on advertisers, and editors showed their scorn of advertisers by requiring ads to be set in small type and permitting no illustrations. Many required a daily change in copy so as not to bore disinterested readers, and all required payment of cash in advance of the ad's publication. But as the revenue from the ads mounted to more sizable proportions, the newspapers lost some of their appetite for the noble fight. Many of the rules laid down to protect the readers were discarded. Illustrations appeared in ads, bold type replaced small type, as the relationship between newspaper, reader, and advertiser changed, with the advertiser moving into a more dominant role. So blatant was the "all-deafening blast of puffery" in the ads for pills, salves, pick-me-ups, and elixirs that Thomas Carlyle charged in *Past and Present* that "the Quack has become God." Sex ads became endemic. The Personals columns were filled with "jolly sports" who looked for "witty, affectionate ladies," "young masseuses" who offered "special disciplinary treatment to select clients," "highly magnetic Parisiennes" who promised "very interesting conversation" in private suites, and "courteous and discreet gentlemen who offered to oblige ladies "in any confidential capacity." Newspapers carried large display ads in which men were urged to apply raw unprocessed bear's fat to nourish their scalps, and ladies to girdle themselves with magnetic corsets whose curative powers "on all the vital organs" rid the body of any and all ailments. Everybody needed a daily supply of Dr. Williams' Pink Pills for Pale People. All manner of wonders was achieved by the mere swallowing of a few small colored pills. Typical was the grateful testimonial of a young woman who before her time suffered from debilitated health. She had tried Phoenix Bitters, Life Pills, Phelps Arcanium, Smith's Anti-Mercurial Syrup, Swan's Panacea, Indian Panacea, Conway's Boston Medicine, Fowler's Solution of Arsenic—to no avail. A friend told her of a new brand. "I am entirely satisfied," she wrote, "that my life has been preserved and my health entirely restored by the blessing of God and the use of Bristol's Fluid Extract of Sarsaparilla." Equally grateful men and women wrote testimonials about their own snatched-from-the-grave experiences. One woman's leg ulcer, which for 13 years was resistant to medical treatment by "over twenty eminent physicians," yielded in "less than one month" to a few dabs by Wolcott's Pain Paint. A man bedridden for 20 years was able, thanks to Holloway's Pills, to run up and down mountains. Henry

Sampson records the ingenuity displayed by a late nineteenth century advertiser who inscribed in large, bold, white letters on the fence surrounding a graveyard: "Use Jones' bottled ale if you would like to keep out of here." And by the go-getter undertaker who drummed up business for his establishment by writing to every sick person he heard about in his city: "Dear Sir, having positive proof that you are rapidly approaching Death's gate, I have, therefore, thought it not imprudent to call your attention to the enclosed advertisement of my abundant stock of ready-made coffins, and desire to make the suggestion that you signify to your friends a wish for the purchase of your burial outfit at my establishment." This letter offered assurance that the funeral would be strictly first-class, and the sick man would have nothing to do except, presumably, to supply the corpse.

Advertisers found to their liking the homely philosophy of Francis Bacon, who wrote in "Essay on Truth": "Doth any man doubt, that if there were taken out of men's minds vain opinions, flattering hopes, false valuations, imaginations . . . and the like, but it would leave the minds of a number of men poor shrunken things, full of melancholy and indisposition, and unpleasant to themselves?" And his conclusion: "A mixture of a lie doth ever add pleasure."

For centuries they dosed mankind with pleasures, if not cures, with U.S. advertisers showing the kind of energy and ingenuity that left their mercantile forebears in England far behind. They filled the wagons of pioneer families as they pushed westward to California with patent medicines of every description. Fortuitously, the pioneer families had no access to doctors on the westward trek, had to administer to their own ailments, and medical knowledge was such, anyway, that the advertisers' elixirs and extracts were relied on to do what the doctors could not. As Stewart H. Holbrook described in *The Golden Age of Quackery*, and Gerald Carson in *One for a Man, Two for a Horse*, it was a golden opportunity which the advertisers gladly seized.

Advertising in the Twenties   3

Aside from a few carping eggheads, criticism of admen and advertising was practically stilled in the 1920's as the nation wallowed in its first rousing prosperity. Nobody listened to the eggheads because everybody was intent on listening to the beautiful music of the prosperity calliope as it rolled brassily down the main streets of every city in the U.S. Aside from coal mining, textiles, and farming, which prosperity somehow seemed to bypass, those engaged in other areas of the economy enjoyed high profits, high wages, stable prices, and a chance to join the merchant middle class. With such a carnival buying atmosphere operating in the twenties, advertisers boosted their promotional efforts between 1921–1929 from $2.3 billion to $3.4 billion.

Illustrative of the temper of the times was the day in December, 1927, when that old diehard, Henry Ford, quit producing the all-black Model T and tried to recapture sales with the gayer Model A. The introduction of the new model was heralded in page ads in 2,000 newspapers for five consecutive days at a then staggering cost of $1.3 million. But thousands of orders were written up for Niagara blue roadsters and Arabian Sand phaetons and Ford again challenged Chevrolet for leadership in the low-priced car field. Newspapers reported how one million persons jammed the Ford showrooms in New York, 100,000 crowded into the Detroit showrooms, and mounted police were called out to keep order in Cleveland. Similar manifestations of the national new-car mania were reported in every big U.S. city.

As car ownership rose between 1919–1929 from 6½ million to more than 23 million, the rise was called by one observer "the most potent statistic of Coolidge prosperity." In "Middletown" the Lynds were astonished at the number of families who owned new cars before they even enjoyed the convenience of a bathtub at home.

Prosperity in the twenties was also stimulated by forces other than the automobile. One was radio, introduced in the U.S. in the autumn of 1920, for which the public soon was spending $60 million annually for sets, parts, and accessories. And that was just the beginning. By 1929 sales soared to $850 million, a 1,400 percent gain for the eight-year period. Other spark plugs of prosperity were refrigerators, cosmetics, cigarettes, rayon, electrical gadgets, motion pictures, all of which entered regularly into family life. Installment buying became widely prevalent, marvelously expanding buying power by mortgaging the future for present enjoyment, and the firm belief gripped millions that not only was it old-fashioned to buy for cash only, but a bit stupid, for installment buying magically produced all the comforts needed to sweeten life. With business booming, the number of U.S. businessmen paying tax on annual incomes of over $1 million rose between 1924–1927 from 75 to 283. In *The Crisis of the Old Order*, Arthur M. Schlesinger, Jr., notes that during the decade profits as a whole rose over 80 percent and "the profits of financial institutions rose a fantastic 150 percent."

The decade also witnessed an evangelical fervor in advertising appeals. In *Only Yesterday*, Frederick Lewis Allen says that the adman was "learning to pay less attention to the special qualities and advantages of his product, and more to the study of what the mass of unregenerative mankind wanted—to be young and desirable, to be rich, to keep up with the Joneses, to be envied. The winning method was to associate his product with one or more of these ends, logically or illogically, truthfully or cynically. . . ." The spirit of unregenerative mankind found expression in Coué Institutes, which sprang up all over the U.S., whose head, Emile Coué dinned into willing listeners his magical formula for personal success: "Day by day, in every way, I am getting better and better." It became a slogan for millions of the faithful to live by.

For giving the country unparalleled prosperity, business was venerated and the figure of the businessman, notes Allen, "ousted the statesman, the priest, the philosopher, as the creator of standards of ethics and behavior." High government officials joined in the veneration. "The man who builds a factory builds a temple," said President Calvin Coolidge, and "the man who works there worships there." So pervasive was this philosophy that the highest compliment was to call a clergyman a good businessman and many churches utilized the general éclat for business as a way of promoting religious purposes. One church offered to those parishioners contributing more than $100 to its building fund "an engraved certificate of investment in preferred capital stock in the Kingdom of God." Another urged regular church attendance on the ground that "Christian Worship Increases Your Efficiency." In an insurance company pamphlet Moses was hailed as "one of the greatest salesmen and real estate promoters that ever lived." The best-selling nonfiction book in 1925–1926, *The Man Nobody Knows*, written by adman Bruce Barton, contained the thesis that Jesus was a great business executive. "He picked up twelve men from the bottom ranks of business and forged them into an organization that conquered the world." Barton was convinced that, if Jesus were living today, he would be "a national advertiser." No better testimony to the nation's solid faith in the "redemptive influence of business" existed than the rapid growth of the business service clubs, the Kiwanis, Lions, and Rotary, which expressed the national idyl that businessmen, gifted with practical vision, nonetheless were dreamers who devoted precious time to thinking up ways of improving mankind.

Not a little of this faith in the dreaming tendencies of businessmen encouraged the two speculative scrambles that are remembered as landmarks of the twenties. The first was the real estate boom in Florida in 1925–1926, built on the dream of seeing the Florida coastline from Palm Beach southward developed into an American Riviera. In a few months some 2,000 real estate offices were operating in the city of Miami alone, and real estate agents buttonholed strangers on the city streets and sold them house lots and acreage. Buyers were ready, able, and plentiful, for only 10 percent of the price of the lots was needed as a binder, which the buyer then turned around and sold to somebody else at a nice profit. Instead of looking over the land, lots were bought from blueprints and practically nobody waited for deeds to be searched and titles cleared. All that mattered was to find a buyer for the binder before the first payment on the lots came due at the end of 30 days, and pocket the profit. Inside lot prices soon leaped to $20,000, waterfront lots to $25,000, and seashore lots to $75,000. The speculative fever became so intense, Allen says, that "one had only to announce a new development, be it honest or fraudulent, be it on the Atlantic Ocean or deep in the wasteland of the interior to set people scrambling for home lots." At the height of the delirium of binders, options, lots, and profits, Miami passed a local ordinance prohibiting the sale of property on a city street, or even the unveiling of a real estate map, because of the traffic snarl that ensued. Finally, when the chain buying of binders ran out of gas in the middle of 1926, those who held binders that nobody else was ready to buy were compelled to default on their payments. If not, they would have been stuck with the ownership of lots whose inflated price was many times the real value. And the Florida real estate boom collapsed about as quickly as it had blown up.

The other speculative scramble that swept the twenties, demonstrating anew the boundless faith of the people in business prosperity as an overriding religion, was in the stock market. Once again the vision of windfall riches seduced hundreds of thousands with modest incomes to take speculative fliers in the market. In *The Great Crash 1929*, John Galbraith recalls that in the final months of the Bull Market *The New York Times* industrials shot up 52 points in June, 25 in July, 33 in August, for a 110-point gain in three months. "Never before or since," he comments, "have so many become so wondrously, so effortlessly, and so quickly rich." The understanding of upwards of a million speculators busily counting daily paper profits in stocks purchased on margin generally did not go beyond the symbols ITT, GL, X as they flitted by on the ticker tape. But did it matter? Everybody was making money. Five-million-share days were commonplace and stock prices practically daily hit new highs. Herbert Hoover's presidential acceptance speech in 1928 saluted his countrymen for getting "nearer to the final triumph over poverty than ever before in the history of our land." Outgoing Calvin Coolidge remarked that even at their high levels stocks were still cheap. John S. Raskob blueprinted in the *Ladies' Home Journal* a plan for national wealth entitled "Everybody Ought to Be Rich." His plan called for investing $15 each month in common stocks, allowing dividends to accumulate, and at the end of 20 years being able to live the life of Riley on an accrued fortune of $80,000 which would throw off about $400 a month. Andrew W. Mellon predicted: "The high tide of prosperity will continue." Professor Irving Fisher noted that "stock prices have reached what looks like a permanently high plateau." Bruce Barton foresaw the economy "on the verge of a great forward movement." The national mood during this surge of the Bull Market was one of certainty that the gateway to fortune stood wide open for everyone.

A 1929 *Saturday Evening Post* editorial marveled at the spectacular profits of scrubwomen, valets, and office boys who rolled up fortunes in a few weeks or months. But the editorial also acknowledged the wisdom of sensible investors who purchased stock outright for the long pull. "Nothing could be safer, sounder, or more wholesome than the well-deserved financial rise of these thrifty, level-headed families and individuals. The beauty of the thing," the editorial could not get over, "is that most of these people who are getting rich so inevitably and so safely know little about the stock market and have nothing in the way of financial connections." Unfortunately the younger generation had been born too late to get in on the ground floor of the stock boom, but the editorial consoled the young people with the prediction that in the future "unavoidable hazards of fortune building will not be nearly so great as they have been. . . ." A scant eight months later the stock market bubble burst.

Advertising was hailed by the American Economic Association in Chicago as an "essential of present-day civilization without which further progress is inconceivable." The few literati who dared criticize advertising were looked on with benevolent contempt by *Printers' Ink*. "The packers have contributed more to the health and general welfare of the country than all the writers combined," it noted. The manufacturer was "more of a benefactor to humanity" than all the writers who ridiculed him. President Calvin Coolidge agreed: "Advertising ministers to the spiritual side of trade," he told the American Association of Advertising Agencies in 1926. "It is a great power which is inspiring and ennobling the commercial world. It is all part of the greater work of the regeneration and redemption of mankind." Admen had a great historical mission. They were the crusaders for the "liberation of a middle-class people from the tyranny of Puritanism, parsimoniousness, and material asceticism," from the archaic attitudes that the craving of material goods was sinful, wasteful, and immoral, as Otis Pease noted in *The Responsibilities of American Advertising*. This attitude was even shared by a few antediluvian businessmen who were properly warned by economist Roger W. Babson in *Collier's* in 1928: "The banker of the coming generation will hesitate to lend money to a businessman who is not advertising. For they know that he is probably due for a deficit."

The twenties witnessed the rise of a new phenomenon—cooperative advertising—in which businessmen in the same industry banded together in an attempt to capture consumer dollars before they were enticed away by another industry. By 1928 some 75 trade associations operated their competitive strategy. Laundries campaigned for the housewife to let the laundries do the family washing. Florists urged people to "Say It with Flowers." Greeting card manufacturers urged people to say it with greeting cards. Soap companies promoted the values of national cleanliness. Orange growers promoted the health benefits of oranges. Coal dealers, ice dealers, lumber dealers, piano manufacturers, photographers, each advanced their own economic fortunes.

Even a cursory examination of consumer advertising in 1929 indicates its congeniality with the wish-fulfillment values of a frivolous decade. The automobile had become the leading status symbol and the car ads traded boasts on their respective capabilities to endow the buyer with greater fashionability. In the *Saturday Evening Post*, Buick claimed "style unsurpassed in motor car history." Dodge offered the "largest, handsomest, and finest product." Willy's-Overland Whippet offered "style creation of master designers." De Soto Six was "distinctly original—and distinctly dashing." Chrysler beauty was so striking that assuredly it was "no chance creation." The Oakland Motor Car Company saw in the "sweep of its flaring fenders . . . the individuality of its radiator . . . the gleam of its wealth of chromeplate" the greatest car yet. Its contours and colors offered "something new in style, something original in design, something triumphantly different from any other car." Hupmobile appropriated 20 years of "mechanical supremacy" and topped it with an idea that was destined to rock the motoring world to its foundations: "The idea that a motor car must be more than comfortable, more than handsome, even more than beautiful—it must be *smart*." Fisher Body appealed to the cognoscenti "who have learned the wisdom of buying cars which set the style—which heighten their pride of ownership." Reo Motors told rising young businessmen that the looks of their retail delivery wagons was "one thing about your business the whole town knows—and judges you by." Auburn fashionability was unmistakably conveyed by a chic young thing in a leopard coat lounging in front of a gleaming 125-horsepower sedan. The caption read: "Standards of living have risen, and people want finer cars." Lincoln sniffed at such pretensions and assured entrenched wealth that *their* car was above the reach of "passing fads and fancies."

Old Briar was pleased that thousands of men had found a new way to show off their affluence: "Like his home, and his car, and his clothes, his tobacco, too, distinguishes the successful man today." La Monte safety paper company suggested such conspicuous evidence of having "arrived" as a bank check with wavy lines: "Isn't there something dignified, substantial—really *distinctive*—about it? And doesn't it by its very look and feel suggest a bank that is drawing its clientele from the top level of businessmen?"

New Haven Clock Co. pointed out that its Tip-Top watch because of its smart octagon case, silver face, and sunken second dial, gave the impression of being at least twice as costly. Upson Company tipped off comers that after preliminary greetings, friends scrutinized walls and ceiling for telltale cracked plaster: "Your home is you! Your friends judge you by your appearance. What does your home say to your friends?" Community Plate tried to ward off a near social tragedy by depicting a distinguished guest confiding to his wife out of the corner of his mouth: "I give you my word, before I try to dissect filet mignon again with a *silver* blade—I'll *starve*." The ad warned: "If your guests have to struggle with a silver-blade knife, conversation will lag."

Smith Brothers endowed stage actress Pauline Lord with a "sixth sense" which told her of an incipient cough in the audience before it broke up a dramatic scene, and enabled her to get off in time a "silent wish—for the cougher's sake and for mine—that somebody hand out a few Smith Brothers' Cough Drops." Luden's singled out the hackers who interrupted "every church service, every lecture, every concert, every public gathering" with coughs. They were reminded that coughing was outlawed by considerate people as a crudity of conduct: "Take Luden's and be civilized."

Another invaluable aid to civilization was the Book of Etiquette which promised expert advice on "what to do, say, write, or wear on every occasion." No social climbers could afford to be without one, could chance the *faux pas* that would humiliate them days on end. Equally important aids were the Elbert Hubbard Scrap Book and Nelson Doubleday's Pocket University, a few minutes daily study of which could step up conversation to brilliance.

The advertising pages were full of manufacturers, some with the most unlikely products, who tried to get in on the success act. Williams Shaving Cream placed a man "head and shoulders above the crowd." Florsheim Shoes put "smart good looks on feet." Vaseline Hair Tonic slicked hair for that look of success. Del Monte canned spinach helped everyone "greet the morning with a smile." Phillips Milk of Magnesia "made life sweeter." Interwoven Socks were "correct in every detail." The Miami Chamber of Commerce boasted how the Miami sun produced healthy bones, teeth, muscles, nerves, increased red blood corpuscles, protected against rickets, against contagion. The Louisville and Nashville Railroad lured the sporting crowd to thoroughbred races in New Orleans—"America's Winter Racing Capital." The flower industry told men to "remember her with flowers and she won't forget you." Sheaffer pens gave "sheer pleasure in writing." Congoleum Rug let no time, trouble, expense, stand in the way of consummate beauty. Mazda Lamps offered new "beauty, power, style, and safety." Ball-Band galoshes blended "charmingly with the season's richly furred ensembles." Palmolive dedicated itself to safeguard "that schoolgirl complexion." Hostess Cakes were a tribute to the smart hostess who served them. Armstrong warned women that nothing hastened the onset of "lines on your face, fatigue in your figure" as much as scrubbing floors, from which fate linoleum rescued them. Ivory Soap's "kindly, comforting foam" put the mind and body in the somnolent state ready for quick entry into the "land of nod."

Pratt & Lambert coaxed homeowners to make themselves "happier this year with color." Haywood-Wakefield breakfast sets furnished the "cheery, colorful atmosphere necessary to the modern home." F. Scott Fitzgerald, John Barrymore, and Cornelius Vanderbilt, Jr., selected the "Twelve Most Beautiful Women Using Woodbury's Facial Soap." Steinway promised fame and fortune to gifted moppets: "Their names will appear upon concert programs, or flash in electric lights." Liquid Carbonic Corp. was pardonably proud that Lou Meyer, noted racing driver, after a breakneck pace of two miles a minute for 200 miles, asked as a first request "for a Carbonated Bottled Drink." McGraw-Hill Publications urged careful reading of its *Magazine of Business* for "a sure course to continued profits."

Expressing the evangelical view of advertising in the twenties, adman Frank Presbrey wrote in *The History and Development of Advertising* that it "probably is our greatest agency for spreading an understanding and love of beauty in all things." Published in 1929 the book stands, if nothing else, as a monument to the decade.

Advertising Under Attack in the Thirties 4

The theatrical mask of comedy which advertising wore throughout the prosperous twenties was replaced by the mask of tragedy as the country toppled into the worst depression in its history in the thirties. Between 1929 and 1933 the Gross National Product (the sum of all goods and services produced in the U.S., a handy, if not too meaningful, measurement) fell from $103 billion to $55.7 billion. Banks failed, factories closed, railroads went bankrupt, farmers fell into desperate straits, the white-collar group was hard hit. In 1933 an estimated 12 million men and women were looking for work.

The federal government undertook unprecedented steps to bolster the faltering economic system. Banks were placed under closer federal supervision, credit was extended to some, others beyond redemption were closed. Farm loans aided individuals in peril of losing their homes and farms, and concerns on the edge of bankruptcy. Billions were loaned to banks, railways, insurance companies, industries whose earnings were dangerously behind their operating needs. Other billions were spent in public works construction which stimulated the building industry and provided badly needed purchasing power to workers. Industry after industry was federally organized in an attempt to stimulate employment, production and sales. Federal laws broke new ground. The Agricultural Adjustment Act authorized reduction of farm production to bring it more in line with existing markets, and create, in the words of Secretary of Agriculture Henry A. Wallace, "an ever-normal granary." The National Industrial Recovery Act aided manufacturing interests whose mountains of unsold manufactured goods were stored in warehouses. The National Labor Relations Act handed labor a mandate to form unions and bargain collectively in matters of wages, hours, and working conditions. The Congress of Industrial Organizations was born and flourished —8 million workers were soon organized into industrial and craft unions. Higher wages and shorter hours were federally fixed in industries traditionally addicted to low wages and long hours. The central government also directly attacked the problems of unemployment, poverty and misery, by providing millions of jobs through the Works Progress Administration and other agencies, and limited insurance against the hazards of unemployment, old age, dependency, and poverty for millions of workers.

The thirties provided bitter, if fertile, soil for the consumer movement to take firm root. An index of its rise was the membership of Consumers' Research, an organization involved in independent product testing, which increased from 12,000 in 1930 to 48,000 in 1936. "Home economics" courses proliferated in the nation's schools: by 1940 there were more than 250,000 students enrolled in such courses. So, too, proliferated consumer exhibits which were set up to teach consumers rational buying and consumption habits, and consumer clubs as adjuncts to labor unions, churches, welfare agencies, and farm organizations. They provided a counterbalance to the blandishments of advertising.

A consumer literature also sprang up which gave this consumer movement an indispensable sense of direction. Arthur Kallet's and Frederick Schlink's *100,000,000 Guinea Pigs*, an attack on useless and dangerous proprietaries, became a best-seller in 1933. It was followed by books of biting social criticism such as *The Joy of Ignorance, The Popular Practice of Fraud,* and *40,000,000 Guinea Pig Children.* Other books ripped into the ethics of advertising and the business community it served. Upton Sinclair's *The Brass Check* tore into the big advertisers and their corruptive control of the mass media. Max Radin's *The Lawful Pursuit of Gain* probed the intrinsically deceitful nature of advertising. And former advertising practitioners James Rorty and Helen Woodward dissected critically their former occupation in book-length confessionals.

In such a hostile environment, advertising was in full retreat as it was attacked on all sides as the unwelcome spokesman for economic waste. "Advertising, installment selling, credit, and high-pressure salesmanship have produced chaos," charged the *Yale Review* in 1931. "So far as advertising goes, we are fallen on evil days," acknowledged adman H. A. Batten in the *Atlantic Monthly* in 1932. Advertising was indeed a favorite sitting duck for those sharp-shooting critics intent on finishing off what they saw was a moribund economic system. The only thing worse than the criticism, from the admen's point of view, was the steady whittling of advertising budgets by national advertisers. Each fall in sales was followed by a sharp cut in advertising. Between 1929 and 1933, as the Gross National Product fell from $103 billion to $55.7 billion—a drop of 46 percent—the advertising budgets fell from $3.4 billion to $1.3 billion—a drop of 62 percent. No matter how loud the exhortations from the trade press that only stepped-up advertising appropriations could reverse the downtrend of sales, advertisers heedlessly cut their advertising to the bone, and then into the bone. As much as the public, they too seemed to have lost faith in the charming power of advertising.

Typical of the general excoriation of advertising was a 1934 issue of *The Annals*, an American Academy of Political and Social Science publication. Called "The Ultimate Consumer—A Study in Economic Illiteracy," each contributor of the joint study provided his own indictment of advertising and the merchandising process. Advertising was considered a tyranny of waste from top to bottom, especially intolerable in an era when everybody was going around tightening his belt. "Whether they want them or not," went the general indictment, "consumers must pay for the perfume in their soap, the flavor in their toothpaste, the expensive container, liberal credit and return privileges, an elaborate display, frequent delivery, and reputation created by advertising. They must even pay for the persuasion and sales talk to which they must for their own protection develop resistance."

Sadly, the industrialization process had played a mean trick on the consumer, for as fabrication techniques advanced he had lost his old thumb-and-finger familiarity with silk, calico, and flour, which had proved invaluable to an earlier generation in making "good buys." Brooms and washboards, those trusty standbys of yesteryear, were so much easier to judge than the vacuum cleaners and electric washing machines that had replaced them. Regrettably, the eighteenth century condition of society as a kind of self-balancing biological aquarium between producers and consumers was dead: in the twentieth century the big fish with the sharp teeth were the producers and the millions of minnow-consumers were swimming wildly for their lives. And advertising was the villain. For by playing on known weaknesses in human nature, by trading on phony values called "style," "this year's model," "modern," advertising egged consumers to engage in a foolish buying race with one another to achieve the transitory euphoria called status. While the race might be needed by producers to shrink their growing stocks of goods, it drew the grim prediction by Thorstein Veblen that in the end it would "bear fruit in the psychopathic wards" for consumers.

Indignation for placing consumers in such a perilous position filled the pages of *The Annals*. Advertising was charged with molesting the consumer on the written page, over the radio, on billboards, in skywriting, by door-to-door salesmen, and by countless unrelenting ways to buy things he did not need, did not want, and to empty his pockets of cash. The consumer was seen facing the "most devastatingly aimed barrage of advertising and merchandising" yet delivered on any generation of consumers. Moreover it was the trickiest for it employed such an insidious concept as artificial obsolescence—"an invention of the Devil to outmode bathroom, furniture, automobile, or clothing . . . before the article in question is worn out." The consumer was a modern David, who stood alone, barehanded, without even a slingshot as defense against the "accumulated momentum of 43,000,000 horse power and their array of salesmen, advertising men, and other jockeys." So much of his money was wasted on the "harmful, ugly, trivial, ostentatious" that one embittered writer opined that the "triumphs of the industrial age seem far less grand and even doubtful."

Each field of consumption contributed to the total indictment of advertising. At the pharmacy the consumer exchanged money for mouthwashes that were either worthless or of no more value than a simple solution of table salt or bicarbonate of soda. They certainly could not deliver the health and social success that the ads promised. Most of the antiseptics he bought were so mild they were not as potent as a simple washing of the open wound with soap and water. Despite the toothpaste ads, which managed to convey the impression that the practice of dentistry was practically obsolete, no consumer could rely on any of the miracle toothpastes to prevent the formation of a single dental caries; the reality was that thousands of dollars went down bathroom sink drains daily. Countless thousands more were sacrificed on the altar of beauty, for women could no more wipe away the lines of age by application of beauty preparations than they could turn back the clock to yesterday. Although harmless, the beauty preparations were scandalously overpriced considering their inability to perform any of the facial magic for which they were bought.

At the household furnishing store, the consumer could come by none but the vaguest information on the serviceability of the product he wanted. If it was a blanket, it was all but impossible to wrest such vital statistics from the salesman as the blanket's heat retentivity, breaking strength, resistance to abrasion during laundering. It seemed to be the most vital badge of honor in the merchandising system to be able to switch the consumer to such flashier things as style and color.

Instead of mechanical and electrical equipment, the consumer bought a collection of "trash": sun lamps that were both a fire and health hazard; toasters that became so hot in use they were positively dangerous to touch; "automatic" irons that burned fine rayons even when set at the lowest temperature; curling irons, vibrators, and massagers that were so poorly insulated that "only a person totally ignorant of the potential shock hazard . . . would dare to use such an appliance." Rather than a small car with low operating cost that he went in to buy, the consumer rolled out of the showroom in a 3,000-pound boudoir decorated with chrome, trick lights, levers, and extra cylinders for high operating cost. Instead of buying a solidly constructed electric iron, the consumer was sold on the importance of a thumb rest, button nook, and yellow handle. "No veteran trader visiting South Sea islanders ever flashed with greater effectiveness his cheap mirrors, bright beads, buzzing toys, or red hats," wrote a commentator scornfully, "than our hordes of salesmen do their chrome plate, match-your-curtains kitchenware, motorized lemonade mixers, and the latest creations in clothes and cars." The consumer's bewitchment with his appliances faded after only a few months as a majority of them either quit working, or became noisy demons, or short-circuited, or burned out. This lamentable state of affairs was not attributable to the engineers who worked up the appliances, but to the sales-bent management which ordered the engineers to spend much of their time building unneeded gadgetry into the appliances.

One critic sneered that the next development in refrigerators might be "doors that open when spoken to and ice that spills itself into a highball glass" (modern refrigerator manufacturers please note). Another argued that the old-fashioned, foot-powered sewing machine was a prime example of an "almost perfect household machine's" debasement by a manufacturer bent on jazzing up its sales appeal. In the good old days, before it was motorized, the sewing machine was commonly good for two or three generations, operating daily without letdown or breakdown. Now, not only could any home needleworker personally testify that the electrically driven machine was not the match of the foot-driven model, but the addition of the motor simply added something that demanded both maintenance care and costly repair. As for the hemmer, tucker, gatherer, shirring foot, and the attachments for pinking, darning, and making buttonholes, all of which came with the motorized machine, while they helped bewitch the housewife into buying the machine, they were actually so much folderol. Rarely if ever would any of these gadgets be used because of the time in fitting and adjusting them and learning how to use them correctly.

Consumers were warned not to be tricked by snappy colors or flashing lights into diverting their attention from the essential points of a product, or into buying items they really did not need. In the words of an author of a booklet called "Prohibiting Poverty": "We all jolly well know the difference between the numerous things we *want* and the few things we actually *need*." Food, clothing, shelter, and nothing much else, made up this writer's list of necessaries, which coincided with most of the nation's Spartan lists drawn up in the rugged thirties.

Confronted by direct and widespread assaults on advertising plus the impoverishment of large sections of the consumers, ad themes in the thirties retreated to the fulfillment of basic human needs. Consumers were forever reassured that their prospective purchases were both prudent and necessary. Examination of *Saturday Evening Post* issues for 1933 shows a spate of car ads outdoing each other in durability and economy claims. Packard, pointing out that the greatest single expense was the depreciation cost when the car was outmoded by next year's model, claimed "no Packard owners ever pays this cost." For Packard lines remained unchanged which saved Packard owners untold "millions and millions of dollars." Tests also showed that a Packard clutch was good as new after 125,000 uses in traffic, its transmission betrayed no visible wear after 50,000 miles of driving, and its motor life was doubled by the installation of a new lubricating system. All in all, it was the "toughest, longest-lived car built in America today." Chevrolet pointed to its modest consumption of gas and oil and suggested that "the money you save on a car like this, in a very short time, is enough to buy several nice accessories—or make a monthly payment or two." Buick called attention to all the Buicks on the road that had traveled 200,000 miles or more and were still nobly serving "after 5, 10, or even 15 years of use."

High-priced items justified their existence on the ground that they were actually longer-lasting and hence less costly in the end. Dutch Boy urged homeowners not to paint with an ordinary white lead, because it was pennies cheaper; because later they would have to pay for burning and scraping away cracked and scaled remains of an inferior paint. Mazda pointed out that a "cheap" lamp, poorly made, was wasteful of electricity and although pennies cheaper to buy, "Mr. Liar Lamp" robbed consumers of an extra dollar on their lighting bill. General Electric offered similar counsel: "You won't take eleven eggs for a dozen —Why pay for light you don't get?" Bostonian shoes wore like iron—"held their shape to the last step." Florsheims at $8 was a better buy in the long run than any "cheap" shoe. Exide warned how a "bargain" battery could wind up frightfully expensive.

Frigidaire proudly announced that its refrigerators operated on as little electric current as an ordinary lamb bulb. Majestic took pains to build refrigerators to last until today's baby marched in his cap and gown for his college sheepskin. Between the Acts little cigars were not for the plutocrats who could afford to throw away a 15-cent cigar half-smoked, but for prudent consumers who would smoke the shorter B.T.A. down to the end and save 7½ cents.

For a nation bedeviled by joblessness and sleeplessness many advertisers solicitously promised partial answers. Absorbine Jr., suggested that a palmful, smoothed on the back of the neck in "slow, firm strokes away from the brain," was good for a night's sleep. Aspirin achieved the same thing with two tablets at bedtime downed with a glass of hot water. Ovaltine promised it in an ad arrestingly headlined: "$10,000 for One Night's Sleep." Sanka's advice to the haggard chap, sitting on the edge of bed at 3 A.M., was drink Sanka.

For those who waked in the morning to face another futile day of job-hunting, many products were available to combat that morning fatigue. Men could use Williams Shaving Cream "to snap out of it" quickly. Chase & Sanborn suggested dated coffee to "sharpen your wits . . . pep up your muscles." A steady procession of bewhiskered foreign doctors in Standard Brands ads prescribed Fleischman's yeast to get rid of a "run-down feeling." A Listerine gargle killed millions of deadly throat germs and guarded against colds and tuberculosis. Squibb vitamins protected against the consequences of wet feet, drafts, overheated rooms, raw winds. Heinz woke up lazy appetites with a condiment that "never fails to make folks hungry." Campbell Soup suggested that everybody keep healthy by eating soup. Spud cigarettes had the happy faculty of lending "wings to anxious moments" of the day. Gold Medal Foods' solution to wives to brighten husbands at dinner was to "put hot biscuits on the table." A paint company advised wives to avoid "trying a man's patience" by making certain they used a fast-drying paint, and putting the furniture back in place before he came home at night. Friendly Five shoes discovered that the "pained look" on Jim's face came not from boredom with his dancing partner but from pinching shoes. Phillips Milk of Magnesia reassured people, plagued by problems, who got to thinking there was something "queer" with them, that it might be a simple matter of stomach acidity. National Casket Company, in a candid chat with an aged man and his wife, suggested: "Let's face the facts frankly. . . . If you know a little bit about caskets before the need arises the selection will be easier and more satisfactory." American Brake Shoe and Foundry Company announced unemotionally that "between six o'clock and midnight, TONIGHT, 31 people will be killed and 861 injured," most of them because of faulty car brakes. Lever Bros. confided to the salesman who could not make a sale—could not even get people to *see* him—what even his best friend would not tell him: he needed Lifebuoy to end "B.O.," even a hint of which was an affront "these days when jobs are hard to get, hard to hold."

Most toothpaste ads enlarged on the painful stance of the times. The dentist in the Pebeco ad said regretfully: "It's going to HURT but that's what acid mouth costs you." The Pepsodent dentist held aloft a just extracted tooth: "Another lovely woman pays penalty of Film." Ipana offered to guard consumers from "Pink Tooth Brush," gingivitis, and Vincent's disease. Dr. West's toothpaste was available for anyone who decided not to take a "needless chance" with other toothpastes. Listerine reversed the field and reassured consumers they would not fall prey to pyorrhea, gingivitis, or trench mouth if they continued using a toothpaste in the 50-cent bracket. But they would be "throwing away about $3 a year." For that tidy sum, Listerine toted up all the necessary items consumers could buy: handkerchiefs, hose, hat, sweater, gloves, knickers, pajamas, underwear, bathrobe, swimming suit, raincoat, sneakers, moccasins, slippers, shoes, rubbers, umbrella, suitcase, traveling bag, book.

The Union Central Life Insurance Company recognized in the mother's wan face, as she brought to her son a birthday cake decorated with five lighted candles, a dread of the "tense struggle that lies ahead for her little son." The burning candles were apt warnings that "her boy's chances would slip away" if the policy lapsed and the tyke was out of his college education. Another insurance company urged a toddler to get his college education on insurance money, and so be in a better position to face "the uncertain world alone."

In general, advertisements in the thirties used the theatrical mask of tragedy to focus and trade on the pain, fear, frustration, and overall unhappiness of people. They spoke to the make-do, get-by, nervous mood of the people. As expressed by a Parke-Davis ad: "The past few years have been years of worry. Fears have walked abroad. Nerves have been harassed as never before."

5 The Postwar Economic Explosion

The ill-fated prediction of Herbert Hoover of two chickens in every pot and two cars in every garage for all American families, promised in the 1928 election campaign, began to come true some 25 years later. What was the butt of anti-Republicanism during the decade of the Great Depression, began to be more of a verity in the postwar U.S. Starting in 1945, the consumers' astonishing appetite for food, clothing, housing, cars, household equipment, and leisure gear has set off the wildest buying spree in U.S. history, or for that matter, in the world. Its astronomical dimensions have challenged, and in many cases defeated, the social scientists who have attempted to measure it and rashly to predict its future shape or trend. With but three brief setbacks in 1953–1954, 1957–1958, and 1960, consumers have seemingly obeyed an urge to buy up everything in sight.

By comparison, the nation's prosperity in the twenties was small potatoes indeed. Consider that in 1929, after a century and one-half, the Gross National Product had edged up to $103 billion. During the depression, of course, the GNP fell flat on its face and did not get up to the $100 billion mark again until 1940, when it acquired a pair of wings. One was war production, the other inflation. As a result, GNP soared to $200 billion by 1944, to $300 billion by 1950, to $400 billion by 1955, and edged past $500 billion by 1960. As Americans soaked up vast quantities of goods and services they continued to upset the estimates of the nation's business oracles.

Gripped by a wild and woolly prosperity, the face of the U.S. underwent a revolutionary change. First of all, the number of Americans took off something like a moonshot, going from 132 million in 1940 to 152 million in 1950 to 185 million in 1961. The nation seemed to preoccupy itself with the business of making babies. Not only did more nubile females get themselves married at an earlier age than ever before, but the postwar crop of first, second, third, even fourth children was staggering, as *Fortune* magazine noted. In 1953 alone, the magazine estimated that they bore 1,300,000 first children, a 47 percent increase over 1940; 1,170,000 second children, a 91 percent increase; 620,000 third children, an 86 percent increase; and 310,000 fourth children, a 61 percent increase. One result of this outstanding display of national fertility was a more rapid growth of population than at any time since the first decade of this century. In the period 1950–1954, for example, more babies were born than were spawned during the entire decade of the thirties. Another result was the stupefication of an entire school of demographers whose gloomy literature, written before the war, uniformly prophesied a virtual standstill population in a few years. Still another result was the formation of new households which grew from under 600,000 annually in 1940 to over 1.5 million in 1950, growing at even a faster rate than the population. Especially in the early postwar years, not only did huge numbers of newlyweds take apartments of their own, but elderly couples, widows and single people joined in the national prosperity by setting up households. Between 1947 and 1960 the number of households increased by more than 25 percent, from 40 million to more than 50 million.

Second of all, and best of all, these families went shopping with pocketbooks that bulged more than at any time in history. The U.S. Department of Commerce figured that the number of households with over $4,000 annually went from 23 million in 1947 to 34 million in 1957 (measured in 1957 dollars). The $4,000 figure held special allure because at about that figure the average family could take care of its food-clothing-shelter needs and start to have something left over for discretionary spending. During the same period of time, 1947–1957, the number of households with $6,000 or more went from 11½ million to 20 million, and the number with $10,000 or more from 3½ to 6 million. All told, buying power was stepped up at least 50 percent between 1929 and 1957, measured in 1957 before-tax dollars, and at least 40 percent in after-tax dollars, a remarkable record.

Assuming that $4,000 to $10,000 represents the middle-income bracket, by Department of Commerce count 28 million households enjoyed such an enviable buying position by 1957. They added up to nearly half the total number of households, and pulled down half the income. In 1929, by contrast, only 8 million households—20 percent of the total—were located in the middle-income range and their incomes (again in 1957 dollars) totaled only $46 billion, or one-third of the total.

This upheaval and redistribution of the national income was hailed by Arthur F. Burns, former chairman of the President's Council of Economic Advisers, as "one of the great social revolutions in history." It won ungrudging honors from the social scientists for bulging the center of the class structure with a teeming middle-income group with money to burn. It won undying respect from advertisers for creating in the middle-income group the power-wheel of consumer demand, the backbone of the U.S.

market, and the prime target for their advertised goods and services.

High wages was only one of the reasons for the spectacular rise of the new middle class, and probably not the most important. What touched off this postwar phenomenon, more likely, was the addition of one or more family breadwinners, in particular wives who entered the labor force en masse after the war. The instant result, of course, of dual pay envelopes was the boosting of millions of families into higher income brackets. The marketplace result was equally instant, as millions of families loosed scads of discretionary dollars unneeded for food-clothing-shelter requirements. The result was apocalyptic.

Probably well over half the middle-income group enjoys its current buying prowess thanks to its female members holding down, full time and part time, industrial or white-collar jobs. Bureau of Labor Statistics figures show the steady entry of such females, mostly wives, into the labor force. Whereas in 1947 the 16 million working females constituted 28 percent of the U.S. labor force, in 1950 the number climbed to 18 million (29 percent), in 1953 to 19 million (31 percent), in 1960 to 22.5 million (34 percent), and it continues to climb. By way of contrast, in 1930 only 10 million females worked (22 percent).

Giving entry to women in the labor force was the mechanization of U.S. production which created primarily office jobs, which the women filled. Significantly, in 1956 the white-collar workers outnumbered the blue-collar workers for the first time. This indicated less that the number of blue-collar jobs had declined than that the number of white-collar jobs had shot up. Bureau of Labor Statistics figures show that for the period 1950–1957, as the percentage of blue-collar workers in the entire labor population declined from 40.2 percent to 39.1 percent, the percentage of white-collar workers moved up briskly from 36.6 percent to 39.9 percent.

Hence, unlike the traditional middle class in Europe, which

is composed of professionals, shopkeepers, and myriads of small entrepreneurs, the American middle class is uniquely composed in the main of working people. They have joined the middle class not by occupation but by virtue of the weekly plural pay envelope. If traditional economists still tend to see them as workers, they do not so see themselves. Any number of studies have shown that in aspiration, in buying behavior, in social habits, they are largely indistinguishable from other middle-class inhabitants, who reside there by virtue of occupation.

It also suggests the precarious nature of the ballooning middle class, for any lengthy business recession probably will mean cutbacks in the numbers of white-collar jobs—which means women. Loss of the female pay envelope will instantly plummet the family back into the working class, aspirations or no aspirations. Should the recession deepen into a full-fledged depression, the miracle by which millions of families have lifted themselves into the heady atmosphere of the free-spending dollar by a kind of national operation-bootstrap will vanish, and the operation will collapse.

Nonetheless, despite its precarious position to which it seems to give scant regard, the middle class has been feeling its oats since the war's end. It led the mass migration out of the cities into the suburbs, moving some 1,200,000 strong as a yearly average to the suburbs between 1947 and 1953. Exchanging three- and four-room city apartments for ranch-type homes, it formed a suburban belt of nearly 33 million. This outward migration of middle-income families got its start in the gay twenties, according to *Fortune*, when about 5½ million people exchanged urban for suburban living. This migratory trickle practically dried up during the depressed thirties and did not resume flowing until after the war when it quickly rose to floodtide. But the migration had undergone a profound change in composition. Whereas in the twenties the upper crust had moved out of the cities and into big, colonial-style mansions, offering a small but luxury market for advertisers, and converting the suburbs into something of an exclusive playground for the wealthy, the fifties witnessed the dotting of the suburban landscape with hundreds of housing developments into which moved the new middle class with its massive appetite for goods and services. This was an idyllic development for national advertisers, if less so for the wealthy who oftentimes lived in sight and sound of the housing developments.

Suburbia became a kind of way of life for millions of Americans in their sentinel-like homes, a kind of national trademark, which drew satire from novelists and worried tracts from social scientists on the dress-alike, think-alike, live-alike uniformity that stamped suburban life. As noted in *The Lonely Crowd* by David Reisman, and by others, suburbanites seemed to sprout sensitive antenna which picked up clues on how the "crowd" was thinking, and which guided their behavior. Individualism took on alarming implications, and was to be avoided.

But advertisers found only pure joy when they surveyed the suburban meccas. The millions of new customers stocked their servantless homes with a wide range of appliances, decorated their well-kept lawns with fancy wrought-iron furniture, delighted in barbecued meals with the accompanying outdoor, sociable life. And, like a magnet attracting iron filings, they attracted shopping centers, department stores, radial highways leading to the suburbs.

The middle-class flight to the suburbs was made easier by cheap and quick financing by such federal agencies as HLB, FHA, HOLC, and VA. In fact, it became almost as financially feasible to buy a suburban home as to rent a city apartment, for it actually took no bigger bite out of the family income. The monthly payment to the suburban mortgagor was about the same as the monthly rental to the city landlord. Instead of thousands of dollars as down payment, 6 to 10 percent interest on first mortgage, and 10 to 25 percent interest on second mortgage, which were the stiff terms commonly prevailing before the war, the VA loan system after the war, for example, enabled a veteran to get a government-guaranteed mortgage at 4 percent without even a nickel's down payment. Banks were ready, able, and willing to advance the building money since the mortgage was guaranteed. And builders, using on-site, mass-production methods, turned out vast acreages of ranch-style housing developments. They used "dry wall" rather than the prewar lath and plaster, preassembled walls, precut frames, and found other prefabrication shortcuts to slice the housing costs, both material and labor. All this helped to drop the price of ranch houses into the $4,000-a-year-and-up family's grasp.

Fortune magazine estimated, for example, that in one big Eastern development the house selling for $10,500, if designed and built to order, would sell for about $14,000, and the $16,000 model for about $22,000. At times the builders could hardly keep up with demand. By 1956 the Federal Reserve Board made the landmark announcement that for the first time more than half the families in the U.S. owned their own homes. Moreover, many of these families got busy improving their homes in the very first years of occupancy. Garages were enlarged to accommodate garden tools, outdoor furniture, bicycles; kitchens were enlarged to accommodate a panoply of built-in appliances; closet and storage space was added, plus an extra bathroom, rumpus room, terraces, fireplace, air conditioning, wall-to-wall carpeting. They neither tired nor ran out of money for more luxurious living, only went into debt.

But debt held no visible peril for them, and none was more worthy than the time-purchase of new cars. For, as *Fortune* says, no other machine ever invented did more to puff up their egos and win them status than the latest-model car. They lavished considerably more than both the lower- and upper-income classes in percentage of income spent on cars, fawned over them, and accounted for more than half of all new cars sold. So long as middle-class optimism continued to bubble merrily, time payments extending over three years were shrugged off, and few even bothered to read the fine-print financing contract which called for steep interest rates. For the new car bestowed on them the highest order of personal gratification. It released them from worldly irritations and frustrations. It offered in one 3,000-pound bechromed and begadgeted mechanism everything the Indian maharajah got out of his rug and Aladdin got out of his lamp. For the novitiates to the middle class, after years of privation and unrewarding labors, this meant everything. Recognizing it, one auto executive noted that the middle class is "willing to chin itself to buy a better car."

By better car he meant one loaded up with power steering, power brakes, automatic transmission, deluxe gadgets, even bumpers to protect bumpers, all of which loaded hundreds of extra dollars onto the car cost. But the deluxe treatment was precisely what the middle class craved for, and as the middle class indulged itself the auto manufacturers engaged in a contest to see who could offer the fuller treatment. In the process, low-priced cars became one of the nation's leading misnomers. The four-door Ford sedan which was $650 in 1929, as *Fortune* noted, rose to $1,802 by 1956. During the same period, by contrast, the Cadillac went from $3,595 to $3,903. Yet despite the sharp price jumps of the popular cars an average of 6 million of them were sold annually, with sales hitting an all-time high of 7,400,000 in 1955.

With something of the car mania of the twenties returning in the fifties, the Federal Reserve Board observed that whereas in 1949 about 50 percent of all families owned a car, by 1958 about 70 percent owned one, and the number of multiple-car families rose from 3 percent to 10 percent. The growth of suburbia, of course, had much to do with this. But the middle-class touch was seen in another statistic—the age of cars on the road. Whereas in 1949 most cars were still of prewar vintage, by 1958 nearly half were less than five years old. And the statistic that kept traffic planners awake at night was the total number of cars choking the radial highways between the big cities and the suburbs, which rose nationally during that period from 27 million to 46 million.

The middle class also liked to eat, and eat well, as indicated by the prodigious rise in the nation's food bill from $20 billion in 1941 to $80 billion in 1960. A considerable portion of this rise was owing, of course, to higher prices, but enough of it was not as to startle both food company executives and traditional economists who previously had accepted without question the hitherto immutable law of food consumption, that as income rises the percentage spent by families on food tends to decline. The law, laid down by Adam Smith in the early stages of capitalism, had said that human wants could all be expanded except one, which was physiologically restricted to the size of a man's stomach. But Adam Smith did not have to reckon with the American middle class. Instead of falling, the part of income allocated by Americans for food, which was 24 percent in 1941, rose in the postwar years to nearly 27 percent, signaling something of a kitchen revolution in which old eating habits were being overthrown and new ones installed. Meat, dairy products, fruit, vegetables appeared more frequently on American plates, replacing the potatoes and grains diet that was the centuries-old mark of low-income families. In a few decades the U.S. per capita consumption of oranges rose from 20 pounds to 58, chicken from 14 pounds to 23, beef from 59 pounds to 72, tomatoes from 27 pounds to 53, ice cream from 9 pounds to 17, and eggs from 318 to 405, according to the Department of Agriculture.

But eating better was only the first stage of the revolution. The second stage was eating more conveniently, a movement in which the entire food industry joined in fervor. As supermarket shelves overflowed with canned, precooked, frozen, individually apportioned, ready-to-eat foods, the job-holding or just leisure-bent middle-class housewives were freed of such nasty kitchen chores as washing, peeling, shelling, measuring, slicing, plucking, cooking. Rather than the five or six hours required of earlier housewifely generations for meal preparation, they now threw together three heat-and-serve meals in about 80 minutes flat.

Kitchen life began to revolve in millions of homes around coffee without the pot, cake without the fuss or clean-up mess, fish without the cooking smell, salad dressing in an envelope. In fact, those who chose the freezer way of life had nothing more arduous to do than the ordering of frozen foods by catalog from one of the 2,500 food-freezer plans in the U.S. It was a far cry indeed from the strawberries-in-December or ocean-fish-in-the-hinterland which was the narrow and somewhat futile appeal of the frozen foods when they first appeared in the depressed thirties. Only the monied few could afford them. But in the prosperous fifties frozen food sales climbed from $655 million in 1950 to $2.2 billion by 1957, almost a fourfold increase. And by 1958 some 60 million frozen dinners, 400 million frozen potpies, 75 million frozen fruit and ice cream pies, and countless other frozen goodies, went down American gullets. The frozen food industry, like many others, was a sleeping beauty awakened by the kiss of prosperity.

Similar to the auto industry, the food industry quickly learned to trade on the middle-class bewitchment with a life of ease. In the words of Charles G. Mortimer, president of General Foods Corporation, the middle class found the "built-in maid service of the convenience foods" irresistible. It gladly shelled out extra money for ready-to-eat foods which, according to the Department of Agriculture, cost about one-third more but required three-quarters less time than meals prepared from scratch. As a result, General Foods passed the billion-dollar-net-sales in 1957 for the first time in its history.

Middle-class buying habits also stood the clothing industry on its ear as middle-class males developed a passion for trench coats with zip-in linings, sports jackets, slacks, a rainbow of sports shirts, tee shirts, lightweight pajamas, and summer suits. Middle-class females helped out by filling their closets with colorful blouses, skirts, mix-and-match outfits, ensembles, and knock-about coats. Both acquired special skiing, golfing, boating outfits, of

which, few if any, found a place before the war in the middle-
class wardrobe. But the informality of the suburbs, the leisure,
the extra cash, conspired to produce a hankering for these special-
purpose clothes. As *Sales Management* magazine early observed:
"Leisure duds have been adopted for all-day wear." Confirmation
turned up in Bureau of Census statistics which showed production of casual clothes up, and formal clothes down. In 1947, for
instance, sports shirts were only 21 percent of total shirt production, and dress shirts 79 percent, but by 1953 their positions were
reversed, with sports shirts grabbing 66 percent of shirt production and dress shirts trailing badly with 34 percent. Sports jackets
moved up from 5 to 9 million in the same period, men's slacks from
42 to 52 million, as business suits slipped from 26 to 22 million.
As for women's clothes, the trend to casual dress pushed up
blouse sales from $250 million in 1948 to $310 million in 1953,
skirt sales from $110 to $190 million. And practically a new industry was created overnight to cater to the subteens who wanted
to dress with the same casual elegance as their middle-class parents.

The very meaning of casual clothes changed in the nation's
vocabulary, no longer signifying the pair of old pants worn while
cleaning out the basement but the new suburban leisure. In a
Chicago *Tribune* survey in 1958, nearly half the men questioned
felt they could properly "go almost anywhere in a sports shirt"
and 63 percent decided they did not need a tie to go "most places."

The only fly in the ointment for the clothing industry was
that suburbanites spent less for clothes than urban dwellers. In
Life magazine's 1957 "Study of Consumer Expenditures," whereas
middle-income urban families averaged $625 yearly for clothing
and footwear, suburban families averaged only $385. Unfortu-
nately, at least for the clothing industry, casual clothes were
also less expensive clothes. But the American Institute of Men's
and Boy's Wear attempted to redress the situation by pushing
a "Dress Right—You Can't Afford Not To" promotion. And,
thereafter, every suburbanite who sauntered into a men's shop

to buy sports shirts or slacks was reminded that dress shirts were needed on certain occasions, and wasn't his supply getting low? The sales picture of formal clothes brightened a bit as a result, as did industry executives.

In its frenetic pursuit of amusement, the middle class became the apple of the travel industry's eye, as fun-loving dollars went freely for travel, particularly foreign travel. Between 1950–1957 the middle class just about single-handedly boosted the nation's travel expenditure from 1 billion to 2 billion dollars. By 1960 the number of new and renewed passports issued to Americans itching to explore the four corners of the world soared to 853,000, about four times that of a decade earlier. In volume, this far exceeds the exodus of Americans even in the heyday of the prosperous twenties, but there was another big difference. In the twenties foreign travel was *de rigueur* for fashionable people of great wealth who spent a leisurely six months or a year on the Grand Tour, accompanied by a dozen or more pieces of fine luggage, governesses, and servants. Postwar prosperity has swept all this away. The Grand Tour has shrunk to something far less grand as today's middle-class tourists sprint in a 17-day race through France, Britain, and/or Italy. Timetable rubbernecking in a staggering number of European cities is crammed into the scant three-week vacation of the 9-to-5, white-collar middle class. The driving compulsion is to do everything up brown.

Boating has become another beneficiary of middle-class largess. By 1958 more than 37 million Americans, mostly middle class, sailed or put-putted around the nation's waterways in 7½ million recreational boats, more than triple the number afloat in 1947. Spending for new and used boats, engines, fuel, repairs, docking, storage, boat-club memberships, hit a record $2 billion, again more than triple what was spent in 1950. Even land-locked buffs used 1½ million boat trailers to haul some of the 500,000 motorboats, 500,000 sailboats, and almost 2½ million dinghies, prams and rowboats to the nearest waterways. The outboard boom of the fifties was faintly reminiscent of the yacht splurge of the twenties.

Backyard swimming pools became the rage in the suburbs, making the home swimming pool industry the second fastest growing industry in the U.S. From 2,500 in 1948, the number of home swimming pools climbed to 124,000 by 1959, an astronomical 4,900 percent increase. Nor was there anything niggardly about the pools, for most of them, a generous 15' by 30' or 20' by 40', were lavished with ladders, filters, diving boards, underwater lights, vacuum cleaners, water heaters.

Blessings were also bestowed on hobby manufacturers. Between 1940 and 1958 sales went from $40 million to $350 million, much of it on home workshop tools, hi-fi's, sporting and athletic goods, bowling alleys, golf greens. And the middle class became habitués, often on expense accounts, of the classier hotels, restaurants, night clubs, country clubs.

In the twenties the idle rich who picked up such baubles as "steam yachts, private railway cars, movie actresses, and hunting lodges," as one writer has put it, had scant impact on the national economy. In the fifties, on the contrary, the middle class which soaked up vast quantities of up-graded, up-priced merchandise spark-plugged the national economy. Because of its largely working-class origin, many of its older members in particular felt that free-spending was a vaguely dangerous and sinful act. But enough of them spent like mad to make them "the most important group of consumers in the nation's economy," in the judgment of the Department of Labor in 1959. As they crossed the Rubicon from working class to the lower-middle class most of them did not look back with any regret at the hard life they were leaving.

The Profusion of Products 6

Nearly 200 years ago Adam Smith wrote that as the economy expands there "arises a demand for every sort of material which human invention can employ, either usefully or ornamentally, in building, dress, equipage, or household furniture." The flourishing postwar U.S. economy provides impressive confirmation indeed of his view. Members of the middle class who reached maturity in the thirties are in a singularly good position to confirm it for themselves.

Today's worries on how to make ends meet have scant resemblance to the worries that plagued them 25 years ago. Mostly they are concerned with how to pay for the second car, the suburban house, the son's college expenses, the family vacation, the orthodontist's bills, as a director of the National Association of Mutual Savings Banks pointed out.

Life in the suburbs virtually requires the owning of one car; some families need two, some three. Practically every suburban home is equipped with a telephone and one or more extensions, and many homes have a separate instrument with its own listing for their teenagers. As the older members of today's middle class will testify, back in the thirties the car and the telephone along with a grand array of products that the average family needs today were in the luxury class for most families.

Prosperity has profoundly, if subtly, transformed attitudes, thinking, buying habits, and what were formerly luxuries are today's needs. And needs are linked endlessly to new needs, particularly for the middle class whose needs have a way all their own of expanding in the sunny atmosphere of optimism. Buoyed by the belief that good times lie ahead, the middle class goes gaily ahead indulging its needs, to the point where the word has probably become the most exercised in the middle-class vocabulary. Frequently it exhibits a surprising lack of togetherness with family income, for middle-class families think nothing of digging themselves deeper in debt to buy the season's new offerings.

Since 1945 U.S. industry has set out forthrightly to meet this challenge of middle-class needs by churning out new products at a fantastic tempo. As part of the jockeying for better economic position, U.S. companies have merged and diversified on a scale hitherto unknown. Many of the founders of old-time companies would undoubtedly be astonished to see the range of products their companies are producing today. Some of the impetus has been provided by a benevolent tax structure which offers capital gains and losses, but by far the most potent reason to pursue diversification and new products has been soaring corporate profits. What board of directors in its right mind would turn its back on a trend that has brought such unqualified corporate year-end cheer? Inevitably, the trend has become something of a landslide. And more and more annual reports today set aside a special section for corporate diversification and new products as of special interest for stockholders, which it is, for they scan it for signs of the company's vigor. Today corporate maps depicting far-flung business operations and product distribution tend to resemble the cross-hatched lines of a Jackson Pollack painting.

Take Philco, for example, which began with the production of storage batteries and radios and then went into freezers, TV's, electric ranges. Or the Longines-Wittnauer Watch Company, which moved into cameras, projectors, and photographic accessories. Or the Borden Company, which found itself in the mincemeat, ethical pharmaceutical and chemical business as well as in the dairy business. Similarly, Du Pont moved from explosives into dyes, paints, lacquers, artificial fabrics, film. Pillsbury Mills, after nearly a century as a miller, dropped the restricting "Mills" from its name when it went into baking mixes, refrigerated products, farm feeds. The Bendix Aviation Corporation, similarly, dropped "Aviation" from its name when it pushed into electronics, computers, machine tools, hydraulics. The Remington Company branched out into cutlery, cash registers, typewriters, firearms. General Mills went into flour, formula feeds, package foods, chemical and mechanical products. The Hercules Powder Company went from explosives into synthetic resins, plasticizers, chemical cotton, cellulose derivatives, paper-making chemicals. Minnesota Mining & Manufacturing found itself turning out some 40 different product lines and some 25,000 separate items. American Machine & Foundry went into automatic pin setters for bowling alleys, tricycles, flip-top cigarette box machinery. The virtuosity of products and forays into other fields was such that when the Hamilton Watch Company began manufacturing fuses and timing devices for guided missiles and rockets, its president expressed the hope in *Printers' Ink* that people would recall that "they still make watches."

Few, if any, big companies today would admit that they do not look to diversification and new products as the main avenue to corporate prosperity. The thinking that domineers corporate board rooms around the nation today is that in new products the American businessman has found a new frontier to open.

One or two merchant philosophers have even expressed the belief that this new product frontier has replaced the territorial one that closed in the 1890's. It promises to act as a seminal, generative force on the economy just as the earlier one did.

The adventurous businessman, they say, is offered the opportunity today to produce in his industrial laboratories the modern equivalents to the automobile, radio, incandescent lamp, airplane, motion picture, all of which so radically altered the nation's living habits in the first 50 years of the current century. The argument has more than the ring of validity, considering the introduction of synthetic fibers, frozen foods, electronic computers, and other economy-shaking discoveries and inventions since the war. Each year the Patent Office in Washington busily registers thousands of lesser brain children, which underscores, if nothing else, the odd recommendation of Henry Ellsworth, the Patent Commissioner in 1845, that the Patent Office be closed because he thought everything useful had already been invented.

Nonetheless, taking nothing away from these momentous events, the plain truth of the matter is that almost all the new products being loosed on the market today are not really new at all. With a few praiseworthy exceptions, they are but trifling modifications of goods now on the market. The chances are overwhelming that they are no more than package face-liftings (a cereal with a new premium), trivial design changes (this year's model), size changes (king-size cigarettes), or color changes (colored appliances). Many bear the label "new" for no particular better reason than that a million-dollar promotion says so. But whatever the reason it does not really matter, for the middle class stands anxiously at the cash register ready to buy what has been so magically designated. Its members clamor for "new products, however good the old ones may be," as the president of the Grocery Manufacturers of America said, with seeming good-natured resignation, and breathes there an advertiser with soul so dead who will not give what the public clamors for? The answer, offered by a cynical marketing magazine, is that a new product is "anything that offers a sales peg on which to hang a buyer attraction."

Measured by this definition, the food business easily qualifies as a new product business. Consider that about half of all the food products on the shelves today were not there eight years ago, and judging by food marketers' plans the pace of new product arrivals will be stepped up in the next few years. A Food Engineering report, for instance, estimates that about 75 percent of the food companies are readying countless new items for the market. The food companies themselves acknowledge that the current rate of new product entry is three to ten times what it was in 1948.

"Almost everyone is getting into the new product race," wrote a commentator in the *Harvard Business Review,* who saw the deluge as "running at an all-time high." All this means is that the entire food business has been converted into a powder keg of new product competition, with each company pressuring its product development people to speed things up. Each seems ultra-sensitive to the industry brooding that new products hold the key to prosperity or demise.

Hence, in 1957 alone, an estimated 6,000 new grocery items were introduced, about 200 per working day. They caused a terrible crush on retailers' shelves and induced not a few of them to recall nostalgically the prewar days when the supermarket, in its infancy, carried about 1,000 items. Today the same supermarket carries 6,000 to 8,000 items. And even with enlarged shelf space and extending gondolas plus the installation of the latest IBM machines to keep track of the swollen inventories, harried supermarket operators still cannot handle the daily flood of new products. For as fast as shelf space is built and gondolas put in place, new items jam them. Moreover, the store clerks have one devil of a time keeping up with the daily changes of prices, brands, packages, sizes. As a measure of self-defense, the supermarket operators rudely weed out most of the new product offerings, as a general rule making room only for the higher profit-margin items. To sweeten the supermarket operators' dispositions the food companies frequently offer a generous advertising allowance.

The laws of space being what they are, shelf room can generally be made only by pushing out other items. "Of eight new products the chain picks up, it drops five," a chain executive told the American Marketing Association. He described as a typical chain's experience the taking on of 4,292 new items and the dropping of 3,725 during a two-year period—a net gain of 567 items. That does not tell anywhere near the whole story. The 4,292 accepted items comprised only one-quarter of all the new items seriously considered during that period by the supermarket operator. The other three-quarters were turned down. Not even included in the count were thousands of items which simply failed to engage the buyer's serious attention and were dismissed out of hand.

From the record, then, it is abundantly clear that quick entry and quick demise is the common fate of almost all new food products. They can enjoy an average life expectancy of two years, a span which is steadily shrinking, a vital statistic which intensifies the mad scramble of the food companies to toss ever more entries into the new product sweepstake. For the jackpot profits are high when one clicks with the public. But the view from the cemetery is dreadful.

The new product race, although at its flagrant best in the food field, is not limited to the food companies. The tobacco companies, for example, between January 1, 1958, and July 1, 1959, came up with such new brands as Marfield, Diplomat, Richmond, Spring, Alpine, Belair, Vanguard, Life, Frappe, and Trim. These crowded into a cigarette market already chaotic with multiple sizes, packs, types. At the same time, confounding the consumer's problem of choice still further, Raleigh began to pack its cigarettes upside down, Old Gold turned out a "spin" filter, Parliament a "hi-fi" filter, King Sano a new "soft" smoke, Hit Parade a filter tip with 40,000 traps (out-trapping Parliament's 30,000 and Viceroy's 20,000), Benson & Hedges a "crimped" seam, and Camel a revamped package.

So, too, with the lipstick manufacturers who originally made lipsticks in only two colors—dark for daytime and light for evening. Then in 1946 a couple of translucent reds were introduced, which caught on, and soon a Pandora's box of colors was opened to tempt milady's fancy. The prewar humble lipstick was reverentially placed on a postwar fashion pedestal and the obiter dictum handed down in the fashion world was that the lipstick color was as important as the right skirt length. The lipstick was no longer sold as an aid to complexion but as an adjunct to wardrobe. And among the lower-middle class, which found itself newly and intensively preoccupied with everything in the world of fashion, the promotional theme scored a neat bullseye. The result: an astonishing range of lipstick colors. And a scouring of the lipstick manufacturers' vocabulary to describe them. The reds, for example, included several true reds, red reds, a primaeval red, the real thing red, pure red, clear red, look-out red, stop red, certainly red, flag red, real-real red, wear-with-all red, never-before-a-lipstick-so-red, etc. The trade press depicted the plight of a Denver druggist who decided to build identity for his store by specializing in lipsticks and soon was up to his ears in 1,200 different ones.

In line with ordinary merchandising practice, as the lipstick was elevated as a fashion item, so was the price elevated. Whereas before the war more than half of the lipsticks sold were of the 10-cent variety, by 1958 more than 80 percent of the lipsticks were in the $1 to $1.35 class. Bringing still more cheer to the lipstick manufacturers was the news that the age of lipstick wearers was moving down to the tenderer years. "Today, young girls of

13 and 14 who wear lipstick are the rule, not the exception," reported *American Druggist.* A high school survey disclosed that 98.6 percent of the girls applied lipstick daily.

The food field offers some more striking examples of new products. Before the war the typical shop specializing in cheeses carried about two dozen vareties. By 1958 the same store stocked as many as 400 varieties and sold them under as many as 800 brand names. The supermarket checked in with from 50 to 100 different ones. A New York department store carried 256. It was up to the housewife to train her olfactory sense to detect the "slightly gamey smell of Camembert, the aromatic odor of well cured Parmesan, the sharp and slightly bitter breath of limburger, the sulphurous whiff of the Roquefort, the heaviness and satisfying breath of the indolent Brie," as a newspaper food columnist wrote. The cheeses also ranged in texture from the "coziest ripeness to hardness that yields only to a saw, the ax, and the grater" and in flavor from "dew-drop mildness to the kinds that can be eaten only with a gas mask."

Bake mixes came out in a host of new flavors. Added to the usual white, yellow, and chocolate mixes were such enticements as orange, caramel, spice, burnt sugar maple, confetti angel food, butterscotch, apple chip, and sponge cake mixes. As each company added to its brand line, and in multiple sizes, entire aisles of supermarkets were piled nearly ceiling-high with the mixes. "You need a whole store just for the mixes," a grocer complained to the *Wall Street Journal.* "Every time a new one comes out, I just have to push an old one off the shelves."

Household pets were not neglected either. Some 27 brands of dog food were carried by the supermarket—a distinct improvement for man's best friend who not too many years ago had to be content with leftover dinner scraps. The canary, too, had its own special menu of eating food, song food, and cuttlebones and gravel for comfort. And the parakeet was entitled to something else, and the lovebirds to something else still. Before the war the retailer carried just one kind of birdseed that seemed to make all the birds happy.

Almost alone, the brewing industry failed to get its fair share of the nation's prosperity. For about a decade the per capita sales slowly shrank as the nation's beer drinkers cultivated a middle-class taste for living with Scotch or bourbon. "You never hear of beer parties any more," a brewer lamented in *Tide*. "Good times have made beer something of an outcast." The brewing industry was not content to cry in its beer and watch its sales decline. The big brewers threw millions of promotional dollars yearly in a counterattack to rout the plebeian image of beer from the national consciousness. Beer ads showed suburban hostesses happily serving beer at lawn parties. But the image of beer as the poor man's drink proved hardy and sales continued to lag. All the brewing millions failed to induce the new middle class to return to its prewar pastime of idling away the hours over a couple of glasses of cold suds. The middle class was too busy fooling around with its car, hi-fi, golf, and home workshop.

Shopping in a supermarket in the postwar years was like walking into an Oriental bazaar. The housewife clutched her shopping list as though she were trying to hold onto her senses as she wheeled a shopping cart down the canyons of multicolored, multisized, and multibranded goods. Everything was "one grand shout," as one researcher described its impact on the housewife. "Her pulse rate and respiration changed. She was poised like a cat, ready to spring when she saw something new and better. Quicker. Tastier. Newer. A better buy. A handier spout. A more promising promise," was the way *The Wedge*, an agency house organ, described it. And since she spent on an average 20 minutes for her tour of shopping, some agency mathematician figured out that some 300 to 400 items a minute clawed for her attention.

In the late fifties a Du Pont study produced as a major conclusion that "spontaneous" shopping was greater than ever before, disclosing that about 75 percent of the housewife's buying decisions inside the supermarket were "impulse" decisions. They were not in her mind when she entered the store. Ten years previously, about 50 percent of her purchases were characterized as "impulse." The trend was gratifying evidence to the high-powered merchandisers that their shockingly colorful displays had forced a further retreat by the housewife from shopping ration-ality. It was hailed as an omen of ultimate victory by one mer-chandiser who urged "more aggressive selling, better in-store pro-motion, and improved packaging," and foresaw the nature of ultimate victory as the automation of the shopping function.

The national advertisers did not have everything their own way, for the supermarkets, chains, and discount houses moved to cash in on the prosperity with their own privately branded items. Located in the suburban giant shopping centers, they were in a good strategic position to wean suburban shoppers to their own brands. A & P, Sears, Safeway, Kroger, Penney, Ward, American Stores, and Woolworth hence began to win sales ground in the battle with the nationally advertised brands and, according to the *Wall Street Journal*, had "the most ambitious expansion plans" for the future. The battle promised to be long and bitter for by the late fifties the national brands still had about 75 percent of total sales, and private brands about 25 percent, but the gap was slowly closing.

Super Market Merchandising described the new development as "the third revolution," the first being the rise of the chain it-self, the second the introduction of self-service, and the third the muscling in by the giant suburban retailers into the manufacturing process itself. For the next logical step for the giant-traffic re-tailer after pushing his own brands was their manufacturing. And some of the retailers did this on a vast scale. In 1959, for instance, of A & P's estimated $5 billion in sales, about $1 billion was in its own Jane Parker, Worthmore, Bokar, Red Circle, Eight o'Clock, Ann Page, and Bright Sail private brands. To produce its own brands, according to *Sales Management*, A & P owned outright some 35 bakeries, 12 coffee-roasting plants, 6 manufacturing plants, 4 salmon canneries in Alaska, 3 cheese plants, 2 milk-processing plants, and a creamery. A & P ranked with General Foods as the nation's largest coffee roasters, one of the five largest bakers, and was steadfastly capturing sales for its own eggs, butter, juice blends, canned and frozen fish, mixes, prepared meats and produce. In many of its stores, in fact, there were *no* competing brands, a survey revealed. And even where A & P was not manufacturing its own brand of something, Borden, Kellogg, General Foods, Ralston Purina, and other suppliers simply affixed A & P's own labels to the something.

The giant retailers also made heavy inroads in non-food items, especially durables. Their appliances, TV's, radios and home furnishings cut deeply into the sales of the nationally advertised brands. In 1959 one private brand tire was on every car (on an average), and about 25 percent of the 50 million sold that year were sold at local gas stations. About half of the 26 million storage batteries sold yearly also were of the private brand variety.

What happened to brand loyalty was a sad story. In 1950 the Brand Names Foundation already noted with alarm that shoppers were given to switching around their brands of dentifrices, cereals, soaps, gasolines, apparel. But as the number of brands, sizes, packages mounted to incredible proportions the shoppers seemed to carry out their function with no sympathy for the millions of promotional dollars so carefully calculated to build sturdy brand images. Yet the result was inevitable, for the shoppers were assailed by advertisers each of whose bold claims canceled each other out. Consider detergents, for instance, which bid for favor with these promises: "No detergent under the sun gets the clothes whiter, brighter"; "Beats the sun for getting the clothes whiter without a bleach"; "Washes more kinds of clothes whiter and brighter"; "Washes clothes whiter without a bleach"; "Gives you a whiter wash without bleaching than any other 'no rinse' suds with bleach added"; "Alone gets clothes whiter than bleach."

Forced to choose among such one-note siren calls understandably reduced the shoppers to a state of confusion (or more probably indifference). A Chicago *Tribune* study, for instance, disclosed that the average housewife just about managed to keep clear the distinction between detergents and soaps. The detergents she considered generally superior in cleaning power, the soaps were judged milder, less allergenic, and productive of "fluffier" clothes. But beyond that, all was chaos. She could not tell one claim from another. She exhibited a chronic inclination to attribute any advertising claim to her favorite cleanser, no matter what it was. Even the placebo claim, "Test after test proves no detergent under the sun gets out more dirt than" dreamed up by the researchers, was credited to her favorite cleanser.

Brand deterioration appeared inexorably in other consumer fields, too. Few car owners replaced tires with the same brand and a shocking number could not even remember the make of the old tire so they could not tell if they were switching brands. About one-quarter of the cigarette smokers switched to another brand in less than two years, about half switched in less than four years, and only one-third steadfastly puffed away at the same brand for as long as six years. Washing machine buyers failed to repurchase the same brand even when satisfied by its performance record. Liquor drinkers were "a fickle lot," according to a distillery executive. About 80 percent of the motorists were convinced that all gasoline brands were about the same and blithely switched brands. In cosmetics, the strong brand loyalty in the early teens stopped abruptly at the college level, where about half the students changed face cream, home permanent, lipstick, nail polish, and toilet soap brands favored before college.

An article in the *Harvard Business Review* came to the conclusion that there were few "loyalty-prone families." At the University of Michigan's Survey Research Center, Eva Mueller came to the same conclusion: "Automatic repeat buying of the same brand is infrequent regardless of previous experience." And a merchandiser wrote glumly of the public indifference: "One brand or another—what difference does it make?"

Ad agencies were browbeaten to come up with distinguishing product claims—never mind that the products themselves were not blessed with such attributes. Ad agencies were somewhat in the same uncomfortable predicament as the housewife, and because they could not come up with some world-beating theme they tended to copy each other's campaigns. "There may have been a day," *The Wedge* advised advertisers in round-robin fashion, "when young brides would take a loyalty oath to Pear's Soap until death should part them. But today the woman who buys your product is likely to be hurried and harried, overworked and underappreciated. As she fights her way into the supermarket with a mass of problems tugging at her mind and a mess of kids tugging at her skirt, she is not thinking beautiful and loyal thoughts about your product. Chances are she has momentarily forgotten just what she is after."

Bereft of brand loyalty, the advertisers fought for the housewife's attentions by another wily gambit. Particularly in the food fields, coupon deals, boxtops, price-offs, two-for-ones, premiums, money-by-return-mail, and other kinds of wheeling and dealing were rife. Between 1955 and 1959, for certain food categories, as sales increased by 30 percent the number of deals increased by 178 percent, according to A. C. Nielsen Co. In 1959 a thumping $1 billion worth of coupons was distributed to housewives. Large chains reported from one-third to one-half of dentifrice sales accounted for by deals, at times as much as three-quarters. A newspaper count convinced a speaker before the National Cranberry Association that "almost a third of all food advertising was gimmick advertising."

Trouble was that many advertisers soon found themselves hoisted high on their own petard. For the housewives, studies showed, were turning by the millions into deal-buyers only.

They bought one deal after another, caring not a hoot about the brand. "The best known brand today," said one adman sarcastically, "is 10-cents-off."

In 1956 Ralston Purina set the cereal world buzzing by its decision to drop all boxtop premiums. It announced its complete surrender on every cereal box: "Look, Ma, No Premiums." It went on to say: "In this box you'll find no trading stamps, space ships, fission guns. Nothing that rips, roars or rolls, goes SH-boom or even pttt. . . . No Venetian poison rings, slave bracelets, or pictures of Yosemite." To the nation's grocers, digging out from an unrelenting blizzard of coupons, Ralston proclaimed: "Grocers of America, Rejoice! No more Cereal Premiums."

Without doubt, every cereal manufacturer cast envious eyes at the Ralston experiment, but none was ready to abandon the tactic by which the giant of them all, Procter & Gamble, had orbited itself into stellar magnitude. The something-extra approach was deemed essential to keep one jump ahead of the competition. A year later, as sales still rose, Ralston still sailed gallantly alone.

With so many new products thrown daily into the struggle for sales supremacy, the death toll rose appallingly high. It was almost a working statistic among advertisers that four out of every five new products failed. The U.S. Small Business Administration discovered that 98 percent fell by the wayside during the first two years. And big companies had a better record than small companies. About 81 percent of their products perished as against the 98 percent for firms of all sizes. But even many of the successful products enjoyed the briefest stay at the top before they were knocked off by newcomers. Of every ten leading brands, three were toppled from first place in a decade by new brands, Arthur C. Nielsen, Jr., discovered.

As the marketplace became one big guillotine for new products, it served the same macabre function for many corporations. And if new product development held out the best hope for survival, it also poised the threat of corporate demise. For the records show that fully two-thirds of the 100 leading companies in 1909 have disappeared, more than half those in 1919 have gone, and of today's 100 leading companies the majority arrived in the past 25 years. The unspoken question that haunted the corporate board rooms around the nation hence was: "Will this company be in business 25 years from now?"

Efforts to ferret out the reasons for new product failures ordinarily turned up shortcomings in process engineering, pilot-plant work, production-cost estimates, and market research. Heard surprisingly often at post-mortems was the charge that company executives worked too often at odds with each other. "Coopera-tion was notoriously weak in many companies and nearly non-existent in some," an across-the-board Booz, Allen & Hamilton management survey disclosed. In the survey some 80 percent of the queried executives called their companies' interdepartment exchange of information "marginal" or "poor." "Pat" organiza-tion thinking came in for considerable scolding.

Too many new products were "nothing more than daydreams of management—a kind of formalized make-believe," said Gilbert Miles, packaging manager of Colgate-Palmolive. Another veteran lashed the common practice of "clients and ad agencies meeting in smoke-filled rooms and snowing each other." Another likened most new products derisively to "the jokesmith's left-handed monkey wrench"—they supplied no genuine consumer want or need. A common plaint that recurred like the down-beat in jazz was that the situation was the case of superfluous products seek-ing to invade fields already overcrowded with superfluous products. To look for anything but an almost unrelieved crop of failures, thus bordered on economic drollery. They "should never have been born," opined Robert M. Oliver, vice-president of Thomas A. Edison Industries.

Several observers expressed the irreverent belief that mar-keting of new products was at bottom a gamble pure and simple. "Picking product winners is a lot like picking turf winners," an engineering executive figured. An ad agency president thought the process was closer to "shooting craps." The Sales Executive

Club heard a new product specialist liken it to "a game of poker. If you see the product is not going well, the trick is to fold your hand as early as possible. Most companies have to play a table-stakes game. With just so many chips in front of you, the sure way to go broke is to stick along for three or four cards on every hand."

But if picking market winners was not exactly a pure gamble, as suggested by the superior playing record of the big companies, it was not scientific by a long shot, as indicated by the $250 million Edsel fiasco. No new product was so well researched, well produced, well marketed, well financed as the Edsel, yet it failed.

Several old-time marketers used the Edsel failure to sound off against the marketing philosophy that gained ascendancy in the fifties. In brief it was that new products must yield a profit after two or three years or be pushed aside for something else. The old-timers were certain that many new products are given up for dead before their time. They argued that marketing history was studded with initial failures that turned eventually into successes. Henry Ford failed with his first two cars and by today's standards he should have given up. In the same way the incandescent lamp, the telephone, the typewriter, were anything but scintillating sales successes when introduced. In fact few important products in marketing history were quick bellringers.

On the other hand, bringing out a new product today is a frightfully expensive business, and getting more so yearly, and few companies enjoy such financial reserves as to eye their depletion with anything resembling equanimity. To stay overly long with a losing product might send them to the wall. In 1959 it cost in the neighborhood of $1 million to market a new grocery product nationally, the U.S. Wholesale Grocers Association was told—and the figure "could run to $10 or $20 million." The amount depended on such factors as how entrenched the competition was and how heavily he was advertising. To introduce a new product meant matching the competition's advertising, dollar for dollar.

The Gillette Safety Razor Company set aside a $3¼ million promotion for its Super Blue blade. The Carnation Company invested $3 to $5 million to gain a national market. Million-dollar sendoffs were given the Hoover Company's electric floor washer, Lanolin Plus's children's hair waving shampoo, Pfizer's drug Diabinese, Johnson's wax Glade, Scott's newly packaged Waldorf tissue, Old Forester's 86-proof bourbon.

In the heavily competitive proprietary drug and dentifrice fields the amounts soar. "We can't get by on a $1 million promotion cost any more; now it takes $5 to $8 million to introduce a product on a national scale," a Colgate executive told stockholders. "Don't expect a $5 million advertising appropriation to buy a large segment of the aspirin market, when the entrenched opposition is already spending $8 to $10 million," a Warner-Lambert Pharmaceutical Company executive advised.

But so long as the middle class exhibited an unflagging eagerness to buy new products, U.S. companies would continue to churn them out by the carload. From less than $1 billion before the war, by 1960 an estimated $9.5 billion were poured into research and development, mostly of new products, according to a McGraw-Hill study. With a new product death toll of 80 to 98 percent the dollar amount that went down the national drain was staggering to contemplate. No figures are available from which to draw a reliable estimate, but a stab is perhaps $7 billion for the year 1960 alone.

This was a stiff price for the nation to pay for its tasty new-product *smörgåsbord*, particularly when the cost of product failures was inevitably loaded onto prices of the products that managed to capture the public fancy. But the middle class, for whose benefit all this was directed, probably would not contain its spending spree even if it knew, for doubtless it would not care.

7 The Meaning to the Middle Class

In the ancient fable six blind men felt the side, tusk, trunk, knee, ear, and tail of an elephant and were separately convinced by their tactile examination that the creature was shaped like a wall, spear, snake, tree, fan, and rope. Today the social scientists find themselves in a position not unlike that of the blind men, for depending on what part they probe, the U.S. class structure assumes differing shapes and meanings to them. If the blind men's limitations were owing to their physical standpoint, the social scientists' are due mainly to their philosophical standpoint.

Before the war and particularly during the Great Depression they were dominated in their standpoint by Mills, Marx, Veblen, the Lynds, and by an economic interpretation of class structure. The nation's social layers were marked out conveniently and neatly according to income levels, which in turn depended mainly on occupation. The pivotal point in this interpretation hence was simply the breadwinner's job.

After the war, millions of working-class families, fortified by a second breadwinner, headed for the suburbs to enjoy their first taste of middle-class life. They liked the taste so well that they cultivated it assiduously. Their homes, their cars, their clothes, their hobbies, their shopping habits, in a few years resembled those of the older, occupation-based middle-class families in the neighborhood. The working-class Rosie O'Grady became almost indistinguishable from the Colonel's Lady, at least in external appearance. "Although there may still be a big difference in the cost of their wardrobes," a Twentieth Century Fund study reported, "it takes a discerning feminine eye to tell them apart." Perhaps because they were mostly nonfeminine, the social scientists were more than a bit baffled at understanding the spectacle of millions of working-class families being absorbed into the middle class. As the economic shackles were struck off, clues to working-class origins could be detected in general only by cultural outlook. It was easier to acquire a new car outside the front door of a split-level than to acquire a new cultural heritage. The new middle class thus betrayed an uneasy balance of working-class cultural habits in the midst of the modish surroundings.

The social scientists had a perfect right to be baffled. For the engulfment in less than a decade of a sizable portion of the working class into the middle class raised general hob with a traditional understanding of the class structure. Nothing like it had happened in the previous 170 years of U.S. history. From a placid specimen readily available for leisurely study and doctoral dissertations the class structure, at least in its vital middle, acted like a thing alive. The big bone of contention was what to call the new recruits to the middle class. As jobs went, they were still working class; as psychological orientation went, they were clearly lower-middle class. Sociologists split over the problem into two antagonistic schools. One held fast to the traditional method of separating the social classes by income or occupation, and to them the millions of middle-class novitiates were still basically working-class. The other insisted that, when you come down to it, social classes actually were no more than handy psychosocial groupings of people, and those who clustered together in practice should be considered in the same social class. There was no question in their minds that the white-collar millions belonged to the social class they and their neighbors considered them to be in. It was all a matter of psychological self-diagnosis subject, if anything, only to the neighbors' consent.

The "psychological" interpretation of the class structure rapidly gained social scientist partisans under the spur of postwar prosperity. And they drew a new social portrait of the U.S. in which, relatively, a handful of families located themselves at the top and bottom of the class structure and everybody else crowded into the middle, particularly the lower portion of the middle. Study after study supported the portrait in that, given an opportunity to choose for themselves, the overwhelming majority of families decided that their new standard of living and their new aspirations entitled them to an honored place in the middle class. One study found 88 percent of the families figuring themselves as middle class, another found 79 percent, another 75 percent. A study reported in the *Journal of Abnormal and Social Psychology* turned up ringing allegiance to the middle class in a variety of occupational groups: nearly 9 out of 10 business executives, professionals, skilled workers, farmers, and 5 out of 6 semi-skilled and unskilled workers considered themselves in the middle class.

The observation was made by many of the social scientists that families generally elevated themselves one notch above the social class where their income alone would have traditionally pegged them. This self-beneficence was found to be particularly prevalent among working-class and lower-middle-class families, about three-quarters of whom up-graded their social status. Significantly, of the two, the lower-middle class seemed to betray the greater psychological insecurity, and conversely the greater aspirations, by not infrequently elevating itself a generous two notches.

The studies, if nothing else, made good copy and were lifted out of the pages of the professional journals and accorded the status of a national credo in the mass circulation magazines. Popular writers acclaimed them as living proof that the nation was a land of opportunity for middle-class Horatio Algers. "Since 1930 not only have the poor become richer," one magazine article noted, "but the rich poorer. The gulf between classes has narrowed abruptly. Big houses are smaller, small houses bigger. Servants are disappearing from the homes of the well-to-do, and the street and sports clothes of assembly-line workers are hard to distinguish from those of the executives." Another magazine suggested to its readers: "Your placement has little to do with any of the old standards of class distinction—money, birth, breeding. What counts is simply how you spend your spare time." The new credo revived the popular image of the U.S. as expressed by European travelers from Crèvecoeur to De Tocqueville to Bryce, that the nation was vitalized by a spirit of "egalitarianism" totally unknown to European society in which class consciousness had been stubbornly rooted for centuries.

Not that the social scientists thought that the class structure was in the final stages of dissolution. It was anything but that, despite the contrary impression that might be gained from popular reading. It was true that the nation's unprecedented prosperity had hastened social mobility, had boosted millions of working-class families into the lower-middle class. But the social scientists recognized that the traditional class structure with all of its built-in covenants at each level of customs, duties, privileges, deprivations, aspirations, beliefs, and discriminations still remained pretty much intact. While millions might shuffle upward from class to class, they were gripped at each level by the dead hand of history, which shaped their transitional behavior and their thinking.

In general, social scientists distinguish three main class divisions—upper, middle, lower—and separate each into an upper and lower portion. It is arbitrary, true, and not all social scientists believe in this division. Nor, moreover, are individuals always easy to classify, for many do not exhibit all the traits of the class. So they require a bit of arbitrary squeezing into social place. What makes the classification burden particularly onerous is that in periods of rapid social mobility, such as has been taking place since the war, millions of individuals are in midstream between social classes and exhibit disconcertingly contradictory characteristics of both classes. Society's class structure, as can be seen, is not as stable as nature's biological structure.

Nonetheless social scientists have determined certain general characterizing traits in each social layer, despite the rambunctious individuals who refuse to exhibit them. Again, not all social scientists agree to the typing, and some assign traits differently from their brethren. But the following is intended as a composite of the six social layers, as drawn from innumerable published studies.

In the rarefied top portion of the upper class—the upper upper—are families which have several generations of money and social position behind them. As inheritors of the nineteenth century's "gilded age," their forebears were probably among the 2,000 prominent and wealthy families whose names appeared in the debut issues of the *Social Register* more than 70 years ago. If these forebears were "rough and piratical," as Dixon Wecter says in *The Saga of American Society*, when they seized the real estate, laid out the railroads, and set up the trust funds, their third- and fourth-generation descendents today live off those economic benefits. They buy fine books and oil paintings, travel, learn about horses and wine, and genteelly cultivate the art of graceful living. They consider it somewhat boorish and crude to display wealth, even to talk about it. It is taken for granted. If through misfortune it is lost, they still are accepted in their exclusive community. They put value on a man's background, not his present accomplishment or lack of it. Genealogy is of critical importance and above the vicissitudes of current events. Consider that even a "traitor" to his class, as Franklin D. Roosevelt was harshly called in the thirties, was not expelled from his club.

Their sons go to Yale, Harvard, Princeton, their daughters to Radcliffe, Bryn Mawr, Vassar. When marriage is considered, family background is a foremost factor. If their sons occasionally get involved with females from the lower social regions, their daughters are more closely sheltered, if only because, unlike sons, they rarely get to play a role in the business world. "This results," writes August B. Hollingshead in *The Annals of the American Academy of Political and Social Science*, "in a considerable number of old maids in established upper-class families."

They spend money, but the results are not publicly seen. They collect art, give to charity, sponsor the arts as patrons, and assume community leadership of events that usually have business implications. They aspire to no higher social class, for none exists. They are born in, live their entire lives in, exclusivity, and wealth alone without lineage cannot buy entry to their circle. "They are the most secure of any that our society produces. They are the most tolerant because they have got everything. They've got family and position, security and money," observes anthropologist Margaret C. Pirie.

But as a consuming group they are the frustration of the marketers, for they go in for what is called "conspicuous non-consumption." They tend to wear the same style hats they wore a generation ago, to drive well kept but old cars. They scrupulously avoid making a show of their purchases. They do not have to. They are not interested in keeping up. They are interested in the past, in their ancestors who are enshrined in oil paintings in their homes, and in class traditions. Their spending habits thus have only a pinprick effect on the economy.

Newly rich families form the brassy lower portion of the upper class—the lower uppers. As a group they are characterized by a stupefying amassment of wealth wrested out of the market-place in a relatively few years. They are dominated, naturally, by the values of the marketplace. They look on masses of great wealth as badges of honor, and the piling up of possessions as a distinguishing mark of business efficiency. Nothing in their lives quite touches the importance of the corralling and displaying of wealth, and each level of their personal fortune becomes, in the words of Thorstein Veblen, "a point of departure for a fresh increase in wealth." They compete with each other in exhibition-ist spending and offer excellent newspaper copy by public displays of conspicuous consumption, more so than any other class segment.

Economic success is ordinarily the crowning and highly personal triumph of the money-making father, and his gratifica-tions feed off its endless process. As a highly successful business executive, he is sought after and elected to numerous Boards of Directors, at whose sessions he rubs elbows with members of the upper-upper elite. But he is systematically, if subtly, excluded from their exclusive country club, and he and his wife are rarely if ever invited socially to their homes. If his wife resents it, because she aspires to be accepted by the established elite, he resents it too, but shrugs it off. As Sinclair Lewis' "Babbitt" put it, he does not "care a fat hoot for all these highrollers." As a self-made man, he proudly displays the middle-class values of his upbringing, and tends to upbraid his wife for "playing the high society game."

However, they spend years trying to break into the upper societal crust. They own all the symbols of great wealth, a man-sion, expensive furnishings, automobiles, clothes, boats, but they do not own the family name that forms the *sine qua non* for ac-ceptance by the elite. "They meet the means test but not the lineage test," as Hollingshead wrote in *The Annals*.

They are an unstable class segment, for conspicuous spend-ing, fast living, contradictory values, among other things, take an uncommonly high toll in divorce, broken homes, alcoholism, and other symptoms of family deterioration. Their wanton spending and behavior patterns are taken by the general public as symbolic of the conduct of the entire upper class, much to the chagrin and anger of the established elite. This further assures their debarment. Because they are relatively few in number, even their splashy spending makes a small dent in the economy.

The upper portion of the middle class—the upper middles—betrays many of the nagging anxieties and aspirations of the lower-upper class—plus a few of its own. If it does not indulge with the same intensity in conspicuous consumption, it is probably only because it has less money. But it buys for the same driving reasons of prestige and social status, and spends much of its time observing the Joneses and making sure it keeps up with them. It exhibits an unbridled passion for what is new, which leads it to buy and discard things constantly. Salary increases that come along are used immediately to throw the family into higher spending gear. Little or nothing is saved, for the upper middles characteristically live close to the end of their incomes. But, also characteristically, they are specially careful about pacing their march to success, for they are thin-skinned about the opinions of neighbors and friends. They would never dream of owning a Cadillac before a prior spell with a Buick. The neighbors and friends might think them "pushy." Nor would they drive around in an old Ford and run the risk of being thought a failure. Their goal is to keep up with the Joneses, preferably getting just a bit ahead of them, but not too far, as William H. Whyte, Jr., wrote in *Fortune*. They avidly read magazines such as *Time, Life, Fortune, Harper's, Vogue, New Yorker*, both to keep abreast of happenings and to learn about new products. New products are their "symbols of achievement," concluded a Hanan & Son marketing study. "Finding them and trying them are their symbols of adventure." As a result they are the target of knowledgeable merchandisers who want to introduce expensive new items. If they don't buy it, nobody will. But if they do, since they act as the taste-makers for the middle class, sales can be expected later to trickle down to the lower middles.

They are the successful businessmen and professionals who stand on the top rungs of the ladder. As such, they do not hold jobs, but occupy positions; they do not work, but pursue careers. The central fact indeed about upper-middle-class family life is the husband's career. The entire family plays a role in its cultivation. The wife furnishes an impressive home as a showcase of her husband's buying power and in which they can entertain his important business associates and friends. In fact, the more she overbuys the more she does him proud for she "puts in evidence her husband's ability to pay," as Thorstein Veblen said. He makes the money. Her job is to display it to best advantage. Indicative of these values was the plaintive comment that turned up repeatedly in a *Woman's Home Companion* study: "My husband says I don't spend enough and don't represent him fairly."

For their part, upper-middle-class children are early taught the inestimable value of formal education, and the standards, educational and occupational, are set so high for them that inability to measure up sometimes leads to psychic disturbances. They "often are subject to neurosis," says Arnold Green in the *American Sociological Review*.

No class segment does more than the upper-middle to bake into American life the widely characteristic care and pride in property, child training, vital importance of career, and planning for the future. "Almost all the good things in U.S. life are its achievement," was the commonly held opinion of the social scientists, with which the merchandisers would chorus a vigorous amen. For the upper-middle class has an ample supply of money, credit when the money runs out, and a compulsive willingness to use both in order to keep up.

In sheer size alone, more millions crowd into the lower-middle class than into any other class segment. Before the war, it was peopled mostly by petty businessmen, petty farmers, semiprofessionals and semimanagerials. They stood on the bottom rungs of the ladder, most of them wore white collars to work, and they looked with condescension at the ordinary wage earner. After the war, they were trampled over by the millions of working-class families which clambered all over the bottom rungs of the ladder. White collars lost their special class insignia as much of the working class donned them.

The established members of the lower-middle class had lived marginal lives, aspiring to the upper-middle class, dreading business reverses which would hurl them to the working-class level, and the millions of new arrivals did not add stability to the class. For they too face sudden declassing if the dual source of family income shrinks to one. The lower-middle class on the whole, hence, enjoys its life on the edge of an economic abyss. It lives in small suburban homes which are kept up by dint of considerable personal labor, and its member families resemble the configurations on the traditional *Saturday Evening Post* covers.

They live by such slogans as "Honesty is the best policy," "Cleanliness is next to godliness," they have a very strong moral code, and they are painfully susceptible to shame and gossip. They worry constantly over what the neighbors think of them, are the most inhibited people of any in the class structure. They hunt desperately for respectability and have moral and well behaved children to show for it. Religious affiliation is not enough for them—they attend services regularly. They think of careers not for themselves but for their children, for they recognize early that lack of professional skills shuts off any real hope for their own advancement. Their children are their link to the future. Therefore no sacrifice is too heavy for the children's formal education.

Because of its imposing bulk, the lower-middle class provides marketers with a mass market for conventional and standardized goods. Unlike the upper-middle class, it is reluctant to try new items before they are generally accepted by everybody. Yet high price is no bar, because it has the money. It betrays its working-class origin by general resistance to time-buying. But unlike the working class it shuns second-hand or hand-me-down items as an affront to its economic independence. It is lumped with the working class in the politician's appeal to "the common man."

As has been seen, the upper class is oriented toward the past and the middle class toward the future. The lower class is oriented of necessity to the present, for it lives just a cut above the hand-to-mouth level. If the wife works, it is to keep the family from falling below that level.

Its upper portion—the working class—holds jobs which are buffeted by the swings of the business cycle and are slowly bowing to automation. It lacks any sort of professional training, so it has no practical hope of finding high-pay jobs. Commonly its children go to work at an early age, because money is always badly needed, so their future chances at high-pay jobs are snuffed out by being forced to leave school. The result is that the children, like their fathers, foreshorten their life plan to a steady job and a modest pension when the job ends. Although a bit envious of the lower-middle class, they scoff at the "snobs" who are so respectable they "don't know how to have any fun." If nothing else, they are psychically freer of inhibitions. Under the pressure of making ends meet, they are largely unconcerned with the niceties of community reputation or children as symbols of family respectability.

As a rule, they are nonjoiners of organizations. Whereas the upper and middle class flock to religious, fraternal, service, recreational, patriotic, political, and cultural organizations, "membership on the part of the lower income class was markedly lower," notes W. G. Mather, Jr., in the *American Sociological Review*. In general they lack the extra money for membership fees, time and energy after an arduous working day, and the class interest in these organizations. Most of them are devoted to middle-class interests, anyway, which imposes a psychological barrier to the working class's joining. The working-class mother thus understandably hesitates to attend a PTA meeting where she would merely put on exhibition her cheap clothes and poor grammar to others who present the benefits of more money and education.

Working-class friendships are ordinarily confined to the neighborhood and include kin. Not infrequently an entire brood of jobless kin moves in, which places still further strain on the household finances. Most companionate marriages—not the most stable kind—are in the working class, which also produces a high rate of desertion and divorce.

Nonetheless the working class still looks for success, not the "family success" of the upper class or the "education success" of the middle class, but the "lucky break." They play the sweepstakes or the numbers as the slim but only way out. While a few break out via sports or entertainment, because in neither field is education a prerequisite, the overwhelming majority are foredoomed to remain mired in their failure-conditioned environment.

Hence, working-class consumption habits provide a steady but unspectacular market for the merchandisers. After food-clothing-shelter bills are paid, there is practically no money left over. Even if housewives are sisters under the skin, and are equally susceptible to impulse buying, the working-class housewife does not have the money. Yet because of its size, Lee Rainwater, Richard Coleman, and Gerald Handel suggest in *Workingman's Wife* that advertisers sell "with an eye on the working class" and that the "behavior" magazines and soap operas are the proper and "clear channels of communication" to its pocketbook.

The very bottom of the lower class—the lower lowers—offers slim pickings indeed for the merchandisers. Its member families live in the city slums or in shacks on its outskirts. They lack education and occupational skills and they fill the leftover menial jobs that nobody else wants. Often as not, they are jobless. Whereas working-class families live just above a hand-to-mouth level, the lower-lowers live just below it. Daily they face the problem of filling hungry stomachs, keeping clothes on their backs, and a roof over their heads. They live by bread alone—and often have to wait for that. They frequent the taverns, the courts, and the welfare agencies. "The girls are always pregnant; the families are huge; incestual relations occur frequently," Hollingshead wrote in *Elmtown's Youth*. Defeatist in outlook, allied to no group or class, they show frequent antagonism to working-class interests, with which they are often in conflict. They represent nearly a cipher to the merchandisers because their buying habits are sparse and unreliable and they are not reachable through any advertising medium. Their only saving grace is their small numbers.

To reach the millions in the upper, middle, and lower classes, to engage their interest, to convert them from readers, listeners, and watchers into customers is the job assigned by advertisers to newspapers, magazines, radio, and TV. In varying degrees all of them have enjoyed phenomenal growth since the war. In 1960 about 1,700 daily newspapers sold nearly 59 million copies per day, 1,100 consumer magazines sold 213 million copies per issue, 3,500 radio and 530 TV stations broadcast during most of the 24 hours. Radio was in practically every home, TV was almost there.

As the prime target of the merchandisers, the populous middle class is commercially laid low by different media. Its upper, more educated, portion is reachable primarily by the printed page. And since the war the highbrow magazines have in fact scored great growth, more than doubling in circulation. Middlebrow magazines—of general interest—on the other hand, have grown about half, while those edited for borderline literacy have dropped about 25 percent in circulation. Radio, and especially TV, have replaced the written word for the less literate.

The educated upper-middle class, on the contrary, is quite casual about radio and TV, and selective about the programs it listens to or watches. It likes news, discussions, forums, serious dramatizations, public affairs programs, serious music, and educational programs. But even these programs are not allowed to upset daily mealtimes or social affairs, aside from an exceptional program. The upper-middle class, placing high store by its self-reliance and independence of taste, conspicuously resists the mass persuasion methods of the air media. It reserves its coldest anger for the hard-sell commercial and is anguished that the most it can do is to turn off the radio or TV set. It likes commercials that make fun of the product or of the sponsor because that kind of selling does not ruffle its feelings of superior independence. In its scheme of things the salesman is a social subordinate who should serve and not try to dominate.

The lower-middle class, on the other hand, loves radio and TV and takes its amusement in extralarge doses. It enjoys the variety shows, comedy, sports, and light drama. It deliberately chooses the frivolous over the serious, fiction over fact, the diverting over the significant, as Leo Rosten points out in *Daedalus*. It hunts down idle-time fillers as an escape from boredom. The soap operas do a fine job for them, for there the conflicting forces of good and evil are simple, and, moreover, breathe meaning and importance into what in fact is petty and meaningless. They furnish millions with an opportunity "to expand their lives . . . to interpret their lives on a more tolerable level," as Leo Bogart says in *The Age of Television*.

TV soap operas are preferred over the radio species because they reinforce the illusion of reality, but for the same reason TV commercials are considered more objectionable than on radio because they so rudely shatter the illusion. In its hunt for entertainment, the lower-middle class has turned dial-twisting into a class activity. It prefers anything on TV to no TV. A heavy TV watcher today, it was a heavy radio listener before TV. A study by the American Research Bureau shows that 25 percent of the TV-equipped families do 40 percent of the watching. In this preoccupation the lower-middle class is joined just as avidly by the working class.

The fact that TV and radio programming is for the lower-middle-class and working-class taste is a source of constant anguish to the upper-middle class. Critic John Crosby expressed the upper middles' feelings in the early days of TV when he said: "The impact of television on our culture is one of the liveliest little topics to come along in some time, much of it conducted between clenched teeth."

In self-defense, TV and radio programming executives say that people want lowbrow fare, otherwise they wouldn't flock to it by the millions. Programming, the argument goes, is thus most democratically determined, for most of the people get what they most want. As it works out, they get more than they bargained for, because of the bandwagon effect of programming. Sponsors like to ride winners as much as anybody else, and when that old Hollywood staple, the Western, made good on TV, they all got on their horses. In 1960, 27 westerns shot their way into the nation's living rooms. The 27 represented 25 percent of the total TV fare, the top percentage for any of the eight program types. But a kind of Parkinson's law seemed to operate here too, for the people's appetite incredibly expanded to encompass all the new "oaters." The Nielsen audience rating for the 27 in 1960, amazingly enough, was about the same as for the three in 1955.

The upper-middle class finds the editing of TV programs to fit lower-middle class concepts of morality bad enough, but when lyrics from stage plays are bleached because they are considered too "blue" for lower-middle-class taste, the upper-middle class becomes incensed. What it finds objectionable is not so much the censorship as the slight to its sophistication, and the fact that this ghastly tampering occurs in its own special province, the theater.

In a study for the Fund for the Republic, Charles Winick uncovered a number of excisions and alterations in Broadway hit productions when presented on TV. For instance, the stage line delivered by a chorine, "He likes me to get to bed early," was modified to, "He likes to get to bed early." The stage lines, "Wouldn't sleep, and couldn't sleep,/ Until I could sleep where

I shouldn't sleep," were rewritten as, "Wouldn't sleep, and couldn't sleep,/ When love came and told me I shouldn't sleep." In the lines, "She messed around with a guy named Smokey,/ Loved him even though he was cokey," the word "cokey" came out "blokey." The lines, "Good writers too who once knew better words,/ Now use four-letter words,/ Writing prose," were altered so that "four-letter words" became, incomprehensibly, "three-letter words." In the general laundering process all the "God-damns" become "Gol-darneds" or some-such, and "sons-of-bitches" are endowed with such more wholesome characterizations as "lecherous" or "treacherous."

Despite the utmost vigilance, however, lines have on occasion escaped the TV censor and touched off a national holler from a squeamish audience. The line, "If he don't come across, I don't come across," brought a raft of protest letters into the station, as did the off-hand suggestion that an unmarried girl could get rid of her inhibitions by relaxing with a drink. Such were the scruples of the lower-middle class that complaints were even registered about the antisocial effects of using lower-case letters in the credits for a major variety show on the ground that this violated the rules taught in schools. So, too, did the outfitting of a criminal in a Santa Claus costume distress a host of viewers who wrote protestingly that Santa should be kept sacred for children. Oddly, TV shows built around a person's physical affliction or the chronicling of human suffering down to the last miserable detail practically never drew a postcard of protest.

The "service" magazines of big circulations serve the lower-middle class something more than the entertainment and commercials of TV and radio. In issue after issue they supply practical advice on the behavior expected of the class. Magazines such as *Good Housekeeping, Ladies' Home Journal, McCall's, Better Homes and Gardens, American Home, Woman's Home Companion* instruct in articles and stories how lower-middle-class families are to furnish their homes, entertain their guests, serve foods, dress, rear their children, meet and deal with community businessmen, lawyers, doctors, schoolteachers. In a very real sense, the "service" magazines function as "trade magazines" for the lower-middle class. They act as the arbiters of taste, guardians of behavior, and the setters of goals. They indoctrinate the millions of formerly working-class families with the values of the lower-middle class, including the enlarged consumption habits expected of them. In this task they are joined by the merchandisers who advertise in their pages the goods and services that go with the higher standard of living. Inasmuch as cues for social and consumption behavior come "even from the illustrations of model kitchens and suburban homes," as a study by Social Research, Inc. points out, advertising in these media takes on some of the force of education. The resentment of TV and radio commercials which rupture entertainment is not present. For the ads are unobtrusively wedded to editorial.

The Built-In Obsolescence 8

The postwar surge of middle-class buying both gladdened and worried the hearts of the merchandisers, for on the one hand the heavy buying very nicely depleted the shelves of consumer goods, but on the other hand it relentlessly shrank the remaining market for such goods. Each sale that pleasantly jingled the cash register at the same time also tolled the removal of one more customer for that item. The merchandisers then had to sit around fidgeting for what seemed an interminable period until the item wore out and the customer returned for a replacement. In the case of certain big-ticket items this wait might well last for 10 or 12 years.

And as refrigerators, washers, dryers, TV's, radios, and other such durable items began to approach saturation of U.S. homes, the steep sales climb of such items began to level off, and the situation in these industries portended an oncoming crisis. The wide application of automation to fabrication methods, if anything, worsened the situation, for it meant that factory production of consumer goods would in the future more easily outrace consumption, and bring the day of glut that much faster. The future looked bleak indeed unless the merchandisers could find some exit from the problem. There was even brooding talk about closed factories, a downswing of the business cycle, and a return to the forbidding days of the thirties.

The exit that many industries found in the fifties was style obsolescence, which had the desired effect of shortening the life of consumer goods and hastening the return of the consumer to the market for replacements. Variations of the venerable Detroit practice of the Annual Model Change became standard operating procedure for a growing number of industries. The sales pictures brightened as the fashion-conscious middle class willingly rose to the bait.

For instance, Frigidaire ended 25 years of uninterrupted production of streamlined white appliances when it switched to "Sheer Look" styling in various color tints. The promotional theme—"Every line is straight, every corner is square; the whole look is sheer"—in the ads was reinforced by depicting pretty models beside the appliances who held their hands demurely to form right angles, symbolizing the new "Sheer Look." The appliances were described as coming in such fashionable colors as Charcoal gray, Mayfair pink, Stratford yellow and Sherwood green. Industry executives depended perhaps as much on color as on restyled lines, for studies had indicated that color was an apt loosener of middle-class purse strings. Color was expected to do its bit to hasten the obsolescence of an estimated 95 million refrigerators, ranges, and washers sold in the decade after the war. And it did, for a survey of the buyers of the new tinted refrigerators showed that four out of five readily conceded the refrigerators being replaced were still in good operating condition. In fact, one out of three acknowledged that the appliance was under five years old.

The success of the promotion induced one appliance executive to enthuse in the trade press that "Color properly merchan-
dised to the public will . . . enables us to reduce significantly the
trade-in span from eleven years to perhaps seven, or even lower."
Another prophesied before the American Marketing Association
the disuse of "white-goods industry" as an appropriate appellation
for the appliances that rolled off the assembly lines. Soon colored
appliances would push white appliances out of the nation's homes.
"I know many people feel that promoting and creating obsolescence is an awful thing for the industry to do," the latter speaker
concluded. But the situation had been forced on the industry and
he hoped that the appliance people would be "as successful as
the automobile people" in forcing sales by periodic face-liftings.

The watch industry, which had been plagued by the durability of its products—"the watches just won't wear out"—also
turned to style obsolescence, opening a promotional drive to
change the public's mind about the desirability of old watches.
"A man will wear the latest in shirt fabrics, the short brim hat,
new striped tie, Dacron shirt, but he will take pride in showing a
watch that's 20 years old and looks it," an executive commented.
Benrus, Bulova, and Gruen—"The Big Three"—looked to style
changes as the psychological lever to push the 12 million annual
watch sales to a more profitable 20 million. The Benrus campaign
made the flat offer of $10 and $20 for old watches "regardless of
age, condition, or make," the Gruen ads called attention to high
style—"The Newest Look in Time"—and the Bulova promotion
urged on consumers the desirability of owning a "wardrobe" of
watches for different social occasions. The onslaught proved
"spectacularly successful." For not only did each company report
a gratifying sales rise, but thousands of old watches were returned
to the companies and thereby permanently removed from the
market.

The furniture industry, too, learned the effectiveness of
wagging a reproving fashion finger at old living room and bed-

room suites. Nothing got sales more perky nor rid of 10-to-20-year-old furniture so fast. The *National Furniture Review*, a trade publication, announced that consumers were "now able to afford up-to-the-minute furniture" and urged dealers to embrace trade-ins, citing examples of successful advertising approaches. A Union-town, Pennsylvania, store had offered "$50 for your old living room or bedroom suite regardless of age or condition"; a San Francisco, California, store had displayed rundown furniture in one window and modern furniture in the other and draped a "Trade-In And Spruce-Up" banner across both; a New York City chain had urged in a series of newspaper ads—"Trade in your old furniture as you would your old car. Now your old furniture can help pay for the beautiful new furniture you've been wanting for years."

The Retail Furniture Association of California heard the novel suggestion that consumers needed a constant reminder that their furniture was getting old. "Let's put a date on our furniture. Stamp the year of a sofa's manufacture on the platform. Burn it into a drawer of a chest."

Reports filtering back to the national trade association from retail dealers around the nation made it unmistakably clear that the trade-in was an effective salesman of new furnishings. Although only 11 percent of the dealers reported that the resale of the trade-ins was profitable, the dealers nevertheless flocked to the practice, according to the National Retail Furniture Association. They willingly took a loss on the trade-ins for the practice "magically facilitates the sale of new goods." By 1960 an estimated 80 percent of the dealers accepted trade-ins, one-third of whom were recent converts to the practice.

The carpet industry, also, began an active campaign to shorten the useful life of its product. The situation, again, was the familiar one of saturation, for two-thirds of the carpets in the nation's living rooms were less than ten years old. Customarily, consumers waited about 15 years between carpet purchases, and even then tended stubbornly to hold off the new purchase so long as some pile was visible on the old carpet. Aggravating the problem, from the dealer's standpoint, was the common consumer practice, after buying a new carpet, of placing the old one on a secondary floor, which eliminated that floor as a candidate for a rug.

The Carpet Institute urged the trade-in as a proved prodder of consumers to "replace rugs and carpets earlier and more often." It would help open up the enormous "carpet replacement market that awaited exploitation in this country." Recommended were such advertising approaches as: "Don't Be Chained to Your Old Rug," showing the plight of a damsel handcuffed to a rug; "Unhappy with Your Rugs and Carpets?" asked of a housewife who was shown obviously miserable over them; and as a "homitosis" cure for homes suffering from old-fashioned rug and carpet styles. Dealers reported a 20 percent rise in new carpet sales. Moreover, the removal of the old carpets via the trade-in was an extra bonus, since secondary floors stayed carpetless and a standby source of another carpet sale.

The home building industry, likewise, tackled the problem of growing homeownership saturation by working trade-ins, and in the process by trading up the middle class from modest to swank homes. "Our present American economy and philosophy of living have created a desire in people to . . . move to newer and better quarters every four years," noted the National Institute of Real Estate Brokers. "The thought of owing a clear home has largely lost its importance. It has been replaced by the desire to keep up with the Joneses and to own the best home that one can afford." The principal speaker at a marketing conference of the National Association of Home Builders urged the builders to make capital of this mood. He urged faster acceptance of Detroit's marketing practice. "How many new cars would Detroit sell," he asked, "if Ford, Chrysler, and General Motors spent their advertising dollars telling motorists how easy it is to fix up [an old car] to be just as good as a new one?" He called unwise the spending of four advertising dollars for every one spent "to tell customers how much pleasanter, easier, and more fun it is to live in a fine new home than in the present old one."

If the trade-in advice was followed, "tomorrow may find trading homes as common as trading cars and appliances is today," editorialized the *American Builder*. "When that day comes, the industry may well be on its way to those 1,700,000 annual starts predicted for the next decade." Pointing the way was a Dallas, Texas, builder who ran his annual sales from $250,000 to $2,250,000 in three years by convincing buyers to swap modest for more luxurious homes. By 1960 an estimated one-third of the nation's builders accepted trade-ins.

Other industries and individual manufacturers, also, turned to style obsolescence as the answer to growing market glut, seeking sales redemption by shortening the life cycle of their products, feeding middle-class ego, and being fed back in return increased sales.

Remington, Ronson, Schick, and Sunbeam advertised trade-in allowances up to $8.50 toward the purchase of new electric razors. Ronson offered a $5 trade-in toward the purchase of its latest table lighter. RCA Victor offered one dollar credit toward the purchase of each classical record. Singer, an old hand at trade-ins, offered a flat $50 allowance toward a new sewing machine. Willoughby's, biggest retailer of photographic supplies in New York City, was quoted in a trade magazine: "Trade-in allowances are the lifeblood of our sales." Johnson Motors acknowledged that half its annual outboard motor sales were spurred by trade-ins. "The Big Four" in swimsuits—Catalina, Cole, Jantzen, and Rose Marie Reid—promoted one swimsuit for the morning sun, one for the noonday sun, and a third for the evening sun. Optical companies promoted the latest style in eyeglass frames. The men's wear industry, eyeing with undisguised envy the traditional fast obsolescence of women's wear, rang in style changes of its own.

Even the sterling silver industry, a time-immemorial symbol

of great wealth and aristocracy, succumbed as R. Wallace & Sons announced the industry's first trade-in program. The reason, disclosed in company sales reports, was that in 1954, for the first time in history, expensive sterling silverware sold just as well as the lower-priced silverplate services. This sales statistic signified more than anything else the challenge by the middle class for ownership of goods formerly considered exclusive upper-class merchandise. As E. B. Weiss, merchandising consultant, observed in a trade newspaper: "Mink was the mark of those who *had* social prestige. Today it is the mark of those who *aspire* to social prestige—which involves a constantly expanding percentage of our total population. Those who *have* social prestige will now be compelled to turn to chinchilla. . . . Actually, it will become increasingly difficult for our native aristocrats subtly to publicize their Olympian aloofness through possessions for the simple reason that more and more millions of families are accumulating incomes and assets that permit them to indulge their social aspirations. . . . This nation has unquestionably embarked on a huge program of keeping up with the Joneses. . . ."

In the mass climb up the social ladder the middle class gave the appearance of being totally blind to high price tags. The trade-in method was such a facile one by which to acquire new goods, and time-payment plans were so quickly and readily available, that buyers accorded scant thought to the total cost of the goods in the process. Few of them knew the true "market value of the articles they gave as trade-ins," concluded a Bureau of Labor Statistics study; in fact, most new appliance buyers figured that "the retailer's allowance exceeded the old appliance's value." This overgenerosity was the result, of course, of the widespread trade practice of marking up the price of the new merchandise so that it more than covered the liberal trade-in allowance. Frowned on by the trade associations, at least officially, it was nevertheless a common practice. As a company executive admitted at a conference of appliance dealers: "We are trying to avoid it, but it goes on every year. All of us have been a party to overpricing." The National Retail Furniture Association duly warned its members that hiking prices "to cover trade-in deals" would damage the retailer-customer relationship if the customer ever got wind of it. But a Texas builder openly advised as a formula for success "the inflation of the new house a few points and fewer deductions from the old house."

By 1960 installment credit pushed over the $40 billion mark, most of it on the backs of middle-class buyers, a figure 26 times as great as installment credit in the depths of the depressed thirties, and 18 times the low reached during the war when durable goods were unavailable. The middle class, of all the classes, paid the least heed to Shakespeare's dictum in *Hamlet:* "Neither a borrower nor a lender be." Installment buying was the wonderful key to the kingdom. If the Federal Reserve Board noted in a Survey of Consumer Finances that consumer debt "reached new highs, largely in connection with purchases of houses, automobiles, and household durable goods," the middle class did not share the federal agency's concern.

Style obsolescence and trade-in brought with it an inevitable flooding of the market with shoddier consumer goods; inevitable because in an economy surfeited with goods and whose salvation in sizable measure depended on abbreviating the useful life of these goods, some manufacturers inclined toward cutting corners, and others followed suit to meet competition. Trade-in was hotly defended in terms of the psychological satisfactions it gave to buyers of the up-to-date, but the production of shoddier goods found no one, except perhaps the philosophical cynics, coming to its defense.

The consumer irritations were vented in angry letters to manufacturers and retailers, to newspapers and magazines (especially the women's service publications), and were mostly directed at automobiles and household electrical appliances. Resentment ran high at glaring examples of slovenly workmanship, poor materials, and careless assembly and inspection. Such was the volume, that Paul Thibodeau warned in *Automotive News* that "the American public will not put up with the missing bolts and nuts, the malfunctioning parts, the squeaks and rattles and frequent return trips to dealers for adjustments—all of which are the rule and not the exception in present American cars." In similar vein, a speaker told the Society of Automotive Engineers: "I just bought my wife a new car, and when I slammed the door the handle came off in my hand. . . . This was followed in rapid succession by a leaky radiator coil . . . failure of the power steering unit." A disgruntled buyer told the *Wall Street Journal:* "Cars are being made to require more and more gas and more and more repair work—and I resent it." Complaints poured in about the frequency of blown-out mufflers, and consumers were in no mood to listen to the car manufacturers' explanation that faster muffler corrosion was a by-product penalty of souped-up engines that gulped high-octane gasoline. They remembered the bygone days when the muffler was just another automotive part and not the $300 million industry it mushroomed into by 1960. Tire manufacturers were hard pressed to explain why tires wore out faster than they once did. They blamed the new cars, which were heavier, and the power steering, power brakes, automatic transmissions, and smaller wheel bases, all of which caused tires to wear out more quickly.

Probably much of the explanation for short-lived durables was attributable to the startling complexity of modern products, particularly household durables, and the haste with which industry churned out new models. The American Home Laundry Manufacturers' Association, for instance, pointed out that the modern automatic washing machine contained 800 parts. A General Electric executive told *Business Week:* "We moved from the plain old electric iron to the thermostatic control, to the snag-proof cord, to the steam iron." Each step posed its own special problems, and multiplied the probability of failure. Indeed, since every alteration, from a new handle, control, dial, switch, to the sheerest gadgetry, opened the door to new mechanical bugs, the annual model changes engaged in by much of American industry offered the bugs a wonderful opportunity to prosper. Moreover, manufacturers who tried to put solid worth into their products found themselves "hamstrung by competitors who don't," an executive observed, which built more trouble for consumers into the appliances.

With an estimated 375 million electrical appliances operating in U.S. homes, and three-quarter million men earning a good living installing, servicing, and repairing these appliances, somehow all the explanations failed to placate irate buyers confronted by balky equipment. "I've always wondered," a housewife griped to the *Wall Street Journal*, "what happened to that pretty girl in the ad—you know, the one who's about to close the door of her new dish washer and dash off to the theatre. Did she come back to find the machine had dumped the dirty dishwater all over the floor—like I did?" Another housewife complained that in the 32 months she owned a clothes dryer, she had the repairman out six times; the vacuum cleaner agency which supposedly overhauled that machine annually pronounced it practically worthless after five years of use; the five-year old TV set ran about $40 a year to maintain after it passed its third birthday; the car emitted a blast of cold air when she wanted warm air, and warm air when she wanted to escape the summer's heat; and her husband had constant trouble with the lawn mower (crucial screws shook out).

"I could put up with miserable service if I got good products, or I could put up with miserable products if I got good service, but to put up with both is too much," wrote a disgusted buyer to a magazine editor. "I've taken to withholding payments as long as possible on any purchase—to keep the dealer interested in any problems I get," wrote another cannily. The *Wall Street Journal* headlined a story on the spawning of inferior goods: "Shiny Dream Products Turn Out as Nightmares for Some Consumers." A rising percentage of the defective merchandise was returned to dealers. "This is the first time in 20 years I've been in this business that I've seen so many returns," a dealer told *Home Furnishings Daily*.

Even the new suburban homes that sprang up by the millions around the nation to house the middle class were often sleazily built. "A Good House Nowadays Is Hard to Find," wrote A. M. Watkins in *Harper's*. He uncovered seven major sources of dissatisfaction and high upkeep in homes: shoddy heating systems, skimpy electrical wiring, short-lived faucet hot-water heaters, token insulation, cheap roofs, cheap plumbing and piping and bathroom fixtures, and poor waterproofing. Much of it resulted from cutting construction corners.

The number of times repairmen entered and left U.S. homes became perhaps the best known, if heart-breaking, symbol of the accumulation by the middle class of household contrivances. "I always have a 'man' coming. One came yesterday, one came today. There will be one tomorrow. It almost seems as if the repairman is a member of the family," a housewife told *Printers' Ink*. Much consumer anger was misdirected at the repairman who was quick to counter by pointing out the loose wires, poor insulation, faulty filters and other inherent defects. One repairman said self-defensively: "Things are made too fast now. It seems as though in the last three or four years appliances are even worse than they were after the war." Another said: "The way most appliances are put together in the factories today, the buyer can expect some trouble for at least one year. If you get through the first year with little or no trouble, you can expect no major troubles for several years."

Slipshod factory inspection of goods, or none at all, was commonly blamed by repairmen. There was the washer and washer-dryer turned out by a major company between 1955 and 1957 which produced two or three times the number of frantic service calls the company anticipated. A trade report stated: "Thousands of housewives complained bitterly that their 1955–

1957 washers and washer-dryers needed six or seven annoying and costly repair calls a year. . . . Company repairmen uncovered faulty clutches, transmissions and filters in alarming numbers." The company made good, repairing and replacing 40,000 units at an estimated cost of $10 million, but no explanation was forthcoming as to how thousands of defective appliances were turned out for three years without detection.

Strangely—or so it seemed to many critics—companies which would not dream of having anything but first-class production machinery in their factories, seemed willing to tolerate the production of second-class consumer goods. Nor did company executives seem particularly unhappy about the apparent contradiction between spending hundreds of thousands of dollars annually on the building of a corporate image as a producer of reliable consumer products, and running the risk of losing the last nickel in the bitter consumer cry: "I'll never buy that brand again!"

Over the years the cost of repairs steadily mounted for consumers. In 1960 a trade magazine estimated that the average family spent $100 to $150 yearly to restore household appliances to working order. A healthy portion of this cost resulted of course from the growing number of appliances in the average middle-class home, for the modern housewife operated in the neighborhood of $2,000 worth of electrical equipment. But a portion resulted from the built-in infirmities of products, many of which could "scarcely hold together for shipment," as E. F. Tangerman wrote in *Product Engineering*.

The situation admittedly troubled some of the merchandisers. *Advertising Age* began to suspect that the principle of obsolescence may have been carried too far: "we are building products designed to start wearing out before the consumer gets them home from the store." Products were not expected to last forever, but they should not be built "so they don't work the first day, or fall apart before they have a chance to get broken in." One adman dubbed the slipshod approach by manufacturers a "what-do-you-expect" attitude and another more inelegantly as "the great goof-off." Reverberations were even stirred in Congress as a Representative charged that so many U.S. manufacturers were cutting so many corners to keep costs down that the nation was in danger of having "shoddy" imposed on it as the national norm. The Representative sympathized with the "millions who find their new gadgets of all kinds falling apart in use." *Printers' Ink* expressed the fear that the "Made in America" stamp on a piece of goods was beginning to mean, at home and overseas, "the highest price and questionable quality."

Of the thousands of industrial designers and engineers who were hired to perform periodic face-lifting surgery on consumer products, many, possibly most, resented the job bitterly. For by training they were equipped to hunt down ways of making useful products still more useful, a training that went largely wasted. Moreover, the textbook precept they lived by professionally that good design was built in, not draped on, was violated daily. They devoted their many meaningful talents to what they considered the less meaningful one of dolling up last year's model into this year's. They acted as stylists, not designers, pursued the impermanent whims of fashion rather than the permanent beauty of art. Perhaps more than most professions they were aware of French playwright Jean Cocteau's definition of the two: "Art produces ugly things which frequently become beautiful with time. Fashion, on the other hand, produces beautiful things which always become ugly with time."

Their work as stylists—a term they deeply resented—muted their professional life's purpose for, as one of them told the American Institute of Electrical Engineers: "It is difficult for a man to get a sense of purpose out of a laborious contribution to a doodle." Many of them argued for a return to technological obsolescence—the genuine article—rather than the artificial kind which, as Henry Dreyfus said, worked by "embarrassing people into buying." They decried what appeared to be a national emphasis on the spurious kind in order to stimulate immediate sales. In *Dun's Review & Modern Industry*, 12 designers joined in predicting, hopefully and fervently, that the American people would eventually get fed up with superficial styling and demand of their products "real quality, value, and ability to perform."

The proliferation of trivial model changes also horrified many of the designers who considered the result to be a "vast debasement" of product design. "There are only so many good ways at any given time of designing a product," said the late Walter D. Teague, Sr. "If you *must* do something different, you are apt to do something bad, something bizarre. That is why car design has grown so extreme in this country." He felt that people bought these "flamboyant jobs" because nothing in "better taste" was offered. And the assiduous restyling of thousands of consumer items in the marketplace acted as a dead weight on American taste.

Aside from the question of taste, there was also to be considered the upward pressure on prices exerted by acceleration of change for change's sake. To begin with, current-model products commanded higher prices because they were current models, but the added expense built into the process of forced obsolescence was also passed on to the consumers. "The cost of continuous restyling," observed Harold Van Doren in *Industrial Design,* tended to "cancel out the advantages of mass production by keeping prices artificially high." This was a sore point to many critics. They regretted the slow loss of low-priced goods to consumers in the country which had first brought these benefits by the widespread introduction of mass-production methods. And it was considered an ironic twist of history that the automobile industry, which had led in their introduction, should be the pied piper that was leading so much of American industry astray.

It should not be thought for one moment that all industry executives felt that forced obsolescence could sustain the nation's prosperity indefinitely, nor that it would even be good for the nation in the long run. In fact, the opposite was probably closer to the truth. A *Harvard Business Review* survey, for instance, turned up a two-to-one opinion among more than 3,000 industry executives that the practice of such obsolescence was getting out of hand, and, moreover, that it was not calculated to help the nation in the economic arena of competitive world trade. However, few knew what to do about the situation.

The situation also troubled many of the nation's nonindustry leaders. When the Committee for Economic Development, a research and educational organization, for instance, asked 50 top-flight social scientists for opinions on "the most important economic problems to be faced by the U.S. in the next 20 years," several raised the specter of marketing practices that "satisfy only frivolous needs." They anticipated a general worsening of the situation as the ability of the economy grew to oversupply consumers with all sorts of goods. They shuddered both at the preoccupation of the middle class with status possessions and the cultivation of this preoccupation by advertisers. For it all led, as one of them said, to "houses with multiple TV sets, automobiles whose sole purpose is to stand at the suburban railroad station to await their masters' return, overobsolescence of durables, silly elaboration of packaging." If no better use is made of our present incomes, another said, "to what futility will we be reduced when our incomes stand nearly twice as high?"

But there were others who argued that such concern was both ill-advised and needless. The board chairman of an appliance company told the American Home Laundry Manufacturers' Association that the worriers were removed from "merchandising realities" of the marketplace. In his opinion, "an engineer's principal purpose as an engineer is to create obsolescence" and "any attempt by various people to toady up to the public saying they are against planned obsolescence is so much commercial demagogy." Aside from the immediate realities of the marketplace, others pursued the more philosophical line of reasoning that there was somehow "a tricky relationship between waste and abundance," a relationship that should not be tampered with. It was explored under the paradoxical title, "Waste Not, Have Not," in *Harper's,* and in *The Beer Can by the Highway,* by John A. Kouwenhoven, who suggested that waste seemed to be necessary in the enrichment process of the U.S., and that "we may not be able to get rid of the [waste] without also getting rid of the abundance."

Both considerations—the pressing one of the marketplace and the sinuous relationship of waste and abundance—were brushed aside by the National Academy of Sciences, whose newsletter expressed, first of all, doubt that middle-class buying would drop off if durables were made more durable. If cars lasted twice as long, consumers would be able to afford two or three cars, or a deepfreezer, or a hi-fi, or a cottage at the beach. If suits and shoes lasted twice as long, more of them would be bought. Consumers will simply be able to expand their buying in new directions.

Second of all, the Academy denied waste its role as a "mainstay of U.S. economy" and urged recognition of it "for what it is—a damper on living standards and a wasting of resources."

It seemed more than likely, however, that neither proponents nor opponents would have any effect on the national drift toward forced obsolescence so long as the national prosperity continued. Should prosperity end, that would be another matter.

The Corruption of Science 9

The itinerant figure of the medicine man who stood on the tailgate of his gaily festooned truck dispensing miracle herbs and potions to the sick and the aged all but disappeared from the prewar landscape. Much of his freedom of action was removed by the Food, Drug and Cosmetic Act of 1938 but even then he was as much an anachronism as the Model T. The *coup de grâce* was delivered to him as to the country store—by the rise of mass merchandising.

Nonetheless he was in a sense reincarnated, except that instead of standing on the rear of a truck he now stood in front of a microphone and TV camera. His spiel was much the same, even if his patent medicines were safer. He no longer claimed that his potions could cure every ailment known to afflict mankind, for the amendment to the Federal Trade Commission Act in 1937 had clipped his glib claims in that area too. Before 1937 he did not run afoul of the law, no matter how outlandish or untruthful his advertising claims, so long as he was not adjudged in restraint of trade; the plight of the consumer was not a factor. After 1937 his nimble words continued to play on the full range of human wishes, but they were carefully chosen words, so that his incantations continued to sell magic briskly in little vials, tubes, jars, and bottles.

He was no longer an entrepreneur but an agent, or simply a spieler, for a patent medicine company. For in the postwar U.S. the patent medicine business became big business, whose packaged self-medications were sold not only in the nation's drugstores but in the supermarkets, department stores, and elsewhere. In 1959 the drug trade estimated that the average family bought $18 worth of proprietaries every month. "By 1970 this will rise to an estimated $24.50," a speaker predicted to the Proprietary Association.

Some of the medicines granted palliative relief to those in distress, others were worthless, yet even the worthless ones were worth something, if only because placebos bring their own kind of psychological relief. Psychological or not, the American people were willing to pay a high price for relief, and the patent medicine companies accorded the public hundreds of private brands to choose from.

If a cold-sufferer walked into one of the nation's 54,000 drugstores and asked the clerk for something good for a cold, perhaps two dozen or so brands would be available on the shelves to do the trick. No drugstore smaller than a supermarket could carry the 341 nationally advertised cold remedies, as listed in the Drug Topics Pink Book for 1960, of course. But the clerk would have on hand most of the best-selling brands and the ones he would recommend would probably be those allowing the biggest markup or the most "push money," as the practice is known in trade argot. It is only fair to add that the ones he "pushed" would undoubtedly be as meritorious as their shelf neighbors, for they were all pretty much alike, so the cold sufferer could not properly feel aggrieved even if by chance he knew of the practice. Shown some of their brand names, he could not fail to be impressed with their efficacy: Cold Fyte, Coldfyters, Coldmaster, Ez-A-Cold, Gesuntheit, Gotacol, Chek-A-Kold, Cold Go, Cold-Eze.

If he had a hacking cough along with his cold he had 644 medications which ranged from expectorants, drops, balm, capsules, compounds, liquids, tablets, teas and syrups to choose from. Such beguiling names were available to him if he was an adult as Cough Master, Bron-Kease, Cheri-Kof, Kol-Kof, Magic Brand, Mastahist, Short-Stop and Stibacol. And if he was a child the choice included such specifics as Babee Cof, Old Dr. Stork's, Tot's and Save The Baby (*sic*).

If the cold sufferer with the hacking cough also had a raspy throat he could seek relief from any of 238 throat aids; if he was seized by bodily aches and pains he could turn to as many as 400 analgesic brands some of whose very names promised to exorcise pain—Counterpain, Pain-Expeller, Kil-A-Pain, Pain Balm, Pen-Trate, Ban Pain, Anti-Pain Pills, Nullpain, Rid-A-Pain.

If he could not sleep at night, he could pick among the 82 sleep-inducers such reassuring names as E.Z. Sleep, 40-Winks, Retyre, Rip Van Winkles, San Man, Siesta, Real Sleep, Shur-A-Sleep, Wunder Sleep, Sleep-Tite, Sleep-Wel, Slum-Bur, Snoozers, Super-Sleep and Sleep-Maker. On the other hand if he could not keep his eyes open during the day he could try 26 stay-awake pills with such eye-opening names as Alert, Be Alert, Driv-A-Lert, Nix-Nap, Nonod, Perk Up, Stay-Alert, Wake-Ettes, Wakeups and Wide-A-Wake.

In 1960, according to compilations by *Drug Topics*, Americans spent $323 million on cough and cold items, $157 million on laxatives and other eliminative aids, $355 million on internal analgesics, $94 million on external analgesics, $86 million on tonics, $61 million on antacids, $122 million on face creams, $373 million on make-up preparations and accessories, $59 million on foot products, $181 million on dieting aids, $417 million on oral hygiene products, $696 million on hair products, $147 million on fragrance preparations, $361 million on personal cleanliness items, $124 million on hand products.

All told, the amount spent on drugs, health aids, and toiletries in 1960 was a thumping $8.5 billion, of which 53 percent was spent in drugstores and the rest elsewhere. Over the years the drugstore was losing out in sales to the supermarket, department store, discounters, specialty stores, and other competition, and an ever-increasing percentage of its income came from prescription items, which the competition could not touch.

The American medical armory was vastly grander than it was at the turn of the twentieth century in the heyday of the itinerant medicine man. It contained almost none of the outrageous and dangerous nostrums that drew first denunciation by Samuel Hopkins Adams in his "Great American Fraud" series of articles in *Collier's* in 1905–1906, and which led to the passage of the first National Food and Drug Act in 1906. The muckrake movement during that period also helped alert the public to the hazards of unscrupulous operators as did the issuance of the first volume of *Nostrums and Quackery* by the American Medical Association in 1911, a 500-page book on the "nostrum evil, quackery and allied matters affecting the public health," and the cleaning by the AMA of its own Augean stable of unscrupulous physicians.

No one would deny that in barely half a century the U.S. had come a long way toward safeguarding the health of the people —at least so far as removing openly dangerous medications was concerned. But the efficacy of these medications was another matter, and suggested that today people could be reasonably assured of the safety of the potions they were taking but not that the money being spent for them was not being wasted. Even a cursory reading of *The Medicine Show*, a Consumer's Union publication, suggests that untold millions are being wasted yearly by Americans and of *The Health Hucksters* by Ralph Lee Smith that the medicine man is still with us. It is also suggested in the fact that up to 1962 a new drug application to the Food and Drug

Administration needed to prove according to the law simply that it was harmless and not that it was efficacious.

Over the years, to borrow a brewer's slogan, the medicine man's hand has never lost its skill. If anything, the laws' strictures have sharpened it. Patent medicines, for one, are sold in accordance with a time-honored formula, consisting of sin and magic skillfully blended by the copywriter. First the copy builds up a sense of guilt and sin in the consumer—as the reason why he is suffering—and then the vial of magic is offered, the act of buying of which expiates the sin and hence ends the suffering. As the game was described by a veteran patent medicine copywriter in a trade magazine: "You, a miserable sinner, are possessed by horrible devils. I, a magician, can give you fast, fast, FAST relief." The sufferer, particularly if he were poorly educated, was highly vulnerable to magic and ready to try anything.

In the postwar era as newspapers, magazines, radio, and TV became mass media capable of reaching millions almost instantly, the artful practice of magic in product promotion grew apace. Moreover, the parade of scientific miracles that came out of the nation's physics, chemistry, and biology laboratories, and the heady publicity given them by the mass media, provided an excellent umbrella for the copywriters' private miracles. The age of science thus fashioned in people its own kind of gullibility. And the exploitation of this gullibility became a prime industry for advertisers. Miracle ingredients, for instance, became a stock-in-trade for copywriters. And a *sub rosa* war of miracle ingredients took over in the advertising agencies. The invention of a miracle ingredient by one ad agency became the compulsion for the agency handling the competition to invent a miracle ingredient of its own. What lent aid and comfort to both sides was the numbing similarity of postwar consumer products which left copywriters with nothing significant to write about their products anyway. So they welcomed the opportunity to invent a mysterious ingredient to which they could attribute their product's superiority.

Besides, it gave them a chance to display copywriting virtuosity, for they were no longer earth-bound to mundane product benefits.

The result was a devastating multimillion-dollar war of the additives: TCP, Activated Charcoal, Gardol, Miracle SLS, M-3, Solium, RX-2, WD-9, Trisilium, Microsheen, Irium, R-51, V-7, Phenylium, Lexitol, Petrox, and so on. They turned up in foods, dentifrices, gasolines, cleaners, hair tonics, cosmetics, cold remedies, soaps, dog foods, in fact everywhere imaginable and some places that were not. So numerous were they, that even their admen progenitors could not keep them straight and a game developed along Madison Avenue to see who could correctly identify the miracle ingredient with the host product. Indicative of the game's complexity, any night of the week the names of 25 or so mysterious ingredients were announced in properly awed tones on TV as the reason for the superiority of one product over all the others.

The ability to believe in magic also kept an estimated 35 million overweight Americans on an all-year hunt for just the right product that would slim them down effortlessly. There was no end to the concoctions and devices they tried out, failed with, and went on to the next. They had available to them bath salts, bath cabinets, and nonporous garments to sweat the fat off. They had soaps, pastes, and creams to wipe it off. They had special girdles and belts to massage it off. They had suction cups designed to pound it off. They had vibratory cushions and chairs to shake it off, and a portable vibrator to remove inches of it from any part of the body where it was unwanted. They also had a variety of internal ways of attacking it. They had purgatives and laxatives to rush the food through the system before it had a chance to add to the avoirdupois. They had materials to swell up in the stomach and leave little room for fattening foods. They had candy snacks to be taken before meals to forestall hunger at mealtime. They had all kinds of drugs, some to stimulate metabolism, others to depress appetite, still others to dehydrate the body.

A favorite was one which miraculously slimmed the body down regardless of what or how much the individual ate. Hailed as an "amazing new drug," a TV commercial depicted a stout woman sitting at a table fading down to slimness, all the while eating like mad. Print ads were headlined: "Eat Strawberry Short-cake and Reduce!" "Lose Ugly Fat . . . Yet Eat Plenty!" "Full-Stomach Reducing Plan." "No-Diet Reducing." The copy went on to describe the lucious steaks, mashed potatoes, butter, bread, pastries that could be put away without putting an ounce on. Rather, the fat "melted right off your body, before your very eyes." The melting process chronicled in the ads was "9 pounds in 10 days, 17 pounds in 19 days, 25 pounds in only 29 days."

The health authorities remained stubbornly unimpressed by these claims, however, for the drug, phenylpropanalomine hydro-chloride, was old hat to them. It had been used for nearly 20 years by doctors in the treatment of obese patients. In *New and Non-Official Remedies*, issued by the Council on Pharmacy and Chem-istry of the American Medical Association, a dosage of "50 milli-grams, two or three times daily for adults" was recommended. In the "miracle" weight-reducers sold over-the-counter, however, the dosage generally was 25 milligrams, for the higher dosage was prohibited by law in over-the-counter products. In the 25-milligram dosage, the AMA said the weight-reducers were about as effective "as an ordinary sugar pill." The nation's overweight hence were in for two surprises. First of all, contrary to the im-pression gained from the splashy headlines about how the fat simply rolled off no matter what or how much was eaten, the package containing the pills invariably included a rigorous diet. "To lose weight, you must eat less," was the burden of the dietary advice. Second, the miracle drug failed to perform the miracle expected of it. The overweight therefore had no recourse but to focus their hopes on the next miracle that came along.

A Congressional investigating committee, after hearings in 1957 on the nationally advertised remedies for obesity, concluded that the whole lot of them were practically "worthless." Food and Drug Administration officials testified that overweight Americans were "fleeced of $100 million a year in their purchase of spurious diet aids and useless mechanical devices." A National Better Business Bureau spokesman said the weight-reducers had been "parlayed into a multimillion-dollar racket." The Postmaster General was concerned that "the use of the mails to promote medical quackery was at the highest level in history." The New York District Attorney, after a 134-count criminal information was returned by a grand jury against a major TV advertiser of a weight-reducer, commented: "In the sophisticated language of Madison Avenue, this was a fraud in depth."

Nonetheless the obese continued to be believers in the magic of the advertisers. They bought hundreds of "dietetic" foods on supermarket shelves, guzzled soft drinks that were advertised as "Refreshing-Without-Filling," ate loaves of bread that were touted as "low calorie," added "low caloric" macaroni to their dinner menus, drank beer that was careful of their "beltline," poured sugar in their coffee and tea on advice from the sugar industry that "an 18-calorie teaspoon of sugar" was an aid in weight loss. Sometimes the advertisers ran afoul of the federal agencies, such as the bread, beer, and macaroni producers, but at no time were the overweight without comforting advice on the advertising pages.

At times in Congressional hearings and in the medical press doctors have speculated on how much health damage the nation's obese have sustained over the years by listening to the siren voice of the advertisers. For heart disease, high blood pressure and diabetes are in common association with obesity, and the inroads of these diseases are irreversible. For those who died prematurely, however, there was no notation on their death certificates: "Sought advertisers' rather than medical advice."

About 10 million Americans, spending between $350 million to $500 million annually on vitamins and other food supplements, provided striking evidence that nutritional misconceptions die hard, and are even harder to kill. In millions of homes the swallowing of one or two vitamin pills became an integral part of the breakfast ritual, for the millions believed that these pills contributed to good health and avoided the perils of something called "vitamin-starvation." Public fascination with the world of vitamins began in the twenties when newspapers and magazines ran feature articles on the link-up of vitamins and human diseases. As more vitamins were discovered the list of diseases resulting from their shortage in the human diet became formidable: anemia, rickets, scurvy, beriberi, eye diseases, circulatory troubles, nervous and mental disorders. Scanning the list was enough to lend a sense of imbalance even to stable people.

Advertising in the twenties, anything but loathe to capitalize on popular fear, promoted vitamins as the miracle pills that prevented the onset of these diseases. And by the time the federal agencies stepped in to curtail the preventive or therapeutic advertising claims, millions were confirmed swallowers of the pills, and a major industry was born. The ads settled thereafter for a permissible tabulation of vitamins and their associative diseases which served nonetheless to trigger continuing vitamin sales among the indoctrinated. Fresh news items and feature articles in the mass media kept the public interest alive and in a buying mood.

Health authorities took a dim view of the vitamin folklore on the ground that unquestionably vitamins are necessary to the human diet, but people generally get enough of them in their daily food. For instance, the AMA Council on Foods and Nutrition never tired of saying that the great majority of people dosing themselves with vitamins were already enjoying a daily diet that had just about all of them the body needed or could use. The superfluous intake of vitamins was simply eliminated by the body as waste and in the judgment of the AMA the money spent on vitamins "could better be spent on food." But this judgment did not sit well with the faithful who refused to believe the medical scoffers who said it would take close to a harebrained diet for anyone to escape his daily vitamin quota, especially with so many food staples currently being vitamin-enriched. The few who indulged in such improper eating habits, according to the medical men, needed their attentions rather than those of the salesman.

Nonetheless the annual sales of vitamins continued to rise, aided by multiplying vitamin advertisers and skillful copy, despite the scoldings by the AMA and public health authorities. For who listens to skeptics when the shamans can ward off evils so easily? Occasionally some of the more aggressive or careless shamans were stopped in the middle of their tribal rites by the Food and Drug Administration. For instance, in 1959 shipments of vitamins, minerals, and other "health foods" valued at more than $1½ million were seized on the grounds that they were unsafe, contaminated, or falsely labeled. But outside these narrow grounds, precious little could be done about vitamin products whose claims were kept under wraps. The vitamin business became "the most widespread and expensive form of medical quackery in the country," according to FDA.

What chafed public health authorities was what the Secretary of Health, Education and Welfare called "the misinformation, pseudo-science and plain 'hokum' reaching the public through books and magazine articles." Granted constitutional freedom of the press, book and magazine publishers printed often with an eye on popular sales, and fragments of inconclusive scientific experimentation were ballooned into remarkable scientific "discoveries." Advertisers could not be expected to pass up the promotional opportunities tailor-made by the "scientific" writings. In an era of mass selling, big promotional budgets ordinarily were made quickly available to exploit the public interest aroused by best-seller books or feature articles in the big circulation magazines.

For instance, *Folk Medicine* by Dr. D. C. Jarvis enchanted a wide reading audience with the idea that unpasteurized honey and apple-cider vinegar could successfully treat or prevent ailments ranging from heart disease to falling hair. While the idea did not gather much support from organized medicine it did enlist the active support of enterprising advertisers who put the mixture up for sale on grocery shelves. Ordinarily the mixture was unaccompanied by claims, but one unwary advertiser sold the product against a display of the book, and FDA promptly seized both on the ground that the book constituted false labeling of the product. More battlewise advertisers were content to cash in on the favorable climate of public interest in the book, made no claims, and hence violated no law.

In the same way the flurry of news reports and feature articles on the suspected relationship between certain foods and heart disease stimulated both the public interest and the advertisers' products. "Fat intake" was the suspected culprit in heart disease and "cholesterol" in the hardening process of the arteries. Although the AMA was far from satisfied that either was guilty of the charge ("only fragmentary evidence that fats in the diet may be implicated in coronary heart disease"), both were pretty much convicted and hung in the mass media. Soon salad oil, shortening, margarine, and other product advertising turned up headlined: "Helps Cut Down Cholesterol." "The Fighter Against Cholesterol." "Lowers the Cholesterol Level in the Blood Stream." "New Skillet Cooking with Your Heart in Mind." The "opportunism" with which such promoters exploited the moment of public anxiety was scored by FDA, which warned that the advertisers courted trouble if they continued to promote unsaturated fats and oils as safeguards against heart attacks and strokes. The federal agency announced that it was prepared to view even the term "cholesterol" on the label of common foods as misleading. Advertisers carefully closed the door to trouble by omitting the implicating word on labels, and fueled the public anxiety by scary reference to cholesterol in ads.

With a national average of three colds per person and an

estimated $5 billion in wages lost from days absent from work, cold remedies had a fine climate of interest in which to operate. Each new cold "cure" that was reported in the news was the signal for advertisers to latch on to the new "miracle." When a *Reader's Digest* article ("Is This Good-by to the Common Cold?"), for instance, reported encouraging results with antihistamines, about a dozen antihistamine brands appeared on the market. The ads lavished praise on the antihistamines for stopping cold symptoms dead in their tracks in only a matter of hours or a day. One advertiser spread the two words, "STOP COLDS," over half a newspaper page, each letter the size of the letter "E" on the optometrist's chart. Another converted the *Reader's Digest* question into a resounding affirmative: "Say Good-By to the Common Cold." In the next months, fortunately in the bad weather season when colds were numerous, planted publicity and feature articles in the mass media hailed the coming victory at last over man's nasty enemy, the common cold. The trade press reported that about $7 million were spent in advertising and by the time the cold season was over the sale of antihistamines hit $15 million. As the public rushed for its antihistamines, one big circulation magazine showed the chairman of a drug company standing alongside a huge mound of nine million antihistamine tablets—his company's one-day output.

Typically, public health authorities were somewhat less than enthusiastic over the new "miracle." They called the value of antihistamines in cold therapy unproved, the research not scientifically acceptable, and the advertising "blatant." A major medical journal concluded that antihistamines could not be counted on "to prevent or cure the common cold." The Federal Trade Commission pressed the antihistamine makers to drop advertising claims that the product cured, prevented, or shortened colds, and insisted that advertising claims could not go beyond the relief of cold symptoms. But by then millions of cold sufferers were swallowing antihistamine pills regularly and, even shorn of strong claims, the antihistamines settled down to enjoy a comfortable $18-million-a-year business.

The flavonoids which arrived a few years later, also timed for the onset of the bad weather season, announced in full-page newspaper ads "Medicine's Newest Weapon for Control of Colds." The ads could barely restrain their excitement as they related how the flavonoids built up the body's defenses in an area hitherto untouched by cold therapy—in the capillaries. The flavonoids were treated just as roughly, however, as the predecessor remedies. The AMA *Journal* dismissed them as having "no significant effect, palliative or otherwise, on the course of the common cold." The medical director of FDA said that "a cold is still a cold" and added astringently that the whole thing might be "a hoax." The *New England Journal of Medicine* was editorially aghast at modern promotional methods which involved a "blast at a gullible public" and a simultaneous by-passing of the medical profession. Doctors who were too busy to read the "morning newspapers or the new *Reader's Digest*," and hence were not up on the latest in cold remedies, were considered something of relics by their patients. Doctors were no more a match for the pill makers than the public.

Advertisers other than the antihistamines and flavonoids also paid solicitous attention to the cold-bleary public. A wide range of choices was available. Anyone with the sniffles could down one brand of Cold Tablets and head for a bowling alley or party, or another brand and enjoy "five stay-in-bed-benefits" without ever going near a bed, or get a "total cold treatment" with Bufferin and Sunkist Lemon diet, or rub on his body an ointment that was better than "any cold tablet," or gargle with an antiseptic that slaughtered millions of throat germs, or go around the house slaughtering them by the billions with a cleansing agent that was touted as "Asian-flu tested." The AMA gave short shrift to all these remedies and methods: they could do exactly "nothing to cure the common cold." The FDA was particularly incensed by the claim that a product could prevent Asian flu—only innoculation could do that—and called such claim "false, misleading and shameful."

The dentifrice makers produced their own succession of miracle ingredients which, if they did not cut down the nation's dental caries, at least helped push up dentifrice sales from $90 million in 1948 to $235 million in 1959. First came the ammoniated toothpastes which were supposed to work by inhibiting the growth of the mouth bacteria believed to cause tooth decay. Sales success came with prodigious advertising and the cordiality of the mass media which hailed the ammoniateds in articles for their doughty qualities in "fighting," "controlling" and "preventing" tooth decay. Practically nobody heard the protesting voice of the American Dental Association that such claims were "not supported by adequate evidence." So impressive were the sales results that the dentifrice makers looked around for a successor miracle ingredient, which they found in chlorophyll.

The public fancy had been touched by a *Reader's Digest* article ("Nature's Deodorant") describing chlorophyll's deodorizing property. The dentifrice makers promptly put the green stuff in their toothpaste tubes and squeezed the last bit of promotional value out of it with massive advertising budgets. In a short time chlorophyll captured one-third of the dentrifice sales, an unheard-of dent in the previously stable dentrifice field. Unforseen trouble developed, however, when advertisers of other consumer products recognized the sales stimulus of the green additive and put it in their own products. Soon it was in chewing gums, mouth washes, shampoos, cigarettes, reducing pills, foot pads, air purifiers, nasal solutions, skin ointments, toilet paper, suppositories, dog foods. As the number of products lengthened practically daily and the wondrous claims grew ever more fanciful the magic almost overnight went out of chlorophyll as a sales-getter. It was literally laughed out of the market. "Never has a substance been so exploited and so prostituted by ridiculous applications," said the American Dental Association.

The next miracle ingredient on which the dentifrice makers put their advertising hopes and millions were the antienzymes. Dental research on the antienzymes was just as tentative, experimental, preliminary—and inconclusive—as the preceding miracles. It revolved around the belief that tooth decay was caused by acids forming in the mouth after sugar and other carbohydrates were eaten. Thus, if the enzymes that formed the acids could be inhibited, the teeth could be safeguarded from acid attack. The fact that the evidence was inconclusive did not stand in the way of the headstrong dentifrice makers. They produced antienzyme toothpastes and again rode the crest of public interest which the big-circulation magazines provided with articles like "A New Weapon Against Tooth Decay," "Good-By to Toothache," and "Found: A New Curb on Tooth Decay." The American Dental Association grimly predicted that the latest claimant would cause "little more than a ripple on the sea of superlatives that have surrounded the dentifrice field since the days of Pliny and Galen." Dr. Leonard S. Fosdick, whose original laboratory research was the jumping-off point for the ad claims, protested against the manhandling of his research in the ads. But by then the dentifrice makers were eyeing their next miracle—the fluorides.

The fluorides had a larger body of research to support them than the preceding additives. In fact, ten-year tests had convinced many public health authorities that adding fluorides to the public drinking water would sharply reduce dental caries in children. The fluorides hardened the teeth and made them more resistant to decay. That was enough for the dentifrice makers who brought out a spate of fluoride toothpastes. The American Dental Association and other public health authorities protested in vain that the available evidence proved only that fluorides were effective in drinking water, or by direct application to the teeth, and not in toothpastes. The ADA warned that the dentists and public were becoming "exceedingly gun-shy" of miracles that failed to live up to their advance promises. But sales of fluoride toothpastes were brisk, with the thunderous promotional campaigns aided again by the drum-beating big-circulation periodicals with their goodby-to-toothache articles, and the dentifrice makers showed no excessive concern with the criticism.

At Congressional hearings in Washington in the late fifties on dentifrice advertising, the dentists were on hand to press their complaints. Testimony pointed to the billions spent on the promotion of dubious dentifrice products and the false sense of security to the public as a result. An ADA spokesman said there were no shortcuts to dental health and "to mislead the public in this regard is to work deliberately against the public welfare." His testimony was denounced by sections of the advertising trade press for the "smugness of the professional boys who see nothing but evil in advertising." The simple truth, argued one publication, was that the dentifrice advertisers had done "more to advance the cause of dental health and the economic prosperity of dentists than any other single group in the population—not excluding the dentists and the ADA."

The publication scolded the dentists for not taking the trouble to learn of the tribulations of the dentifrice makers every time they introduced a new ingredient. It meant they had to revise their marketing strategy from top to bottom every couple of years, for they had to come up with a new product (with a winsome flavor), design a new package, work out new prices, check the product in test markets, strengthen distribution, worry about trade relations (and especially the overstocked druggist), and come up with a bright new advertising theme. And they faced competition that did the same, and fickle consumers who stayed with the new product only until a newer one came along.

Furthermore the stakes were exceedingly high. An ad budget of $10 million and another $10 million for giveaway samples was not exceptional, and then the companies had to wait two or three years before the investment started coming back. Rarely indeed did a company reap the kind of windfall of Procter & Gamble, one of whose toothpaste brands was accepted by the ADA as a caries-preventive agent. It was a curious windfall, anyway, for it was not immediately in counter sales but in the stock market. P & G stock shot up 13¾ points within three days of the ADA announcement, which added some $360 million to P & G's total worth, which was more than $100 million in excess of the total annual sales of all dentifrices. This was indeed a first-class miracle. The sales spurt came later.

The cigarette advertisers have for most of two decades been on the firing range of the Federal Trade Commission which, in 1942, ordered advertising claims stopped by several of the tobacco companies. Ordered stopped were claims that Old Gold contained "less nicotine, tars, resins than any other brand," that Lucky Strike was "easy on the throat," that Philip Morris' diethylene glycol protected smokers from smoker's cough, that Camel would "never harm or irritate the throat," that Chesterfield would have no adverse effect on nose, throat, or other organs. With one fell swoop FTC attempted to lay low these claims by taking the position that there was "no significant difference" between the brands in nicotine, tars, or resins, and that the smoke from all of them was equally irritating. In hearings that were protracted over the years the FTC fought for an elusive victory. For as soon as one claim was struck down another, as obnoxious in the FTC's eyes, took its place, and the administrative and legal tussles with the tobacco companies gave promise to be endless.

By 1954 the FTC decided to try another gambit and proposed to the tobacco companies an industry-wide advertising code to eschew any claims that cigarette smoking in general, or the smoking of any brand in particular, was noninjurious to the smoker's health. Nor would ads be permitted to claim less nicotine, tars, or resins unless such claims could be fully proved scientifically. Although some tobacco companies griped about infringements on freedom of speech, they signed the code. The pressure to sign came from two sources. First, the nation was by then in the grip of the first big cigarette-lung cancer scare, and cigarette sales had dived, for the first time in more than a decade. The American Cancer Society had issued a report on the smoking habits of 187,766 men between 50 and 70 and established a high statistical correlation between smoking and lung cancer. Heavy cigarette smoking doubled the death rate from coronary diseases and more than doubled the death rate from lung cancer, and even light cigarette smoking was associated with a death rate rise. Second, the tobacco companies, aware of the alarm among cigarette smokers, had worked themselves in a corner in their ads and were, in effect, promoting brands on a my-brand-gives-less-cancer-than-your-brand basis.

Shortly thereafter the tobacco companies joined in a full-page ad headlined "A Frank Statement to Cigarette Smokers" which was placed in 448 newspapers over the nation. In the ad smokers were reminded that for more than 300 years tobacco had given "solace, relaxation, and enjoyment to mankind," and were offered the reassuring prediction that the cancer charge against tobacco would eventually be abandoned for "lack of evidence." But the tobacco companies were unmistakably worried.

So were the smokers. For they ran in such numbers to the presumed safety of the filter-tips that one executive termed what was happening "one of the greatest upheavals since Americans first started smoking cigarettes." Whereas in 1954 only 10 percent of sales were filter-tips, five years later 50 percent of the smokers were puffing through filters. The filters offered dubious protection. The *AMA Journal* reported after testing the filters: "In all cases, the fraction of nicotine removed by the filters . . . is small." But the public did not get to read the *AMA Journal*, and put its trust in the filters. It was also put under heavy sedation by the public relations program of the tobacco companies which effectively cushioned every piece of unfavorable news about cigarette smoking with standardized rebuttals.

For about two years after appending their signatures to the FTC's code, the cigarette brands sparred with "mildness" claims. Camel and Lucky Strike were "mild," Chesterfield was "much milder," Dunhill was "far milder," Pall Mall came up with "mildness you can measure," and Philip Morris with "tasty mildness." But under the spur of competition for the filter market, the brands soon began to slug it out in earnest. Typical of the ads: "Kent filters best." "Parliament with recessed filter is best." "New Hit Parade has America's best filter." In the crossfire of claims and counterclaims, virtually every brand established itself as lowest in tars and nicotine. And every brand proffered the findings of "independent testing laboratories" as proof of its claims.

Thus the FTC code went up in smoke as lung cancer deaths mounted to what Dr. Alton Ochsner, professor of surgery at Tulane University, called "epidemic proportions." From 3.08 per 100,000 in 1930, deaths climbed to 42.16 per 100,000 by 1958.

It became an open question who was going to get hurt most in what was dubbed along Madison Avenue as the "tar derby" —the racers, the public in the stands, or the "umpires." For the racers chopped away at each other's claims to their common immolation, the public might be getting cancer by the carton, and the ubiquitous "independent testing laboratories" risked the charge of prostitution by issuing findings that contradicted each other. It raised the obvious questions about their "independence" and the propriety of their "science."

The trade press gave indications that the testing outfits were generally unhappy about their predicament. They did not like to yield their scientific standing by performing tests along the client's specifications, which often were designed to make the client's product come out ahead of the competition. But as servants to business they had scant choice in the matter. As *Printers' Ink* noted, theirs was the touchy problem of "reconciling . . . the ethics of science with the ethics of business." Regrettable though it was, nonetheless "doing business with business makes a scientist a businessman."

Thus the distortion if not the wholesale corruption of science proceeded with gathering momentum as a characteristic of mass merchandising in the postwar U.S. Grants by companies to universities, foundations, and other scientific bodies for experimental laboratory work often provided the basis for runaway claims which the watchdog federal agencies were in no position to challenge, for they lacked the money and personnel to do so. By the time they got around to testing the products and disputing the claims, the companies had dropped these claims and were off on another tack. Moreover the law put the burden of disproving advertising claims on the federal agencies, which guaranteed that they would take second place in the race with the advertisers.

No wonder, then, that ads promoting the dubious virtues of black strap molasses, wheat germ, Royal Jelly, "happy" pills, tranquillizers, arthritis and rheumatism remedies, so flamboyantly crowded the mass media. Many constituted "outright quackery," the AMA charged. In the *Wisconsin Medical Journal* an editorial titled "Hucksters and Hoaxes" noted that "despite the sad moral tone of this kind of advertising, few advertising agencies or media have found the strength to refuse to touch it." The editorial concluded that "as long as people have tooth decay, indigestion, headaches, sleepless nights, running noses, middle-age spread or cigarette cough, the gray-flanneled medicine men will prey on their fear and offer the security of self-administered panaceas." The medicine men had learned to operate profitably within the "general respect in which science is held by most people."

The Giveaway 10

As an agent to speed up the consumption of consumer goods the giveaway became almost endemic in postwar merchandising. Something-for-nothing offers broke new highs annually as the practice spread from soups and cereals, where they originated, to a wide range of consumer products. That the giveaway boosted sales was undeniable, for apparently it touched the larceny deep in the hearts of consumers, although many wary consumers insisted "you never get something for nothing."

In the thirties advertisers were chary of spending promotional dollars until federal pump-priming and the passage of time had put money back into pockets and consumers in a buying frame of mind. In the fifties, on the contrary, advertisers freely threw in extra promotional millions to encourage free-spending consumers. Advertisers, like fishermen, head for the stream when the fish are running and produce all their promotional lures when there is something worthwhile to lure.

It might be stated with accuracy that the sales efforts indeed of the entire merchandising system moved into high gear. Even factory and office workers, unconnected with sales, were caught up in it. For a variety of continuous company contests stirred them to greater job interests and productivity. Of course company contests had for generations been used in employee-relations programs, but in the fifties more contests were employed by management than ever before, according to *Management Review*. For instance, General Motors ran a "My Job and Why I Like It" employee contest, Westinghouse a "What Owning Stock in Our Company Means to Me," Western Union offered a prize for the best slogan describing a new company service, Reynolds Metals for a snapshot, Alcoa for an industrial design. So great was company interest in contests that the Dartnell organization issued a brochure "How to Promote a Know-Your-Company Contest" and many management consultants urged the introduction of contest-fun into the nation's factories, to harness the yearning for sudden riches that compelled 40 to 50 million adult Americans to enter contests yearly. Among company prizes to lucky employees were refrigerators, ranges, washers, freezers, TV's, automatic irons, and cash.

Management paid special attention, of course, to its selling arm—dealers, jobbers, salesmen. To get extra effort out of them, more than a half million dollars was spent annually on sales contests for them, a trade magazine estimated. A speaker told the New York Sales Executive Club that salesmen were like storage batteries in cars—always running out of energy—and that it was management's responsibility to recharge them periodically. The company contest was a sure-fire way to do this for reasons, as Zenn Kaufman wrote in *How to Run Better Sales Contests*, that were heavy on the psychological side. Even more than the prize, the salesmen coveted the honor of winning. They were boys at heart who would rather play than work, and would play harder than they would work.

They were thus spurred in the postwar era to new sales records by such lures as hunting trips to Africa, around-the-world jaunts, cruises to the Caribbean, ocean voyages to Europe with a limousine and liveried chauffeur waiting for them at the docking pier. Commonly the companies paid for everything, from hotel tips and travel insurance down to the maid for the winner's wife and the flowers that were pinned on her. Some companies even threw in the cash with which to buy souvenirs.

All this benevolence paid off for the companies, of course, for not only did sales spurt during the contest but winners returned to their jobs with the kind of fresh enthusiasm that is ordinarily mustered only by recent college graduates for their alma maters. Even the losers harbored scant resentment for having worked so hard in vain, as several surveys showed, but many companies took the precautionary measure of giving token awards to the also-rans. As sales contests became big business, one company specializing in handling them for many giant corporations was reported in *Newsweek* as having handed out $40 million in prizes in 1959.

Dealers came in to their own brand of red-carpet treatment. Some two million of them were instructed, inspired, and entertained at 89,000 conventions and national sales meetings in 1959, according to *Newsweek*. Many were posh affairs, not in the same league with the company-produced theatricals that pepped up sales meetings in the thirties, or even the vaudeville shows staged by professionals that took over in the forties. In the fifties the grandeur of the sales push called for nothing less than full-fledged Broadway musicals, produced for the companies by "name" writers, lyricists, producers, and cast. The staging of such extravaganzas became the specialty of a handful of show packagers, one of whom put together 25 to 30 yearly with the tab running as high as $1.5 million, said *Business Week*. Typical of them was the gathering of 1,300 department store buyers in the grand ballroom of the New York Hotel Statler where they were shown the latest creations of a fabric firm and entertained by a Broadway musical. To make sure that they arrived on time, poodles, silver fox stoles, and two Thunderbirds were given away as door prizes.

The biggest giveaways of all, however, were reserved for the nation's consumers. To this end, the airways became the special communication medium to the get-rich-quick impulses that seemed to stir in everybody. When $64,000 Question captured an astonishingly high rating in 1955, quiz and contest shows moved heavily into network programming. Soon it was money, prizes, and games all day and night and each show miraculously pulled down a high rating. As soon as one showed signs of faltering it was replaced by another money-showering format that clicked. On TV even faster than on radio the shows kept multiplying. In a short time the giveaway shows rode into second place in network programming, hard on the heels of the fast-shooting badmen and sheriffs. Surveying the airways' fare, a staff writer for *Advertising Age* quipped: "It hardly seems worthwhile going to work, when you can stay home and play bingo for thousands of dollars, or name a turtle for a diamond ring, or have a go at a dot game for a refrigerator."

The giveaway show had long fascinated the American public. Such shows as Pot of Gold, Double or Nothing and Take It or Leave It in the early days of radio had given away $100 to housewives for no more arduous a task than answering the telephone. Then in 1945 Stop the Music came out of nowhere and hit the jackpot by giving away carloads of merchandise to merchandise-hungry consumers at the end of the war. But such money and merchandise prizes looked piddling compared to the gold rush that began in earnest in the midfifties. The hundred dollars that looked like a tidy fortune in the lean years yielded to tens of thousands in the fat years. As advertisers fought each other for a larger slice of the audience they seemed to vie in seeing who could give away the most money. The dollar bait for the audience grew more munificent yearly. When the quiz shows hit their stride in

1955 the grand prize was $256,000 and rumors spread up and down Madison Avenue that the next prize plateau would be a cool half million. There was no end to the amount of money advertisers would spend to prevent the restless audience from twisting the station dial. As they raised the ante on each other, *Advertising Age* worried that they were engaging in "a race towards bankruptcy."

In 1958 the television networks programmed so many quiz shows that the electronic marvel of the age appeared to the casual viewer as one big guessing game. Among the big-time shows there was Lucky Dollar, a word game based on the old parlor game Ghost, Twenty-One, based on the old card game, and Top Dollar, based on the old dollar bill number gimmick. And there were endless variations on the theme: Make Me Laugh, a game in which comedians tried to make unwilling subjects do just that, who were paid at the rate of a dollar for every second they kept a straight face; Dough-Re-Mi, a musical game in which contestants tried to name the song after listening to a few bars (if they missed, they could risk part of the bankroll and try again); High Finance, which depended on shrewd "trading and bartering" and in which a contestant could win up to $75,000 in cash plus generous prizes; The Most Beautiful Girl in the World, which offered a comely lass with acting, singing or dancing ability, plus brains, a chance to win $250,000; Dotto, an audience-participation game in which TV's, refrigerators, and mink coats were awarded to telephoned watchers who correctly identified a dot-sketched picture of a celebrity; Do You Trust Your Wife, which pitted two couples against each other with prizes of a swimming pool, gasoline for 10,000 miles and a piano as part of the loot; Your Hit Parade, which required the folks at home to view the show and smoke and like (in 25 words or less) Hit Parade cigarettes.

Also astride the airways were $64,000 Question, The Big Surprise, Tic Tac Dough, The Price Is Right, You Bet Your

Life, People Are Funny, Brains and Brawn, Treasure Hunt, Truth or Consequences, Haggis-Baggis, Music Bingo, The Big Game, Win with a Winner, Concentration, Anybody Can Play, Bid 'n' Buy, $64,000 Challenge, Name That Tune, The Big Payoff, Play Your Hunch, For Love of Money. Certainly nobody with a TV set at home could have failed to have been impressed with the marvels of knowledge—at least with its windfall aspects.

Some of the quiz shows wilted temporarily in 1958 under the heat of the rigging scandals. In short order Dotto was unceremoniously dumped by its sponsor and $64,000 Challenge followed a week later. It left Madison Avenue in a dreadful state of cliff-hanging uncertainty, guessing how many more shows would also be dumped. In the balance, should the public show its disenchantment with the isolation booth geniuses and the show ratings slide, were some $20 million in agency billings. Few admen were concerned with the moral questions involved in the rigging of shows. Far bigger was the question whether the hanky-panky would end the public's interest in them. If ratings slid, that would signal the death sentence for all of them, for nothing survived on TV without a good rating.

During this period of uncertainty quiz sponsors and packagers mostly reassured themselves that their properties would not be seriously affected. Some resorted to the "one rotten apple" bromide, some thought "crank" mail would zoom, but most were convinced the shows would ride out the storm. Indeed some of the impresarios were affronted by the widespread unfavorable publicity, and considered it somewhat unfair. A few saw in the indignation of the press nothing more than the foul mouthings of a rival communication medium. It was no secret to anyone, they pointed out, that showmanship was the vital consideration in a good quiz show, for it was intended to entertain, not instruct. How could drama be built up if one contestant after the other could not shoot back the answers? How could the sponsor build up goodwill for his product if one contestant after another failed to walk off with the mink coat, the trip to Europe, or the $64,000? To find proper contestants the quiz show packagers were put to considerable time and effort to hunt down personable people blessed with photographic memories. When they were found, the show tried to hang on to them, especially when the show grew "hot." The question of "honesty" or "morality" hence had no relevancy to a quiz show appraisal, for the one real yardstick was the size of the audience attracted. That—and only that—was the measure of the packager's ability, and what the sponsor laid down his money for.

Actually the quiz show offered the sponsor one of TV's best economic bargains. An *Advertising Age* staff writer calculated that $64,000 Question gave away, on the average, only $14,000 weekly during its first 21 months on the air. Generally it took four or five weeks for contestants to get into the big money brackets, and then some of them could always be counted on risking the jackpot, and losing (and driving away in consolation Cadillacs). The production cost of such a show, moreover, was low compared to other shows attracting an equivalent audience. On a cost-per-thousand basis—a method commonly used by sponsors to figure cost, because it was so easy—no other type of show offered the opportunity to keep brand names on steady display and allowed such a steady stream of commercials. What was more, even the luxury merchandise given away as prizes was frequently part of an arrangement with other advertisers, who contributed their products in return for "plugs" during the show. Several companies were around for the specific purpose of supplying the giveaway shows with merchandise, in return for the proper "mentions." One such company rounded up $3 million worth of merchandise yearly, according to a trade press report. It was a happy arrangement for everybody, for the sponsors who kept their costs low, for the collateral advertisers who got their free plugs, and for the in-between brokers who got their cut. And the audience was treated to a lot of high-tension excitement and the pleasure of seeing an ordinary mortal beat a big company out of a bundle of money and other prizes.

The sponsors and show packagers were quite right in their faith, for the quiz shows sagged only briefly following the skul-duggery exposure and a huge audience continued to be fascinated by shower-the-wealth programs. The few criers of doom proved to be not only premature but unrealistic.

The Federal Communications Commission was unhappy about the ubiquitous quiz shows but there seemed to be nothing the agency could do. Back in 1949 when the radio giveaway shows began to pour their bounty on the nation, the FCC tried to deliver a knockout blow to such shows by promulgating a rule that banned them as lotteries. Even before that the agency had tried unsuccessfully to get the Department of Justice to take criminal action against the shows, and had similarly failed to get Congress to amend the law to prohibit them. The three networks promptly challenged the FCC rule, took the battle to federal court, and won the war in the Supreme Court. The FCC con-tention that the giveaways were "nothing but age-old lotteries in a slightly new form" designed to "buy" audiences was dismissed by the Supreme Court as stretching the definition of a lottery "to the breaking point" and making such programs "a crime." The 1954 decision thus opened the radio and TV floodgates to the giveaways. *Advertising Age* was moved to caution networks, sponsors, and packagers to show more restraint than was "nota-ble in the past"; otherwise, it warned, "Santa Claus is going to be a year-round visitor and Christmas may actually settle back to being a religious holiday." The trade newspaper's fears were groundless, for neither has happened.

Another major manifestation of the national acquisitive in-stinct in the fifties took place in the avid collection of trading stamps. Starting in 1953 when the supermarkets took on the stamps, so rapidly did the contagion spread that by 1960 more than 40 million families—four out of every five—were busily pasting the tiny gummed rectangles into books. Nobody knew how many stamp companies operated nor the dollar volume of sales, but trade estimates ranged from 250 to 500 stamp companies which did from $600 to $800 million in stamp business. Stamps figured in at least 10 percent of all retail sales, and the printing presses were turning out trading stamps faster than the U.S. Post Office was turning out postage stamps. In 1960 Sperry & Hutchinson, the oldest and largest stamp company, serviced about 60,-000 accounts, operated more than 600 redemption centers, and claimed more than 25 million stamp-savers. Nine of the nation's ten largest food chains gave stamps (and the holdout A & P succumbed the next year). Indicative of the thumping good business was the $30 million in stamp sales racked up by one company in its first year of operation, the printing of 30 million redemption catalogs by another (probably the largest single print order ever placed), and the lavish color spreads that graced the big-circulation magazines for the competing stamp companies.

The craze signified another step in the disinterest of consumers with price and their growing love for shopping centers with wide merchandise assortments, big parking lots, air conditioning, kiddie corners, carry-out service and—trading stamps. All sorts of surveys showed that housewives often knew they paid more at stamp-giving stores but did not care. For they had their eyes on the pop-up toaster, TV set, chaise longue, barbecue set, matched luggage, mink coat, or trip to Europe, all prizes which were theirs—for nothing—when they brought the magic number of stamp-filled books to the redemption center. They patiently waited months, even years, to hoard the proper number of stamps, for they got one with each ten-cent sale and it took $150 of spending to fill a 1,500 stamp book.

The psychologists said they got a feeling of being virtuous and thrifty over saving stamps, for they were able to pick up luxury items for "nothing" that their consciences would never have permitted them to walk into a store and buy.

As for the retailers, they sometimes had the feeling they had a bear by the tail. Sales jumps from 30 percent to 50 percent were not uncommon when a retailer first introduced stamps in a community. This not only offset the cost of stamps—2 percent of gross—but threw off a handsome profit from the boosted sales. But as the other retailers—food, gasoline, drug, dry cleaning, and so on—got on the stamp bandwagon the sales curves tended to flatten out and they were left with the residue of the stamp overhead. There was just so much money around to be spent. Unless overall spending increased, the retailers faced trouble.

One disillusioned supermarket operator wrote in *Super Market Merchandising* that the end result was "exactly the same as putting a 2 percent tax on everything sold in food stores." Some retailers got out from under by raising prices on some items, dropping "loss leaders" and shopping day "specials" and gravitating to higher-priced merchandise lines that afforded more comfortable profit margins. But they could not get rid of the stamps themselves. They were stuck with the gummed pieces of paper so long as competitors had them, for they were fearful that being the first to drop the stamps would also lead to a drop-off in sales. Many said they would gratefully drop the stamps if the competition would do the same. "Stamps are a necessary evil," wrote a food retailer in *Premium Practice*. "As long as other stores have them, I will have them; if others drop them, so will I."

Few merchandising gimmicks ever raised such a hullabaloo in the merchandising world. Those for and against stamp plans were at each other's throats. A Chicago retail merchants' association branded stamps "prostitution at best, economic insanity at worst." They were "the worst cancer that ever hit the food business," hollered another association. The New York State Merchants Association condemned them as "economically unsound." A Brooklyn food association laced into them as "nothing but a racket." Another retail association charged them with perpetrating "a hoax on consumers" which was in effect "no more than legalized robbery." Even Madison Avenue, the ringmaster of promotional lures, sniffed suspiciously at stamps, probably because advertising budgets were axed by some retailers in the frantic effort to cut down overhead.

Defenders were mainly the stamp companies and a phalanx of retailers who enjoyed thriving sales increases from stamps. Rearguard support came from millions of housewives who demonstrated a 'till-death-do-us-part affection for them by marching resolutely on state legislatures which were debating the advisability of inflicting crippling restrictions on stamp plans, and by defeating one state referendum after another aimed at outlawing them. In their camp, the stamp companies had an Indiana University study which found scant evidence that stamps pushed up food prices, and confirming articles in the *Harvard Business Review* and *Dun's Review*. Wide publicity was given a Department of Agriculture study in 1959 which showed that food prices in stamp-giving supermarkets were only $6/10$ of 1 percent higher than prices in stampless supermarkets; and the point was stressed that the 2 percent merchandise redemption value of stamps more than compensated housewives for the small increase in food prices. But the stamp companies subdued the Department of Agriculture caution that "the time and trouble . . . to save and redeem stamps" was worth something. And they were utterly silent on the observable point that housewives were inveigled by the stamp plans into paying for, even partially, merchandise they were not prepared to go out to buy.

Mass media, federal agencies, merchandising associations—all looked into the trading stamp fracas. The *Journal of Commerce* found the retail food industry rocked "in the most bitter competition since the depression days of the early 1930's." A *Reader's Digest* article acknowledged that stamps brightened the lives of shoppers but found "overwhelming evidence" that "stamp savers usually pay for their premiums—and then some—through higher retail prices." *Life* depicted the "staggering" impact on the shopping habits of Americans "and on the tempers of American businessmen." A *Dun's Review* article conceded they were poison ivy to many retailers yet a potent stimulus to sales. *Fortune* said, "Logically, the whole idea should come unstuck." Investigations were afoot by the Federal Trade Commission, antitrust division of the Department of Justice, Department of Commerce, and the Senate Small Business Committee. New Mexico, Denver, and Indiana universities were inspired to analyze the significance of stamps in the economy and even the psychology of collecting and redeeming them. The Bureau of Labor Statistics weighed whether to include stamps in its price index. The *London Economist* was moved to comment that stamps were "the most discussed, the least understood, and perhaps the most potent new sales device in the U.S. today."

One reason for the ferment was what happened in Denver in the early fifties when stamps were issued in wild profusion and led retailers to their slaughter. For innocent as they looked, stamps represented a potentially uncontrollable economic force. They could lead to nightmarish price wars, which separated them in kind from all the other sales-inducers in the promotional armamentum. Denver merchants learned this the hard way. Stamps came to Denver in 1951 and within a year four of the six food chains had them; a few months later the fifth succumbed. As stamps lost their novelty value to consumers and sales value to the chains, a few merchants broke with standard practice and offered triple stamps on Tuesday, Thursday, and Saturday. Other stores followed. Soon triple stamps were offered on three shopping days and double stamps on the other days. One thing led to another: quadruple stamps, price-cutting, advertising sprees, giveaways, and an all-out war broke out. When the smoke cleared, the number of food stores remaining in the Denver area was cut drastically. Whereas in 1945 about 1,400 food stores served the

485,000 people, by 1955 the population had grown to 750,000 but only 1,035 food stores remained.

Another reason for retail bitterness was the windfall reaped by the stamp companies from unredeemed stamps. Retailers were in hot disagreement with the stamp companies over the percentage of stamps that never turned up at redemption centers to claim merchandise. No military secret was ever more closely guarded than this, and the most the stamp companies would say was that the percentage was not more than 5. The retailers insisted 20 to 30 percent was closer to the truth. Considering the $600 million to $800 million in annual sales, either percentage represented a juicy sum. What stuck in the craw of the retailers was that stamp companies fattened off their sales.

Retail trade associations hence pressed for protective legislation, and every year all sorts of bills to outlaw or restrict trading stamp operations were thrown into state legislative hoppers. Some required trading stamps to be redeemed either in cash or in merchandise, others imposed stiff license fees or taxes on stamp companies or on retailers dealing in stamps, still others simply escheated to the state the cash equivalent of unredeemed stamps. In one such attempt the State of New Jersey was denied by the New Jersey Supreme Court in 1960 the right to seize under its escheat laws some $7,615,000 in unredeemed stamps as "unclaimed personal property." The action was brought against Sperry & Hutchinson and was figured on the stamp company's 5 percent estimate over a period of years. Crippled as it was in many states, the stamp giant refused to be slain.

The something-for-nothing psychology operated in every nook and cranny of the merchandising process. Aside from trading stamps, premiums were almost endemic, and were considered a major prop holding up consumer sales. In the fifties the amount spent by companies on premiums went from $1 billion to $2¼ billion. A 1956 study by Dr. Arnold Corbin of New York University found that of those companies using premiums one out of seven spent more than $100,000 a year on them. More than three out of five coffee roasters and tea packagers dealt in premiums, according to *Coffee & Tea Industries*. Of the 20 leading food advertisers 14 trafficked in premiums and other coupon deals, according to Arthur C. Nielsen, Jr., and one in every four food sales was affected. The food field was particularly vulnerable since it dealt in high-turnover items.

A growing percentage of housewives began to shop on the basis of the accompanying premium offer, and ever more merchandise began to enter U.S. homes via the premium route rather than by direct purchase. Indeed the Premium Advertising Association of America estimated in the late fifties that the premium trade consumed 30 percent of the chinaware manufactured in the U.S., 15 percent of the enamelware, and 10 percent or more of the aluminumware. More and more manufacturers allowed their well known brands to be used as premiums, encouraged their use, in fact: Ansco, Burpee, Columbia Records, Detecto, Eastman Kodak, General Electric, B. F. Goodrich, International Silver, Johnson & Johnson, Lionel, Polaroid, RCA, Revere, Ronson, Silex, Sylvania, Westinghouse, Zenith.

As the bewildering array of models, sizes, packs, brands were pumped into the heavily freighted economy, the premium emerged as the backstop to consumer buying. It emerged practically a more vital marketing tool, in terms of money invested, than any other. And the $2¼ billion spent in 1960 seemed destined to grow, if only because brand sales tended to slump when the premium was discontinued. It acted like any other narcotic, moreover, by requiring ever more attractive and costly offers to keep the sales going. The 10-to-25-cent premium bracket of the early fifties hence all but disappeared, except in juvenile offers, and was supplanted by the half-dollar-to-dollar bracket, with most premiums at the higher figure. Even such big-ticket items as appliances, fur coats, TV's, radios, sporting goods, luggage, bicycles, silverware, cutlery, hardware, furniture, dishes, glassware, lamps, clocks, turned up as premiums. For brand-name advertisers found that premiums were an aid in holding list prices. As an executive told the Premium Advertising Association of America, consumers seemed bewitched by premiums and "did not ask for price cuts on merchandise."

Nonetheless a new species of consumer emerged in the low-priced field who had a highly developed nose for premium deals. For instance, a study on cake mixes by the Market Research Corporation of America discovered that 15 percent of the cake mix buyers walked off with 55 percent of the deal merchandise, disregarding brand. What little was left of brand loyalty thus was still further eroded by premiums. As an adman on a breakfast cereal account wailed: "We're only as good as our last premium."

Enterprising collectors learned to fill their homes with an astonishing array of useful and oddball premiums by diligently filling out boxtops, coupons, sidepanels, and adding a few dollars in cash. Every day the mailman delivered to them such items as nylon gloves, wastepaper basket, kitchen towels, parakeet book, dog training book, corn popper, pencil box, brush dishwasher, dishcloth, paring knife, world atlas, silver service for eight, measuring spoon, 60 miniature flags, 107 articles of Boy Scout equipment, nylons, baby set, steak knives, cocktail glasses, comic books, razor blades, serving table, sporting goods, garden seed, Indian belt, dolls, can opener, aprons, beanie cap with charms, orchids from Hawaii, miniature TV set, coonskin cap, ballpoint pen, horoscope date book, Western bracelet, Christmas cards, paint set, model trains, fishing equipment.

A Park Forest, Illinois, building firm gave away a $1,800 bank account with each home purchased, and reported 147 sales in one week. A Midwest auto dealer gave away 5,000 trading stamps to anybody who brought in a customer. In the hunt for unusual premiums, three coffee companies began to pack genuine money inside the coffee cans. A food company brought over ten tons of stone from the grounds of Blarney Castle and dispensed Blarney Stone chips and four-leaf shamrocks. A soft drink bottler offered —of all things—a free bottle cap, and was startled to receive 12,-500 postcards and letters requesting one. Some of the requests came from a bemused public, and one respondent wrote, according to *Advertising Age:* "My Chris Craft cruiser, Brooks suit, Mercedes Benz and genuine Zippo lighter have failed to impress my aristocratic friends. But your Dr. Pepper bottle cap, I am confident, will finally open the door." A cynic who could not resist wrote: "I think this is a test to see how 'loco' people can get, but here is my name and address."

Children found themselves specially courted, for any number of surveys paid them high testament for their capabilities in persuading parents to change brands, try new items, or call on local dealers for demonstrations. They were a highly vocal and combustible lot and when they wanted something, likely as not there was no peace at home until they got it. The ordinary run of flesh and blood was no match for them and parents bowed to keep them happy, or at least quiet. In recognition of their awesome power, many companies made a point of offering child-appeal premiums. For instance, General Electric offered a 60-piece circus, magic ray gun and space helmet to moppets who corralled their parents in for a demonstration of new refrigerators. Sylvania dangled a Space Ranger kit, with space helmet, disintegrator, flying saucer, and space telephone in front of youngsters as an inducement to have their parents in for a TV demonstration. Nash gave away thousands of toy service stations for similar juvenile service. Kellogg enclosed a replica of a TV-famous character in each Kellogg box and urged children to start a collection: "Start with the one inside, collect all 12." General Mills countered with millions of Lone Ranger masks in Wheatie boxes and millions of comic books about that hero in Cheerio boxes. Quaker Oats arranged to have five tons of dirt dug out of the Yukon, shipped to Anchorage, Alaska, from which exciting point a prospector's pouch of the dirt was mailed to children in return for a boxtop and 25 cents. Standard Brands offered coloring cards in its pudding boxes, Armour encouraged an appetite for frankfurters with baseball buttons, Colgate pushed a name-the-puppy contest with the winner's mother being awarded a year's supply of Fab.

The premium was not all trouble-free as a promotional device for in general it looked better in the color ads than when the postman delivered it. This led to a certain amount of disillusionment, especially in children, and a vocal manhandling of the company image in the privacy of millions of homes. A survey of 10,000 families, for instance, turned up one-third who harbored some grievance against premiums. The most frequent complaint was hurled at the shoddy quality of the premiums and at the phoniness of come-on advertising. Next came complaints about non-receipt of premiums, damaged premiums, an excessively long wait for them, and incredibly poor packaging of them. A 1959 study by *Premium Practice* drew the judgment that half the premiums were inflated in retail value or had other major defects, and a *Consumer Reports* study concluded that premiums were a "doubtful bargain at any time." *Printers' Ink* reminded the premium-showering companies that disillusionment with advertising would make it tougher to sell the youngsters when they grew up, and offered the watchword: "Don't bamboozle children."

Nonetheless, despite such cavalier treatment, millions of adults and children continued to send in ever larger mountains of boxtops and coupons, indicating, if nothing else, the validity of Alexander Pope's "Hope springs eternal in the human breast."

Hope also sprang as a result of consumer contests which became a sizable business in the fifties. Some $500 million was spent on the promotion of contests and $50 million was dangled in prizes in 1958, according to *Printers' Ink*. In that one year there were contests to fit everybody's tastes—crossword, jigsaw, word-building, recipe, popularity, talent, beauty, versifying, letter writing.

The most popular of the contests were those which asked contestants to tell in 25 words or less why they liked some brand, or to suggest a slogan for something or other, or simply to write their names and addresses on a postcard and enter a sweepstakes contest. Americans seemed to have the inclination to benefit from sudden wealth but almost no energy to be put out to do so, and those contests which required of the entrants nothing much more than breathing drew the most contestants. Recognizing this, contest promotions carried perpetual assurances that artwork or elaborate presentations would not count. The rules avoided overtaxing the contestant's physical capacities by asking for no more than one boxtop and the flagging of his interest by confining contests generally to three to six weeks.

As for prizes, money, lots of it, proved the biggest attraction and drew many more millions of entries than automobiles, jobs, travel, life insurance, rent-paid-for-a-year, and other gimmicks. In answer to the question, "What type of prize appeals to you most?" asked in a Bruce, Richards Corporation study, 80 percent of the women and 90 percent of the men said money. The study also showed that most of them were up on their mathematics enough to figure out the remote chance they had of winning the top prize, so they preferred contests which offered a few big prizes and lots of smaller ones—in cold hard cash. That was all right with the contest promoters, for they used the big money prizes to engender enthusiasm in the contest and the smaller money prizes as convincing evidence that there was a good chance to win something.

The promoters had their own way of classifying the contestants. Those who scanned the mass media looking for a contest to enter were professionals or hobbyists, with the pros trying to make a living from winning contests and the hobbyists going in just as seriously but for the excitement. Eugene C. Pomerance reported a study in the *Journal of Marketing* in which he found less than 1 percent to be professional and 25 percent hobbyist;

everybody else who entered a contest went along for the fun of the ride.

P. T. Barnum who ran the first contest in this country in 1850 to promote the Swedish nightingale, Jenny Lind, would have been proud of the virtuosity of the contest promoters in the fifties. Canada Dry, for instance, promoted a contest over TV in which the winners got all the silver dollars they could shovel in several minutes. Elaborate preparations for the contest included the gathering of 250,000 silver dollars from the Federal Reserve Bank, the hiring of three Brink's guards to transport the treasure trove to the Waldorf Astoria's Grand Ballroom, the hiring of four Pinkerton men to keep an eye on the silver mountain in the ballroom, some careful calculations by a corps of engineers to make sure the 7½ tons of silver coins would not crash through the floor, a couple of doctors to examine the contestants to make sure they could withstand the strain of shoveling, and a bevy of beauteous creatures to counterbalance the grim-visaged guards for the gaping TV millions. In trial runs the Canada Dry executives had figured that about $15,000 could be shoveled in five minutes, but the winner who had practiced shoveling metal washers in the basement of his home managed to shovel up $37,500 of the silver dollars. The extra cost was considered a trifling matter to Canada Dry executives since hundreds of newspapers gave the contest a bonanza in publicity.

Dole Pineapple ran a "Treasure Bottle Sweepstakes" which drew two million entries, some of which were chosen at random and placed in a revolving drum. From the drum ten were drawn under the watchful eyes of Burns International Detective Agency, placed in ten sealed bottles, all of which were then thrown into the ocean off Hawaii. The incoming currents washed the bottles up on the beach, and the name in the first bottle that hit the beach became the winner of $10,000, a two-week stay at a luxury hotel on Waikiki Beach, plus $500 in pin money.

Mission Orange ran a "Silver Dollar Contest" during which

a salesman drove through city streets each day stopping at a certain number of homes, and if the occupant could show evidence of a Mission Orange purchase, he could grab a handful of silver dollars from a bucket.

In celebration of its 75th anniversary the Dr. Pepper Co. gave away a genuine diamond doorknob, valued at $8,000, which was attached to a $30,000 house. Other prizes dispensed as part of the celebration were cars with diamond-studded keys, swimming pool, furniture, hi-fi sets, movie cameras, appliances, and sports equipment.

Schenley ran an "Own-a-Toll-Booth" contest whose winner got the day's receipts on a Staten Island ferry, the runner-up pocketing a day's receipts of a Triborough Bridge toll booth. Lesser winners had to be content with 24-hour ownership of subway turnstiles, penny gum machines and other mechanical money-grabbers.

Renault promoted a "Teacup Grand Prix" to determine how far actress June Havoc could drive a Dauphine on one teacup of gasoline with the winner getting a round-trip jaunt to Paris.

Kayser thought up an oddball "Historic Ladies" contest which revolved around guessing what six antique-looking ladies might have invented or created. Among the zany responses, one said: "This woman made history because she was the first to drink Beethoven's Fifth." An unconfirmed trade press report said the winner turned down free tickets to a Broadway musical in favor of six psychoanalytic sessions for his unsuspecting spouse.

Among the hundreds of contests that enlivened the print and air media and spread a rainbow with a pot of gold at the end of it, there was the one by Dial Soap which gave away an oil well, by Motorola which offered a romantic vacation in "a Castle in Spain," by Gulf Oil which offered an equally romantic vacation "in a palace on the Riviera," by Piel Brothers which donated a tropical island of five acres in the Bahamas, by Remington Rand which gave away one share of every company listed on the New

York Stock Exchange (then valued at $44,800), by Kentucky Club which offered a thoroughbred race horse, by Puss 'n Boots which offered the winner the weight of his cat in gold (at $35 an ounce, the value of gold). For those who wanted a taste of a millionaire's life, one contest offered the winner free butler service and the use of a Cadillac for one year, and another gave 5 percent interest on $1 million for one day, a chauffeur, Cadillac, butler or maid, baby sitter and a night on the town.

As he surveyed the wondrous landscape of popular opportunities, Marshall S. Lachner, president of B. T. Babbitt, was moved to poetical homage in *Contest News Bulletin:* "The dreamers of promotion, the architects of the contest, the designers of the giveaway, are the men who give flavor to the special kind of wonderful life that we live here in America."

11 The Packaging Revolution

Not until the fifties did self-service merchandising, which had been introduced in the twenties, have a
rendezvous with history when the nation's supermarkets, drugstores, five-and-dimes, discounters, and department stores turned
to help-yourself buying. As the retail sales clerks began to follow
the cracker barrel, the butter tub, and the sugar bag into oblivion,
the package began to emerge as a dominant, and sometimes only,
selling force in the store. Whereas the prewar package was considered to be nothing much more than the carrier for the product,
to the postwar package was entrusted the vital mission of charming the housewife into buying.

Food advertisers especially catered to her freshly awakened
middle-class interest in an easier life by introducing a steady stream
of conveniences into their packages. They tried to catch her
shopping eye with such temptations as fruits and vegetables in
see-through polyethylene envelopes, preseasoned and precooked

foods of all kinds, squeeze-bottle sauces, whipped cream in pressure cans, easy-to-open ziptapes and spouts, complete frozen dinners tastefully displayed and individually apportioned in aluminum trays that simply required heating before serving, and foods that were boiled in the bags they came in. Much of the work was taken out of the food before it ever reached the kitchen. With a wide array of prepackaged skills of master chefs at her disposal, even the newlywed could not fail to impress her husband with the facility with which she prepared such sumptuous dinners.

More than 165 kinds of consumer products were in convenient push-button containers in 1960, which ranged from cream soaps to candy-flavored vitamins. With the handy aerosols the housewife could paint her furniture, spray her hair, wash her windows, shine her shoes, extinguish fires, mothproof her closets, cedarize her chests, fragrantize her bathrooms, wipe out insects, de-flea her dog. She was occasionally irked by the minor tragedy of spraying her husband's shaving cream into her hair, but her faith in the wonderful world of ease, though momentarily shaken, was soon restored.

The packaging revolution caught up with hardware stores too, and attractive packaging of tools, parts, and even heavy equipment lured the do-it-yourselfers. They helped themselves to screws in plastic containers, nails in fiber cans, washers in fiber tubes, calking compound in handy-to-use cartridges, drills and bits in bubble-packs, assorted screwdrivers in plastic bags. They even found such unlikely objects as power mowers and gasoline engines and rose bushes handsomely and conveniently packaged, and in some of the larger self-service hardware stores shopping carts à la the supermarket.

The packaging revolution also swirled around the drugstore whose self-service shelves were loaded with packages dressed to sell. In many ways the drugstore took on the carnival aspect of the supermarket—its deadly foe—and in the merchandising changeover the pharmacist lost much of his identity, for he no longer compounded drugs in the back alcove of his store but counted out precompounded drugs in capsule or tablet form. *Drug Trade News* reported several studies showing that some 90 to 95 per cent of all medical prescriptions, for which the customer was told by the pharmacist to return in a few hours, were simply decanted from a bulk container into a small one in a matter of minutes; either that, or the pharmacist simply affixed his own label to the prepacked bottle of the drug company, which took even less time. But the pharmacist, most likely regretting his changing role, resented the usurpation of his function by the prepacked drug, and the demeaning of his professional training by the pretense to the customer. As one of them characterized the transformation in *Tide:* "The proud old druggist is gone like the cigar store Indian."

Behind the "multicolored, flip-topped, squeezable, pressurized packaging boom," as *Newsweek* called it, was the willingness, almost eagerness, of the middle class to pay a higher price for a product packaged to convenience. In one study, cited by Harrison Young, marketing consultant, packages that featured convenience enjoyed a sales rise of 124 percent between 1952 and 1956, while competing items with little or no convenience rose only 10 percent. In another study, by *Sales Management*, the conclusion was reached that rather than a special treat to the housewife, packaging convenience was "fast becoming her birthright." On her weekly shopping forays she kept a sharp eye out for the latest in packaging convenience. She filled her shopping cart with aerosols, hand lotions with pump dispensers, roll-on deodorants, toilet water with cut-glass atomizers, knowing that these items cost more because of their packaging, even suspecting (correctly) that the packaging cost more than the items, but not particularly caring. Because she did not care, these products were "the success story of the fifties," as a speaker told the American Management Association, for they fed the insatiable middle-class desire for more luxurious living. *Printers' Ink* extracted from the "literally thousands" of items on the marketplace which commanded higher prices by virtue of packaging, the extreme example of the small picnic shakers which sold by the millions at a price 1,700 percent higher than salt in the conventional package.

With packaging emerging as a sharp-cutting marketing tool, its control was removed by management from the hands of production men and cost accountants and placed into those of the merchandisers. Taking a fresh appraisal of the situation, many advertising agencies rejuggled their tables of organization to make room for a packaging department. By 1960, a speaker told the Association of Advertising Men and Women, nearly half of the agencies were in packaging. Years before, in 1952, the package designers had hailed their own growing importance by founding the Package Design Council.

The lusty growth of the industry was suggested by its annual dollar volume which went from $2 billion in 1940 to $7 billion in 1947 and to $17 billion in 1960. It considerably outpaced the growth of the Gross National Product and several speakers at packaging forums had no hesitation in predicting that the figure would touch $27 billion by 1970. True, the acceleration of trends, up or down, always brings forth the prognosticator instinct even from the most cautious human beings, but there seemed to be ample evidence for such optimism.

For by 1958 the packaging industry had raced to ninth in industry dollar volume and was surpassed only by such giants as the automotive, petroleum, and aircraft industries, according to *Sales Management*. It gobbled up vast quantities of the nation's basic raw materials. The Assistant Secretary of Commerce told the Packaging Institute that in 1959 the industry consumed about 50 percent of the national output of paper and paperboard, 85 percent of its aluminum foil, 99 percent of its cellophane, and 90 percent of all glass except flat glass. It had developed into the third largest user of steel and was a customer for a tenth of the lumber.

The Fibre Box Association drew a dramatic picture for its members when it said that if all the fiber boxes produced in only one year were laid end to end they would encircle the earth at the equator more than 13 times. The 600-odd plants in the U.S. produced enough fiberboard in one year to "make a lid for the State of Delaware, cover the District of Columbia, and keep the sun out of the Grand Canyon." There was no end to the apocalyptic configurations that could be worked out given such gargantuan production. The food industry, incidentally, used up nearly one-third of it.

It was probably inevitable that package designers became in their own right something of merchandising oracles, if only because management seemed to be overawed by the general éclat for the package. Every time a housewife went shopping, they said, a package contest took place in which the package that went out of the store was the only winner; there were no runners-up. The package, all by its lonesome, had to catch the housewife's eye and make the sale, and it had but a scant two or three seconds to do so. For it took no more than that for the housewife's fleeting eye to scan the piled-up competitive brands on the supermarket shelf. Those two or three seconds represented for each advertiser his moment of truth. Within such fragment of time the color, size, shape, and symbolism of the package had to win sudden empathy with the housewife: reassure the economical homemaker in her that the quality and price were right, feed the middle-class yen in her that it was a token of gracious living, touch the romantic woman in her that the lovely package was created for her alone.

The package that failed to communicate all this was likened by the package designers to somebody "talking into a dead telephone—he was speaking, but no one is listening." In their trade sessions they dedicated themselves to the creation of more articulate packages. And in their sessions with the big advertisers they conveyed their unshakable belief that, more often than not, it was the package more than the product that produced the sale. Indeed the package became known in packaging literature as the advertiser's "second product," a positional diffidence that appeared subject to correction in the future, and not without justice. For a food advertiser admitted in *Printers' Ink:* "We're not selling products these days as much as we're selling packaging." An editorial in the *Drug Trade News* acknowledged that the package was "the most important factor in drug, toiletry, and cosmetic marketing during 1960." Marketing studies frequently made the same point.

To reconnoiter the hidden perils of inarticulate packages, the package designers went themselves and sent emissaries to prowl the supermarkets to learn which package "personalities" failed to hit it off with the consumer. In their laboratories they worked up some impressive equipment with which to test a package's love song on housewives. They rigged up a Distance Meter to measure the distance at which a package and its design elements could be identified; a Flash Meter or Tachistoscope to determine the speed of recognition registered by the housewife; a Threshold Illumination Meter to test the readability of typefaces; an Eye Movement Camera to record to the split second the order and length of time that package elements caught and held attention; an Angle Meter to show how a package appeared at various angles; a Color-Form Meter to record the strength of a package's personality in the color bazaar of the supermarket; even an Apparent-Size Meter to find out how large the design on the package made the package appear to be.

It is probably a fair statement to say that no professional body of oculists ever assembled more equipment to test the movements of the housewife's hazel eyes than in the package testing laboratories. Certainly no oculist was ever called upon to make such awesome decisions over color hues and delicate lines. Nor were the decisions even that simple. For the package designers also had to struggle on the one hand with the tricky aspects of psychological symbolism and on the other with the stark fact that myopic housewives, of whom there are many, would not be able to see anything but the big type on packages (studies showed that vanity precluded their wearing glasses while shopping). It was enough to turn the package designer's hair gray overnight.

The upshot was that the riddle known as the housewife frequently made disconcerting beelines for packages which by laboratory tests should have gathered dust on the shelves. Nonetheless out of the packaging laboratories came the brightest and shiniest packages that men and money could put together. Soap and detergent packages glistened with optical brighteners and the multicolored cereals gave the supermarket shelf a billboard look. The package that scored so highly in laboratory tests and communicated so glamorously to guinea pig housewives became tongue-tied when surrounded by such scintillating company. It was a problem of everybody talking at once and deafening the poor housewife, a problem which the package designers called "the blends." Likely as not, the housewife who paused momentarily in front of a shelf piled high with gaily colored packages was looking glassily right at the brand she wanted but could not see.

The package designers were so chagrined at the packaging world they had wrought that in the late fifties many of them subdued the package decibels in the hope that a soft compelling voice would attract more attention in a roomful of screamers. They produced more subtle hues and worked in materials and shapes that they calculated would impart the necessary feeling of empathy. Cake mix packages came with flavorsome photographs of the individual cake flavors they contained, cellophane wraps turned up more frequently, cosmetics were treated to foil coverings, and oval shapes became more fashionable as the oracles decided that women liked oval shapes better than any other kind. Tissues, napkins and higher-priced cigarettes came almost diffidently packaged, with the advertiser's name printed on a cellophane overwrap which slipped off leaving the product standing

in nameless modesty. What was formerly a face-tissue carton became a beauty box dispensing tissues with equal grace in the
boudoir, bathroom, or living room.

As elegance joined convenience in the package, it became
eligible for sharing in some of the millions spent by gift-giving
Americans on each other. Whereas only a sharp-eyed shopper
could find a gift package before the war, the retailers' shelves
in the postwar era assumed a permanent state of holiday dress.
Men's belts were packed in jewelry boxes, electric razors in handsome traveling cases, standard drugs in apothecary jars, whiskey
in decanters, kitchen spices in miniature cabinets, blankets and
other soft goods in elegant open-windowed cartons. Even hum-
drum items were uplifted by the query as the cash register rang:
"Shall I gift-wrap it?" The merchandisers discovered that gift-
wrapped items not only "flattered the purchaser into believing he
has good taste" but encouraged the urge "to spend conspicuously," as one of them said.

Christmas, Mother's Day and Father's Day, the traditional
gift-giving days, were joined by the somewhat less than world-
shaking Secretary's Day, April Fool's Day, Sadie Hawkins' Day,
and Groundhog Day. With the adaptability of a chameleon, the
packages on the retailers' shelves turned appropriately red at
Christmas, green on St. Patrick's Day and purple at Easter. But
the extra sales were well worth the cost of the packaging change.

Not only did the postwar package move toward convenience
and elegance but, like Stephen Leacock's horseman, it moved in
other directions too. In fact, the other directions were opposing
directions, for it moved toward larger "economy" sizes and simultaneously toward smaller "personalized" sizes. Proprietary medicines, soap powders, detergents, beverages, and toilet tissue led
the march to giant packages, while table salt, facial tissue, crackers and cereals led the retreat to diminutive packages. Yet, oddly
enough, the aim of the merchandisers was in both cases the same
—to increase consumption. For, as William R. Mason wrote in

Business Horizons, the aim of the merchandisers in pushing for package giantism was to get the consumer to maintain larger product inventories at home than necessary to meet the household's immediate needs. And the aim toward diminutive packages was to get products to penetrate more points of use in the home —to put facial tissues into purses as well as on the vanity, to get table salt on the breakfast and dining room and barbecue tables as well as on the pantry shelf, to move different types of breakfast cereal into the home instead of one.

Two things happened. First, the merchandise was moved out of the space-choked supermarket and into the home for use, and the home became in a sense an auxiliary warehouse. Second, the merchandise was used. Not only it was used, but it was freely used, for as one trade magazine said: "The more of a product a housewife has on hand, the more she'll use it." There was something about opening a giant-size detergent or soap powder that induced the housewife to pour it with a lavish hand. She used a tablespoon where a teaspoon would have done the job. The same magnetic force operated to get a giant toothpaste tube used up proportionately faster than the small size. Every summer's day many parents were dimly aware of the principle as they watched children guzzle the large-size carbonated beverage with the same facility that they once guzzled the small size. Enamored with the simplicity of the principle that availability forces consumption, the advertisers gave it a big play in the fifties.

The handy carry-carton of a half dozen or so cans or bottles was a variation on the theme. When the multipack was introduced in the thirties, it made no headway with a generation of housewives compelled to guard their budgets. But when revived by the brewers in 1947, it caught on, so that by 1956, according to *Tide,* more than half the beer and soft drinks came in multipacks. With the visible determination of the merchandisers to put an end to the consumer habit of the single purchase, multipacks turned up for auto parts, cigars, cosmetics, drugs, film, fruit juices, hardware, pet foods, and even paint.

The invisible elf that aided merchandisers in the force-feeding of consumers became a gremlin only insofar as the trend toward dwarfism was concerned. For the diminution of package size led directly to an increase in pilferage. Retailers had long accepted pilferage as a chronic evil of self-service merchandising, but as the shrinkage of packages simplified the matter of theft the legions of light-fingered Annies multiplied. Supermarket operators complained in the trade press "they are stealing us blind" and losses in 1959 were estimated at $500 million. To add to the woes of the retailers a new breed of consumer was spawned by the giveaway age who specialized in label larceny. *Super Market Institute* pondered vainly how to deal with housewives who ripped labels from food cans, boxes, and bottles for the redeemable coupons that were attached. It was not the value of the stolen coupons that bothered the retailers, for the amount was negligible, but the mess as a result of products bereft of their identifying labels that was estimated at $25 million annually. Some conscienceless shoppers even went in for cap-switching—putting the lower price-marked cap on the larger bottles—but they were stopped by changing the neck size of the small and large bottles. The pilferage problem was partly solved by blister- and skin-packaging of small items, but the retailers stood helpless before the label larcenists.

As sales quickened as a result of convenience, elegance and size variety in packages, most advertisers became convinced that Americans liked change. And whereas before the war package changes were ordinarily made when printing plates wore out or inventory was low, the postwar period saw package change when sales began to slip or when the competition came out with a new package or just to freshen the consumer appetite. In the late fifties a *Dun's Review* survey found a diverse range of advertisers, from food to fasteners, lathes to lingeries, with package change in the works; a Better Packaging Advisory Council study found more than half of 1,200 advertisers on the verge of change; and a *Sales Management* probe into the reasons for change turned up a 75 percent response—"to pep up sales." As one of the respondents said: "Today you have to run like the wind just to stay where you are."

The inevitable result, of course, of the advertisers' race for package change and the consumers' expectancy—and desire—for it was the shortening of the life of the average package. Although some lasted as long as 18 months, *Food & Drug Packaging* estimated that "six months is often more than the life span" of new packages.

The packaging pundits developed the rationale that modern shoppers looked for "youthfulness" in everything they bought, and would shy away from packages that weren't face-lifted periodically, which sounded at times close to a plea for change for change's sake. But perhaps it was because each change stirred up the need for the next change. At any rate, the packagers warned the advertisers that unchanged packages ran the risk of looking like flappers out of the twenties—"out of style, out of step, and soon out of the market."

The surge to repackage America's products ran to an estimated $25 billion at the consumer level by 1960, according to trade sources. And that was not the total tab, for package changes not infrequently were accompanied by massive advertising to alert consumers for the new package. For instance, when Marlboro cigarettes switched from the conventional soft-pack to the "crush-proof" box, hardly anyone in the nation could have escaped having firmly implanted in his consciousness the lilting jingle about "filter, flavor, flip-top box."

Not every package change was a smashing success. For consumers sometimes hankered after the old package. Marlboro, for one, learned this and returned temporarily to selling cigarettes in the conventional soft-pack, acknowledging with rare candor from an advertiser, that some smokers simply did not cotton up to the new flip-top box. Camel also learned the hazards involved in modifying the familiar when it made what its advertising agency called "a few minor changes" in its package design and brought down a storm of protest on its head from the curmudgeons who refused to accommodate to design progress. Camel went scuttling for the nation's newspapers to assure its army of smokers in ads: "We're putting the pyramids right back where they were." Consumers comprised a tricky species that ordinarily took to newness in stages, tended to reject the radically new package as a slight to its emotional attachment to the old, so advertisers had to find the proper mixture of the old and the new to make the new package socially acceptable.

More serious consumer packaging criticism in the late fifties probably put the first suspicion in the minds of many advertisers that elegance, convenience, and modernity represented not quite the packaging paradise they had ordained for consumers. A Nesbitt Associates study, for instance, discovered nearly 40 percent of the housewives voicing complaints about leaky milk and juice cartons, nearly 20 percent felt that oversized cartons were a bit dishonest, about 25 percent griped that many cartons were not brimful, nearly 10 percent were annoyed at the "overstating" of the number of servings in food packages (the "serves four" often left four hungry people at the table). Moreover, the dotted guide lines and "press here" triangles and semicircles at the top of the box too often proved more than a match for finger pressure or even the jab of a spoon handle. They yielded only to a resolute attack with a kitchen knife.

A *Sales Management* study turned up similar grousing among 1,089 homemakers, who were sometimes brought to the end of their patience with box-tops that seemed destined to stay glued down for good, jars hard to reseal once opened, and evaporated milk cans whose flat rimless tops were immune to the ordinary can or beer opener and required the ministrations of something like an ice pick. Indeed *Sales Management* came up with the bruising statistic that some one-quarter of the housewives were convinced that "a new improvement in packaging is often a change for the worse."

The operation of opening a can with a key was described at a Food Packaging Council symposium with all the derring-do of the Perils of Pauline, replete with the hazards from the jagged metal edges to the disappearance of the key while the children were playing and the frustrating impossibility of opening the can.

A newspaper food columnist toted up for the American Management Association the many wayward packaging customs that she felt irritated housewives. First, they could not understand why so many advertisers carefully packed their products in glass and then proceeded to conceal the contents behind an all-enveloping label. Second, they failed to see the wisdom of packaging bleach, shampoo and baby care products (which were used often when hands were wet) in the slipperiest containers. Third, they thought the advertisers "absolutely nuts" for packaging toys "in the flimsiest boxes man can make" when the toys obviously were going to be used by the destructive element in the family. Fourth, they were riled by the packaging of stationery, candy, cosmetics, shoe polish, furniture wax, crackers, and so on, in boxes, bottles and jars that were far bigger than the contents warranted. The food columnist prophesied in conclusion that more housewives were going to question the need for "squirting everything in sight," would look suspiciously at the aerosol valve and remind themselves how often it went bad. "The end of the honeymoon may be coming," she warned.

A marketing consultant scoffed at the belief that consumers could afford the luxury of fancily packaged foods as "a most dangerous myth." While it might be true of nonfood items, he told the Food Packaging Council, the notion that consumers wanted sophistication in food packaging was "a lot of balderdash." They wanted good food at low prices. He twitted the designers who pressed for continual package renovation by pointing to the high sales of Campbell soup, whose cans have remained virtually unchanged for 50 years, to Hershey cocoa and chocolate, A-1 sauce, and the host of other products that have flourished by means other than package refurbishing. He chuckled at the blue-and-green can of Heinz beans, which horrified the designers for its poor color combination, yet which failed to sell as well in a more congenial color scheme.

To avoid taking issue with the old saw that wrath has no greater fury than a woman scorned, it might be said that a woman cheated comes a close second. Packaging deception, or what looked like it, produced howls of rage even from the most middle-class housewife. Yet it was inevitable if only because of the vagueness of the Food, Drug and Cosmetic Act which prohibited containers "so made, formed, or filled as to be misleading" without specifying any standards to make that determination. Marketplace competition being what it is, there soon was a perceptible movement to retailers' shelves around the nation of larger packages with the same content, and less content in the same sized packages. With rare exceptions, advertisers scrupulously adhered to the law by specifying the number of ounces on the label, but only housewives blessed with 20/20 vision and a mind for detail could read the minuscule type and know how many ounces were in the package. What added palpably to the confusion in the supermarket was the handiwork of the designers who created packages that optically looked larger than they really were.

Hence few housewives were probably aware of the shift in the early fifties of can sizes in which fruits and vegetables were packed. The trend was away from the No. 2 can (19.7 fluid ounces) to the No. 303 can (16.2 ounces), without any general reduction in price. In 1955, citing figures by the National Canners Association, *Printers' Ink* traced the movement of green beans, corn, peas, apricots, and peaches into the smaller can. Whereas in

1947, for instance, 74 percent of the green beans were packed in the No. 2 can, by 1953 some 65 percent were ensconced in the No. 303 can. Without placing the two cans side by side, the difference in size was practically undetectable.

The artful practice of deceiving the consumer reached such proportions in the late fifties that *Consumer Reports*, printing a number of complaints from its restless subscribers, scored it as "one of the most rapidly expanding shady practices." Although *Food & Drug Packaging* expressed the opinion that the problem was being publicized out of proportion, it conceded that "too many of the reader criticisms possess frightening validity." It chided the few advertisers who were engaged in "juggling quantity and price and using the container as a vehicle for their practice," for blackening the name of all. A marketing consultant warned at a National Food Packaging symposium, attended by food manufacturers, packagers, and ad agencies, that the housewife would be jolted into disenchantment if the manipulation of packages continued.

The Food and Drug Administration sent out the word to every advertiser who would listen that it had uncovered far too many packages with improper weights. An FDA survey of 32,225 packages had found short weights in 39 percent of them. Most of the short weights were less than 2 percent, but ½ of 1 percent came out short by 5 percent or more. Some spaghetti shortages were as much as 17 percent. Offenders ran the range of corn meal, butter, sugar, oleomargarine, farina, oatmeal, macaroni, frozen fish, vegetable shortening, liquid salad dressing, and rice.

What restrained the federal agency from cracking down on the situation was the manifest difficulty of successful legal prosecution. The agency still smarted under three successive defeats in "slack fill" cases sustained in the years immediately subsequent to the passage of the Food, Drug & Cosmetic Act in 1938. Thereafter, for the next two decades, the FDA turned its attention to the more rewarding fields of drug potency and purity, apparently abandoning the packaging aspect as unenforceable. But by the late fifties the FDA decided that something had to be done. Alarmed at the general "backsliding" of packages, it chose as a test case a packager of mints and charged that the appearance of the package was likely to induce consumers to anticipate more mints than the package contained. A federal court was unconvinced that consumers expected any particular number, and ruled against the agency. On appeal, the case was remanded back to the federal court for reconsideration, on the ground that the question was not whether a purchaser expected any particular number of mints, but whether he expected more of the box to be filled. The court of appeals cited as an example the person who bought a crate of apples and found it only half filled: he may not have expected any particular number of apples, but he was deceived for he expected to find a full crate. On reconsideration, the federal court again turned back the agency. And the FDA had to content itself with widespread seizures of products, many of which were heavily advertised national brands, on the ground of short weight and improper labeling. In 1961 a Congressional subcommittee held a three-day session which crackled with consumer indignation at the unrelieved growth of package deception.

Manipulation of package sizes had brought such joy to so many advertisers that 12 liquor distillers petitioned the Alcohol and Tobacco Tax Division of the IRS for permission to cut down the size of bottles. The frank goal of the distillers, according to the *Wall Street Journal,* was higher prices, but since current prices were about as high as they could go, a slightly smaller bottle would serve the same purpose, and help restore the profit margin which had slipped from the peak 1950 level. Accordingly the distillers petitioned for a new bottle rule—one that would permit switching from the fifth (one-fifth of a gallon) to a sixth (one-sixth of a gallon). In support of the petition, the distillers' brief pointed out that "packaging to price at the retail level is an accepted merchandising practice in the food industry." Most packaged cold meats come in 6-ounce packages, instead of quarter, half, or pound sizes. Salad dressings come in 6- or 7-ounce packages instead of the former half pints. And packages of crackers have diminished up to 25 percent while maintaining the former price. Even razor blades, formerly 21 to a container, now come 18 to a container—at no reduction in price, of course.

Although organized sections of consumer opinion expressed indignation at the widespread packaging shenanigans, they were pitifully small, and the millions in the middle class wended their way down the supermarket aisles oblivious or not caring. In general the postwar shoppers had eyes only for the convenience of a product, not its net contents, their ears heard only the love song of a package, not the cash register ring of its higher price. Their weekly food bill ran higher because they willingly paid more, and because the food industry concentrated on feeding their middle-class egos with package elegance as much as it fed their middle-class stomachs with fancier foods. They were to a large extent even mindless to cheating.

"How has it happened," wondered *Consumer Reports*, "that a population which is aware of the odds against drawing an inside straight, which is accustomed to the handicaps in sports, which is familiar with Dow Jones averages, seems unable to remember how many pints there are to a gallon or how many ounces to a pound." The answer, *Consumer Reports*, is that when you have the money you let the advertiser do the menial counting for you.

The Image Builders 12

The multiplication of products, brands, and packages made the art of consumership increasingly difficult to practice in the postwar period. Increasingly the marketplace was dominated by symbolic buying and selling, with the sellers of goods engaged in selling the symbols of goods rather than the goods themselves, and the consumers buying these symbols over the inherent product values.

Advertising symbols were as old as advertising itself. Fifty years ago, for instance, there were hundreds of advertising symbols that served consumers in the identification of products. Among the most popular were the Gold Dust Twins, the Old Dutch Lady who chased dirt, the Victor dog listening to His Master's Voice, little Miss Muffet who sat on a cake of Fairy Soap, the Buster Brown boy for children's shoes, and the Red Cross symbol for women's shoes.

163

But identification was not enough in a marketplace jammed with competitive goods, none appreciably better than its shelf neighbor. Symbols were given the job by advertisers to convince consumers that their products "are better than those of the competition even though they aren't," as researcher Pierre Martineau told the Newspaper Representatives Association of Chicago.

The gospel spread up and down Madison Avenue that products by themselves were no longer intrinsically interesting to consumers. The admen found a fresh merchandising truth in the *My Fair Lady* philosophy that the difference between a flower girl and a duchess is in the way she is treated. It was all in the mind. "What makes one product different from another is how people feel about it," a speaker told the National Industrial Advertisers Association. Consumers had to be cadged somehow by advertising into feeling more kindly disposed toward one product than another. If products were the same, their images could pose as different.

The fifties witnessed the largest planting operation in history by advertising agencies in the minds of the nation's consumers. The images were nourished by untold millions in advertising but because the human mind lacks infinite warehousing capacity countless numbers of the seedlings perished. The holocaust was worsened by conflicting images and the *ad hoc* way in which they were planted.

Nonetheless the ad agencies rushed to abandon the so-called scientific principles of advertising which had dominated agency thinking for over two decades and which had been laid down by Claude Hopkins in *Scientific Advertising*. Hopkins had preached the finding of some dramatic peg, relevant or irrelevant, on which to hang the ad, and he himself had invented such things as "mucin plaque" on teeth which Pepsodent alone could remove, cereals "shot from guns" which distinguished the Quaker Oats Company product, and bottles "purified" with "live steam," which set Schlitz beer apart. But the Hopkins' principles were now considered inapplicable for the most part in an economy of abundance.

Since pictures were the fastest and easiest method of image-building, the ad agencies became avid followers of the old proverb, "One picture is worth ten thousand words." The ads that filled the print media in the fifties were domineered by large and striking pictures. In full-page ads especially was this true, for perhaps four out of five of them contained a big picture and no more than a few lines of copy, almost as an afterthought.

If nothing else, the trend pointed up something of the intrinsic futility in trying to sell products in a glutted marketplace. It was an open invitation to some social scientist to reduce to a neat mathematical formula the new *modus operandi* of advertising: the less to be said for a product, the bigger and more striking the picture and symbolism to be used. Yet because the admen were nearing their wits' end in dreaming up winning appeals for their clients' products, they gladly espoused the opportunity to operate on the symbolic level.

The terms "corporate image" and "product image," freshly minted in the fifties, received wide currency in the trade press. Scores of articles and editorials made the point that a favorable image of the corporation, or of its product, or both, gave the consumer an extra reason to buy an item, without which today's product is marked for oblivion. The concept of image building intrigued top management brass as much as it did many of the ad agencies. It "captured the imagination" of business executives, observed *Printers' Ink,* "won fresh and sometimes wildly enthusiastic recognition," according to *Sales Management,* handed management "one of the keenest tools" for merchandising, said *Industrial Marketing,* and was an "unexplored advertising horizon," in the words of *Advertising Agency Magazine.* Speakers and trade writers hailed it as a new "third dimension" of advertising, and its values were explored by Paul M. Dauten, Jr., and Robert D. Gieselman of the University of Illinois in the *Journal* of the American Society of Association Executives. Clay Buckhout, advertising director of *Life*, predicted "more and more image building" as products continued to multiply.

Many research organizations, recognizing an area for fresh diggings, offered as a service to corporate clients the measurement on a continuing basis of the public's attitudes toward both corporations and their products. Subscribing to these continuing audits were such giants as U.S. Steel, General Motors, Du Pont, General Electric, Union Carbide, Ford, and Westinghouse. The interest of the mass media in image building also quickened. The Television Bureau of Advertising produced a study which showed how TV was useful in creating and maintaining favorable acceptance for a business and its product. *Editor & Publisher* told "How Newspaper Ads Develop and Protect Corporate Image." Magazines urged advertisers to protect their image in magazine pages.

Dun's Review was awed by "the rush of businessmen to the mirror to see what kind of an impression they are making on the public." For what was happening had no precedent in U.S. history. Certainly the nineteenth century steel, oil, railroad, and other big business buccaneers would have been a bit bewildered by the frantic efforts of their corporate descendents to cultivate the public favor. In their day they had amassed vast power and fortunes without indulging in much sentiment for public opinion. Even the institutional advertising of the early twentieth century by many of these corporations was totally unlike the new image advertising. Those early ads ordinarily featured a bewhiskered photograph of the founder or showed the smoke pouring from the smokestacks of a brick factory; the purpose of those ads was to convey to the public something of the solidity and fidelity of the company and its products. In those days the admen followed the advice in the ditty: "When the client moans and sighs/ Make his logo twice the size/ If he still should prove refractory/ Show a picture of his factory." And the contemporary "tombstone advertising," as it became known in ad circles, was an apt expression for the cold, graven images that were printed in the public mind.

The selfsame corporations in the fifties seemed to be swept up into the Dale Carnegie world of *How to Win Friends and Influence People* and went around posturing before the public as civic-minded business entities whose highest duty was to dispense aid to needy widows and orphans. Although the mechanism was unclear, corporation executives believed that even a billion dollars was not too much to spend on image building if it led to a favorable balance sheet. Behind their thinking was the belief that the principle explored philosophically by Kenneth Boulding in *The Image*—that human behavior depends on the accrual of images—somehow had carry-over validity for the marketplace. Just as man could be conditioned to go through his workaday rituals, so could repetition of a kindly corporate or product image affect his behavior in the supermarket. By steady playing, a groove could eventually be worn in the consumer's mind that would condition his brand selection.

The big question that occupied the best management brains was whether to push the corporate or the brand image. Advertisers like U.S. Steel, Alcoa, IBM, Du Pont, and General Electric, with multifarious products, many of which were incorporated in other manufacturers' products, decided to push their corporate images. Advertisers like Procter & Gamble, which built success on promotion of individual products, pushed brand imagery ahead of corporate imagery. The automobile industry, on the other hand, had a tougher problem and followed a middle-of-the-road policy of promoting corporate and brand images simultaneously.

Hard as the decision might be, most management brass seemed committed to the principle that selling images to the public was necessary to business survival. The private utilities were worried over the encroachment of public ownership of power—between 1938 and 1958 the government had increased its share of power production from 8.5 percent to 23 percent, according to the private utilities. Banks felt they must make a favorable impression or lose more business to the 30 percent interest set; the day of the platinum watch fob, marbled walls, and cold money lending was over, and the bank had to convey the impression that "for all its strength and dignity [it] is as human as any institution can possibly be," as a speaker told the Financial Public Relations Association. Other business enterprises had similar problems.

What disturbed business executives was the undercurrent of distrust and antagonism toward the motives and methods of big business that turned up regularly in soundings of public opinion. The public associated big business with monopolies, trusts and cartels and held misgivings about the social, economic and political ideas of businessmen in general, according to a contributor to *Developing the Corporate Image*, edited by Lee Bristol.

Getting their noses rubbed in what the public thought of them was unpleasant enough, but with business expansion and diversification proceeding on a huge scale the public was needed to supply staggering amounts of money. The public held the biggest reservoir of funds, and the tapping of these funds by the sale of corporate stock provided the companies with far more operating money than retained earnings or loans. Hence, as Keith Funston, president of the New York Stock Exchange, said, good image building programs were perhaps the most critical factor in obtaining such funds.

It was common knowledge in stock brokerage circles that the reason why one stock sold well above its book value and another with equal merit sold well below lay in the image that financial analysts and investors had of the corporation and its products. As J. R. Pershall told the Midwest Stock Exchange, when investment brokers were asked: "In your opinion, does corporate advertising favorably affect the sale or the stability of a company's securities?"—more than nine out of ten unhesitatingly answered yes.

If further comfort were needed on the value of corporate imagery, Pierre Martineau wrote in the *Harvard Business Review* that in his opinion the reason the government failed to whip up public feeling against Atlantic & Pacific stores in its antitrust suit was that people did not see the A & P as some powerful corporation. Rather, he said, people were acquainted with individual A & P stores in which lettuce was trimmed, aromatic-smelling coffee was sold, and whose employees obligingly carried out heavy bundles of foodstuff. The lesson of the public's friendship was hardly lost on the nation's business executives.

Nonetheless, especially in the early fifties, image building ran into snide skepticism by some merchandisers and even stonewall opposition by others. For instance, after listing all the fads that had swept public relations over the years, a trade journal ended with cordial, if tongue-in-cheek, hospitality: "welcome to the corporate image." One speaker told a group that he saw image building as "a kind of cross between poetry and adultery." Another attacked the phrase as "dangerous because it sounds so specific and tangible, which it isn't," and because it implied that a corporation's image had an isolated life that could somehow be manipulated by fooling with a mysterious set of symbolic knobs. Another wrote in *Sponsor* that "to hear some admen talk, you'd think that an image is a kind of crafty cosmetic" that could be applied to a corporate face "like lipstick, mascara, or false eyelashes." Another insisted there was nothing new about the concept of the corporate image "except the silly label."

Much of the dispute over the importance of corporate or product image rested on exactly what it was everybody was talking about. It was hard to get at. A public opinion researcher told the American Management Association, "I don't know what it is, but I'm sure it's important." An adman wrote in *Printers' Ink* that the image business was "a little like Zen Buddhism—easy to believe in so long as you don't have to explain it." A *Business Week* query to the presidents of the nation's largest ad agencies and to the ad directors of the biggest corporations produced "as many versions of what corporate image is, as there were respondents," according to Bayard E. Sawyer, associate publisher of the magazine. In his opinion it was not only "sheer nonsense" to set aside the advertising of what a good product could do for the consumer in favor of other aspects of the company image but "a good way to commit business suicide." To gain a larger slice of the market a good product *and* a good reputation were needed: "In other words, it takes two to tango."

By the late fifties, however, a survey of corporation executives revealed the grip that the image approach had on the imagination of management. In answer to the question whether a favorable corporate image was "the most valuable single product your company has to sell," 37 percent said yes.

Defining this most valuable single product was no easy matter. A newsletter described it as "basically what people see in their mind's eye when the name of the company or product is seen or heard, or brought up in conversation." An American Management Association speaker called it an "abstraction of your reason for being." *Sales Management* divided it into two parts—at its simplest it merely meant the corporation's personality, its business profile, the style, manners and the way it combed its hair; at its most complex it was the climate and the psychological setting in which the corporation did business. There they let it rest.

On examination there seemed to be as many aspects of the corporate image as there were activities of the corporation. It seemed to be made up of the corporation's advertising, showrooms, community relations, letterhead, buildings, trademarks, employee relations, logotypes, annual reports, company colors, salesmen's cars, and ad infinitum. It seemed to be a vaporous distillation of a mishmash of information and misinformation about a corporation that was stored in the public's mind, or the last contact that the public had with a representative of the corporation. That was what so frightened executives—that the corporate image could rise or fall on such things as the receptionist's voice over the telephone or the makeup on some secretary.

Worrisome and illusive as the problem was, nonetheless many

executives were convinced that a corporation could no more avoid creating an image than a person could walk in the afternoon sun without casting a shadow. Hence it was only the better part of prudence for the corporation to go ahead fashioning the image it desired for itself. And it was no job to be left for junior executives: the public mask had to be created by the firm's top executives. Something of their intense dedication to this *magnum opus* is suggested by the words of an Esso executive, as quoted in *Printers' Ink:* "It has never been out of my mind. It has never been out of the minds of a great many other people from the moment we come into the office at nine o'clock until we leave at five o'clock in the evening; and as we go through Grand Central station and get on the train we think about it, and we think about it until we come back to the office the next morning."

There was plenty to think about. For if the problem of what the corporate image was seemed hopelessly knotted, the problem of selecting the image the corporation desired of itself was only slightly less so. Since the purpose of the image was to humanize the corporate entity in the public mind, the next logical step was to consult the dictionaries and other language repositories for a list of applicable human traits. There the first difficulty arose, for there seemed to be no end of adjectives. One research company on behalf of a corporate client was reported in the trade press as having gone through some 60,000 words in Webster's *Collegiate Dictionary*, then some 52,000 words in *Roget's Thesaurus*, and finally Webster's *Book of Synonyms*, in the running down of adjectives that could reasonably be applied to a corporation. It came up with a final tally of 58 corporate traits. Another research company was reported to have rummaged through dictionaries and the literature of psychology and to have come up with 30 appropriate adjectives for its client.

The management was then called on to try out the adjectives on the corporation for size, and to weed out the unbecoming ones. The outfitting of the corporation with a personality was a lengthy process, particularly when each of its products had to be similarly ornamented. It may be of passing interest to note that considered appropriate for corporate and/or product image, according to one compilation of adjectives, were aggressive, avant-garde, benevolent, conscientious, daring, efficient, farsighted, giddy, honest, ingenious, jolly, ladylike, modest, neighborly, old-fashioned, proud, quaint, quality-minded, reliable, snobbish, sophisticated, thrift-minded, urbane, virile, witty, young, zany. It was up to management to put together the appropriate raiment for corporation and products. For instance, an advertiser of women's shoes might want to choose for his line such word cluster as avant-garde, daring, sophisticated, young, urbane. An advertiser of men's shoes might settle on such words as honest, proud, quality-minded, reliable. As for the corporation itself, the management might decide that it should appear aggressive, farsighted, ingenious, virile. In the play-acting that went on in corporate conference rooms, the Walter Mitty qualities of the participants must have been given free rein.

Some of the adjectives proved more troublesome than others. Aggressive, for instance, might be a desirable trait to some people, but obnoxious to others. Similarly, conservative pulled in opposite directions, depending on viewpoint. So cautious advertisers exhibited a tendency to tone down the word-image, to make it more readily acceptable to a wider audience, although the image-researchers warned that this threatened their corporations and their products with a neuter personality. "No capon ever rules the roost," as one of them warned. "Neuter brands get no place in today's market."

As a help to management to decide what kind of personality to be, the researchers went out to find what the image of the corporation and its products was in the public mind. They developed a battery of tests ranging all the way from the simple thermometer kind, which indicated the degree of feeling for or against the firm and its products, to depth interviews which were pored over by psychologists to determine if the public held any deep-seated bias on the unconscious level.

An index of the seriousness with which U.S. corporations viewed the image business was the movement toward trademark alteration that swept through much of corporate America. Mc-Kesson & Robbins, Abbott Laboratories, General Foods, Westinghouse, and hundreds of other giants embarked on expensive and time-consuming programs to introduce new trademarks. "In this country trademark alteration has grown to the status of a major operation," commented *Business Week*. McKesson & Robbins was reported as spending a million dollars and several years on the introduction of its new insignia, and in some cases the business press noted that the cost ran to $15 or $20 million. In a report to the American Management Association on a trademark analysis of 100 of the nation's largest industrial corporations, designer Walter P. Margulies warned that 75 did not measure up to the highest standards of memorability, recognition, appropriateness, and uniqueness.

In *The New York Times* designer Henry Dreyfus wrote that whereas originally members of his craft were retained to work on a company's products, they "now find themselves working on the offices and showrooms where the product is sold, the trucks and railroad cars that deliver the product, even the stationery and other forms on which the sale is recorded."

Although at no time were the researchers able to establish that the image concept was validated by consumer behavior in the marketplace, nonetheless hundreds of big corporations pursued image-building campaigns, which in some cases were exercises in corporate narcissism.

Esso, for instance, tried for greater public recognition of its research efforts ("Esso Research Works Wonders with Oil"); United Gas linked the image of its growth to the South's growth ("Keeping Ahead in the Growing Gulf South"); General Motors pictured itself as a friend of small business ("General Motors—

Good people to work for—Good people to deal with"). The Bell Telephone System—the parent company—emphasized its people, while its manufacturing affiliate, Western Electric, focused attention on its products. Some companies sought prestige for all their products by special promotion of one, as Ford did with its Thunderbird, General Foods with its gourmet line, and Corning with its Steuben Glass.

Du Pont took up the cudgels against the specter that haunted the board rooms of many of the giant corporations—public antagonism toward big business. Mindful of the "Merchants of Death" epithet with which it had been tarred in the thirties, and which took a king's ransom to remove, Du Pont executives foresaw the public's distrust of big business as a threat of such magnitude that it might ultimately lead to the "dissolution of our company," a spokesman told *Advertising Age*. As a countermeasure, Du Pont sponsored "Show of the Month" and carefully portrayed itself to 35 million viewers as a major producer of high-quality products at moderate cost, as a company whose stock was proudly owned by people in every walk of life, as a major contributor to the economic health of the nation, and as a possessor of a strong sense of social responsibility. Attacking the idea that it was a monopoly, Du Pont pointed to the competition it faced in every field. Consonant with its projected image, Du Pont's president toured the country making speeches on the social utility of big corporations, typically "Big Business Is Essential to Our Economy." A considerable portion of its $30 million annual advertising budget was devoted to this campaign, which seemed to pay off, for studies revealed a progressively more understanding and kindlier public.

General Electric picked up a $5 million tab annually to get across a six-sided image to the 30 million viewers of its General Electric Theater—leadership in research and development, product reputation, customer treatment, concern for individuals, employer role, and defense contributions. The "human" qualities of

GE were brought out in discussions over the air of the company's science fellowship program for teachers, the community contributions of its employees, the retirement benefits of its pension plan, and as an employer of the physically handicapped. Continuing studies by Opinion Research Corporation turned up growing favorable attitudes by steady viewers of the TV program, although undisclosed was the degree of image deterioration that resulted from GE's joint conviction in 1961 with 28 other major electrical manufacturers of illegal bid-rigging and price-fixing.

Armour set out to develop an awareness on the part of businessmen that in addition to consumer food it also was a major producer of mineral plant food, fatty acids, soaps, leather, adhesives, and pharmaceuticals. The image sought was "an aggressive group of innovators and a dynamic source of supply for some of the essential tools of industry," as a spokesman depicted for *Advertising Age*.

Borden called on Elsie and members of her bovine breed to push the Borden image. Elsie, in more animated and more human form, appeared as the corporate symbol on over three million consumer packages each year, while her husband Elmer appeared as the corporate symbol on Borden's industrial products.

Western Union turned its efforts to the erasure of the unpleasant image that had built up over the years that a telegram brought only bad news. It promoted the idea that telegrams could be fun by providing stock telegrams for Christmas, Valentine's Day, Easter, and for practically any happy occasion. One of its recent efforts was the Bunnygram for children—"The Easter bunny is on its way, so be a good little boy every day."

The First National City Bank of New York showed who came first in its heart by modifying the commercial on the 11 o'clock news from "More People Bank at First National City than at Any Other Bank in New York" to "*You* Come First at First National City."

Shell Oil ran ads showing photographs of interesting and

ancient shells and reminded people: "When you see the sign of the shell, think of it as the symbol of the quest for new ideas, new products, and new ways to serve you." Container Corporation of America ran a "Great Ideas of Western Man" ad series to advance its image as original, resourceful, and design-conscious. General Dynamics, the nation's No. 1 weapons maker, pushed its nonviolent image of vision, scientific creativity, and product triumphs. U.S. Steel's "Operation Snowflake" managed to cut that segment of the population critical of steel companies by half.

Standard Oil, a holding company coordinating the operations of affiliates in 135 countries and dependencies, ran ads amounting to hymns of praise for the lands in which affiliates operated. When proofs of the ads were taken to the respective embassies in Washington "it was like going to see children with enormous boxes of candy," David Ogilvy told the Public Relations Society of America. "I've never seen such happy Ambassadors."

Ogilvy, an evangelist in the corporate and product image movement, also had a hand in changing the image of Puerto Rico in the public mind. Surveys in this country had shown that the island was believed lacking such native assets as cleanliness, fun, good climate, romance, scenery, beaches, and popular prosperity. A lengthy series of ads typically captioned "Falling in Love Again with Old San Juan," "Puerto Rico Will Enchant You," "Puerto Rico Invites You to the Ascot of the Caribbean," "Puerto Rico Will Surprise You," "Suddenly Everybody's Going to Puerto Rico," plus some hard sell about tax exemptions for new business ventures, helped restore Puerto Rico's allure.

Ogilvy also was the chap who put the patch on the Hathaway shirt model's perfectly good eye in 1951, and thereby induced imitators to bring forth a flood of distinguished gentlemen, all British to their fingertips, with an assortment of monocles, four-button suits, waxed moustaches and bowler hats to grace the ads for dozens of products. A careless reader of the advertising pages might even have gained the erroneous impression that the leading

British imports at the moment were members of the horse-show, riding-to-hounds set. Not only were Americans introduced to an impressive Commander Whitehead who sauntered down the steps of an airplane and on to a red carpet, looking like an important foreign dignitary rather than the commercializer of a tonic water, but to a Tetley Tea Man, a possessor of infinitely delicate taste buds, and to a host of lesser snobs. The Commander's luxurious beard, incidentally, was reported in the trade press as insured for $100,000 (could any other beard make *that* claim?).

As the advertising pages were converted into an image-building Donnybrook, the cigarette companies entered with some of the most virile-looking males ever to squint at the consuming public. First came the Marlboro Man with a crew haircut, squared-off jaw and provocative hand tattoo who was supposed to erase from the public mind that the Marlboro cigarette was a tainted female brand. The Marlboro Man soon had rugged company in the Viceroy Man who thought for himself, the L & M Man who lived modern, the Chesterfield Man who liked his pleasure big, and the Lucky Strike Man who knew a real smoke. It became almost a physiognomical impossibility to tell what brand the craggy character was smoking on TV until he announced his allegiance after a satisfying puff at the cigarette. But he undoubtedly entranced millions of desk-bound white-collar males and females with the immense benefits of the great outdoors.

Among the farmers, truck drivers, cabbies, steelworkers, divers, jet pilots, loggers, construction workers, ski patrolmen, Coast Guardsmen, firemen, and cowboys who puffed satisfyingly on one brand or another, the cowboys seemed to emerge for the tobacco companies as the epitome of American manhood. Indeed the cowboys seemed destined to become the leading authorities on whiskeys, automobiles, and many other products, as they became the hired hands of an increasing number of advertisers. A staff columnist on *Advertising Age*, who patently took advantage of his anonymity to criticize the rugged cowboys, objected to their aggrandizement in U.S. life. The particular cowhands he had met, the columnist said, had excited him chiefly for their resemblance, intellectually, to the animals they husbanded. They were no doubt an outstanding symbol of masculinity—at its worst and lowest form. Considering their exaggerated pleasure in personal ornamentation, drinking, brawling, and regarding females largely in the herd, the columnist wondered how "civilized" admen could parade them before America as individuals "whose habits are worthy of copying."

The first Maidenform bra model who sallied forth into print in 1949 with the unlikely declaration—"I dreamed I went shopping in my Maidenform bra"—was followed by subsequent admissions over the years that she dreamed she played Cleopatra, won an election, was a private eye, sang Carmen, was a vamp, and covered the Paris collections. In all she dreamed more than 100 ads and in each she dreamed in a white bra (the color most women bought) and in enough titillating circumstances to boost sales. The dreamers of the dream had "a particular penchant for a theme with a double meaning, as long as it's decent," observed *Advertising Age*. The most successful of all such *double-entendre* ads, the trade publication added, was the one of the model in her Maidenform, a cowboy hat on her head, and a gun pointed at the reader in the approved style of a Western "wanted" poster, captioned: "I dreamed I was wanted in my Maidenform bra." With sales up from $14 million in 1949 to $35 million in 1960, and women now dreaming in their Maidenform bras in 110 countries, dreaming has become a most profitable commercial pastime.

With advertising agencies on an intense hunt for imagery and symbolism, ads appeared more frequently whose chief puzzle for the reader was to decide what they were selling. Arnold Gingrich, publisher of *Esquire*, was unsettled to see so many ads in his magazine showing golf pros blasting out of sandtraps. Although the ads were for sport shirts and slacks, the casual reader might be pardoned if he concluded that they were ads for sports equipment. In some of the ads it could not be said for sure if it was furniture, a new cocktail, or a vacation resort that was being advertised. In fact one ad ostensibly advertising men's wear brought inquiries about the hi-fi dominating the illustration and another about the liquor decanter in which the merchandise was shown in reflection. In *Advertising Age* one men's wear ad was reproduced with the tart comment: "This is not an ad for binoculars. It only looks like it. It is an ad for men's clothing, but the manufacturer thought that men with $250 to pay for a suit are more interested in a pair of binoculars than in good clothes."

If much symbolism was lost on the consumer, at least he was kept amused and guessing about the growing number of bizarre and outlandish ads, which gave to advertising something of the flavor of old-time, slap-stick vaudeville. Liquor companies seemed to have special relish for the incongruous. In some of the ads, a man in a superbly tailored dinner suit sat backwards on a white horse, a statue wore spectacles, a bandanna was tied around a dog's nose, a plaster-gloved hand held aloft a whiskey jigger, a man sat on the floor indoors under an open umbrella to keep his martini dry. These promotional postures lent to advertising an air of "studied lunacy," commented Russell Lynes in *Harper's*. In *Reality in Advertising*, adman Rosser Reeves laid the whole absurdity to copycatism. What started out as an original bid for attention, he said, turned into an empty fad, devoid of meaning. One eyepatch bred a procession of eyepatches, one beard on a Commander Whitehead became a thousand useless beards.

But the drive for bizarre effects like a *deus ex machina* could not be halted. It infected wide areas of advertising. An air conditioner company, for instance, depicted the leaning tower of Pisa, with a comic strip balloon emerging from an upper story, containing the words: "What if it does? Carrier can air condition anything." Another Carrier ad presented a mud hut in a jungle compound with a voice coming out of the hut, again in comic strip balloon: "Who needs a patio, Celeste? Carrier can air condition anything." A Woolite ad showed an unsavory male in his undershirt beside his wife who was studying a racing form; the ad had no copy, only a box of Woolite stood on the table. Another copyless Woolite ad showed a bearded male taking care of half a dozen of squirming youngsters, a box of Woolite on the sink.

A Quaker State motor oil ad showed a glamorous female in chinchilla coat preparing to enjoy a sumptuous dinner with a waiter's hand pouring some motor oil on the roast. "We do not suggest you drink Quaker State," reassured the copy, "but it is definitely one of the finer things in life for your car." A series of coffee ads depicted a young stalwart in medieval suit of armor, holding a cup in his mailed fist, who exhorted readers to "Strike a blow for freedom" (for coffier coffee).

Another lover of freedom, Capezio, rallied the females of the nation to fight against the "pea-pod philosophy where one young lady is distinguished from another only by the thickness of her eye-liner." Capezio's call to freedom was in ads acclaiming a nondescript orange-and-yellow creature called the Polka-Dotta, which wore an outsized Uncle Sam hat and whose battle cry was: "Liberty from conformity for all." The ads urged readers to subscribe to the Capezio Declaration of Independence which was guaranteed to strike off the "surly shackles of the *status quo*." A State of Capezio was proclaimed, the Polka-Dotta creature was promptly appointed its secretary of the treasury, and "mad money" was its official currency. An ad in *Seventeen* invited readers to write in for some "Mad Money to throw around," which some 8,000 libertarians reportedly did. Another ad offered "something nice" to all Capezio partisans who clipped the sample mad money out of newspapers and stuffed it in their shoes. Some 45,000 females complied, and trooped into stores selling Capezios for the "something nice," which turned out to be a Polka-Dotta charm. The State of Capezio apparently also banned the traditional use of measurements, for Capezio shoes were sized smaller than other shoes hence making feet "smaller," a not displeasing result for most women.

As the number of uninhibited radio and TV commercials increased, *Advertising Age* commented that they were "zanier than ever." For instance, one coffee commercial dialogue went: Query to grocer—"Do you handle any other coffee besides Wilkins?" Answer—"Yes, I handle . . ." *Bang.* The grocer is shot dead. Another commercial, for Dodge, had a husband waking his wife at 4 A.M. and telling her to "start packing, dear. We're moving out." "Moving? Now? It's four o'clock in the morning." Hubby explained that everybody in the neighborhood had the new Dodge but he. "I'm so ashamed. Grab the other end of the davenport, dear." Still another, for the Volvo, took place in a rocket ship headed for Mars, where on arrival the Martians were found to be driving the Volvo. The astonished earth scientists were assured that the Volvo was "the family favorite on all progressive planets."

As Madison Avenue filled the nation's mass media with more and more ads with symbolic and bizarre themes it undoubtedly was with a sense of welcome relief that the public occasionally discovered some ads which presented the good old-fashioned verities of home, mother and child.

13   The Language of Madison Avenue

As the nation's prosperity forced Madison Avenue to grab increasingly at the public's attention with imagery and symbolism, the copywriters—whose forte was persuasion with words—seemed to fall on evil times. First of all, they seemed to be losing out in the ancient battle with the Art Department as to whether the copy or the illustration was more important to the success of an ad. Second, with advertising nearly quadrupling in dollar volume in 15 years, even with the lessened use of copy in ads, they had the killing burden of finding fresh selling words and phrases. Under mounting agency and client pressure for "something different from the competition" they not unnaturally fell to the use of lingual contortionism. This drew the occasional scolding in the trade press that they were devoting too many efforts to selling the agency brass and the client on their creativity, and that the resulting ads probably won admiring and amused glances from the public but made few sales. Too often the copywriter's tricks were calculated to "entertain, startle, or humor himself, his intellectual friends, and the client," Alfred Politz charged in the *Journal of Marketing*. Nonetheless, in fairness to the copywriters, it should be noted that much agency brass silently assented to the use of show-off copy for it generally tranquilized the client.

What most humbled the copywriters in the fifties, however, was the group-think sessions that became quite the rage among many of the larger agencies. In the course of these sessions the copywriters' efforts gained the benefits of the collective thinking and surgery of Creative Committees. Sometimes the surgery was minor and bloodless but more often it was a major operation and sometimes at the end of it nothing was left but the copy corpse. Understandably the copywriters had scant love for the Creative Committees. One of the copywriters labeled the Committees "groups of men afraid of an idea," another said they were shot through and through with "caution, compromise, and fear," still another was heard to mutter as he left the conference room where his work was torn apart: "The score for today, Lions 3, Christians 0." Robert Pritikin attacked the group-think sessions before the American Association of Advertising Agencies in these words: "It's now time for the slaughter . . . the great conference room free-for-all. Everyone's invited. It's opinion time. . . . It's time to converge on the scripts and nibble at the words; it's time to hack at the layouts."

But even after the Creative Committees put away their sutures and their scalpels the copy operation was still not over. For the ads then had to go to the client for approval, which often was not forthcoming for weeks during which time the ads went back and forth between client and agency with both making additional excisions and grafts. When the ads were finally approved, said Mr. Pritikin, they were loaded up with "inanities" that ran the gamut of ridiculous ideas ("Don't let romance fade-fade-fade away") to pompous ideas ("They said it couldn't be done") to braggart ideas ("The greatest name in rubber") to innocuous ideas ("Summertime is sandwich time"). It made advertising look as if "90 percent of it was written for boobs—or by boobs."

"If you were selling toothpaste over the counter could you look a person right in the eye and say, 'Don't let romance fade-fade-fade away'?" Mr. Pritikin demanded. "You'd get smacked right in the choppers." Hal Stebbins also demanded at a copywriters' Creative Workshop that the agencies and the clients "quit pawing copy to death." He pleaded that they leave alone what Browning in "Paracelsus" called the "imprisoned splendor" of words.

Many clients and ad agencies found explicit justification for the "inanities" in the finding of psychologists that the mental age of the average U.S. soldier in World War I was about thirteen. Although the trade press occasionally carried indignant protestations to the contrary, many advertisers and ad agencies were undoubtedly guided in the preparation of their ads by the thinking that grown-ups were simply children grown large—mentally and emotionally they were still children. Despite the official protestations, it was certainly true that the ads in general memorialized this belief. Occasionally someone raised his voice in tart criticism —"the consumer is not a moron, she is your wife"—but he was virtually alone. Admen generally shrug off any attack on the inane and corny language of the ads on the ground that "hell, yes, it stinks but, chum, we're not writing for smart guys like you and me but for the peasants and that's what they go for," as William H. Whyte, Jr., observed in *Is Anybody Listening?*

According to the gospel, the corn kept the peasants credulous; it kept them buying hair tonics to restore lost hair, vitamin pills to renew energy, creams to restore bloom to skins, perfumes to find or beguile mates, ablutions to keep them young. Indeed corn-fed peasants were capable of credulity in the face of denying reality. The reality for them was the dream, the hope, the wish, which were kept alive by the nourishing corn in the ads.

The only problem was how much corn the peasants would go for. There was a danger that it would be carried too far. A speaker told the Fashion Group of New York, for instance, that women welcomed "a little immoral support" from advertisers in the nurturing of their daydreams, that the truth had to be "razz-matazzed." But, especially in the selling of cosmetics, the problem was how high the promise could be pushed and how low the performance could fall—without inviting trouble. There was growing hazard in "bringing out the same old nail enamel formula under a new name and telling women it will make their nails longer and stronger when we all know it's the same old stuff and it can't and it won't." Growing hazard, because under stress of competition the tendency was for advertisers to push the promises up and strip the truth down. Truth had to be "razz-matazzed," the speaker warned, but not so far that it burst the bubble of be-lievability. In the argot of Madison Avenue, the speaker "touched all bases" by giving the double title to her talk: "Promise her anything but for God's sake give her *something*," and "How to succeed in the cosmetic business without really *lying*."

A McCann-Erickson house ad put the truth manipulation another way. Milady's new dress was more than a combination of fabric, thread and buttons—it was an extension of her per-sonality. Because she felt like a beauty in it, "perhaps she is," and her belief fully justified the ad-dream promises. If ads con-centrated on reality alone it would be like looking at a pretty girl through glasses that magnified the pores. "The girl you love may be 70.2 percent water, 25 percent oxygen, carbon, hydrogen, and nitrogen, and 4.8 percent mineral, but it makes a lousy love song."

Apparently there was a bit of peasant among the high-income and more educated too, for it was hard to withstand the siren calls of the make-believe. But most sophisticated adults were simply bored or amused by the corny ads, according to studies by The Pulse, Inc. Low-income and less educated adults, however, were bitter when on occasion they were disillusioned with ad promises for to them the unmasked claim was in the same class as a hit-and-run driver.

The biggest problem for copywriters, of course, was provided by the glutted marketplace. The sheer volume of goods left the copywriters at a loss to describe them individually. So the temptation to shout down the competition became almost overpowering. A kind of Gresham's law operated in which milder claims were driven out by wilder claims. Copywriters found themselves indulging first in the use of the "little lie" and later in the "big lie," as Walter Weir wrote in *On the Writing of Advertising*. Hence every drug palliative soon promised the fastest relief, every soap claimed to give the whitest wash, every detergent insisted it was best for automatic washers, every cigarette delivered the mildest smoke, every dentifrice promised the fewest cavities—and the public was left bewildered by the whole show.

In fact the public had to learn how to deflate superlatives, which it did, and the words which copywriters upgraded were automatically downgraded as they entered the mind. The public automatically downgraded the word "regular" to "antiquated," "new" to "regular," "totally new" to mean maybe the carton or bottle was new, "new new new" to mean not more than six months old, and "miracle" to mean it worked, as Allan B. Goldenthal told the American Association of Advertising Agencies.

In the war for consumer favor ordinary standards of measurement quickly became inadequate. Giant Economy Size became the normal in package size and Large became the smallest unit on the shelves. Olives started with the "Giant" size and moved up quickly to "Mammoth," "Jumbo," "Colossal," and "Super Colossal." Low-line tires were "De Luxe" and moved up to "Super De Luxe," "Super Champion," and "Super Super." The pint was no longer a pint but a "large pint" and a gallon was no longer a gallon but a "big, big gallon." The quart and the pound similarly were found wanting and items were sold at such-and-such a price for "a full quart" or "a full pound." So fanciful and meaningless did the size and grade nomenclature become that *Printers' Ink* was editorially alarmed that consumers were in danger of being "hopelessly confused" and E. B. Weiss saluted them in *Advertising Age* for "truly astonishing shopping ability."

In the same way distances became "a long foot in length" when dealing with material and "a short mile to the railroad station" when selling a house, and minutes also were lengthened or compressed depending on what was sold. Cooking minutes were the shortest and were generally referred to as "little" minutes or "brief" minutes. As the time to prepare the family dinner shrank in one ad to "a meal in a minute," an adman scoffed, "Hell, it takes that long to open the can."

As copywriters put increasing pressure on the language, the adjective by itself was considered no longer potent enough for the proper understanding of consumers, so adjectives were lined up tandem fashion to provide that extra tingle to consumer senses. A shampoo was a terrific new Lanolin shampoo, a cake mix became an amazing new Golden Mix, a dessert was a marvelous new taste treat. If it did not partake in the collective strength of other adjectives, the lonely adjective sought the security of an adverb. The shampoo left the hair radiantly alive, the carbonated drink was deliciously different. Copywriters seemed to think there was "something naked about an adjective not clothed with an adverb," Clifton Fadiman observed in *Holiday*.

The hyperbolic spiral worried *The New Yorker* which found 312 "finests," 281 "world's bests," 58 "America's onlys," and "47 other bits and pieces of improbable nonsense" in an analysis of its own pages over a six-month period. The magazine undertook to wage "a long, lonely, and losing struggle" against the spiral which it acknowledged "gets longer, lonelier, and losinger all the time." It circulated a plea for self-restraint among the ad agencies which drew the prediction from *Advertising Age* that "improbable nonsense will not perish from the earth."

Sometimes advertisers were hoisted on their own spiral petard, as Gillette was when the company was ready to introduce its Super Blue Blade. As a company executive admitted in *Business Week:* "Over the years the language has been so beggared by extravagance that superlatives have lost their impact. We ourselves have not been overly modest in advertising our Blue Blades. Now we have a radical improvement. What do we do?" The problem was how to get across to the customers that "this time we really mean it." The way out that Gillette tried was a series of subdued ads in which the virtues of the new blade were understated. With customers deafened by the previous barrage of shrill claims, Gillette hoped that a whisper would now carry conviction.

Semantic trickery took an honored place in the language of persuasion. In general favor was the "floating" comparative which produced "32 percent more medicated vapors" for a chest rub, made a laundry soap "22 percent better," made a tire last "10 percent longer" and all and sundry products to work "faster and better." The claim may have left some customers idly wondering about the referent: the product worked faster, deeper, better, longer than what? For their benefit it may be said that the referent ordinarily was the worst product in the field, or a nonexistent product, or a collateral feature of the product unrelated to its efficacy. The copywriters hoped that the customers would be generous and unthinking enough to supply the name of the major competition.

Some minor grammatical aberrations also put in frequent appearance, such as the commas, dashes, semicolons, and colons which were displaced by a series of ellipses. To the commonplace user of the English language the ellipses signified of course that something was omitted, but the copywriters found new use for the three dots as punctuation for selling points. Even this use did not satisfy some copywriters who threw in an extra dot or two apparently for emphasis. Possibly second to the ellipses in favor was the asterisk which ordinarily found its place next to the boldest claim in the ad, and was intended to modify that claim at least enough to keep the federal agencies off the advertiser's neck. The asterisk hence permitted the advertiser to go poaching without worrying about the game warden. As for the customers, "the trick is to so bury the reference that the reader will go nuts trying to find it," as a copywriter wrote in a trade publication.

Grammatical aberrations of more serious magnitude found some of the more finicky copywriters balking at their widespread use. The most celebrated example was the "Winston Tastes Good . . . Like a Cigarette Should" slogan which set some teeth on edge. "The brutal fact," wrote one aroused copywriter in *Advertising Agency Magazine*, "is that Ad-Grammar is spreading *ad nauseam*." He charged that the Winston slogan not only was committing "grammatical murder on a coast-to-coast scale" but that it was unnecessary murder, for the slogan would be equally effective and more grammatical by the substitution of "as" for "like." Most admen rose to the defense of the slogan, however, on such varied grounds that a shocker was good in an ad, that it was the way the man-on-the-street spoke, and that language was a living thing and should not be strangled by slavish attention to the rules. *The New Yorker*, referring to a writer supporting the "living language" position, said "Winston cigarettes, of course, backs him to the hilt, like a cigarette should" and went on to prophesy that "along Madison Avenue, bad grammar, as an attention-getter, will soon be as popular as mutilation—which started with an eyepatch and rapidly spread to arms and legs."

Also grating on the nerves of the grammarians was the "travels the smoke further" slogan of another cigarette for its blithe transformation of an intransitive verb into a transitive verb. They argued that a person or a thing could travel but you could not travel a person or thing. Moreover, you travel "farther" not "further."

Less noticeable because it was more subtle was the way the comparatives "better" and "older" were upgraded by the copywriters into positives. The public was advised that certain classy products were sold only in the "better" stores—not in the "good" stores or the "best" stores but the "better" ones. "We must admit," Roy H. Copperud commented in *Editor & Publisher*, "that the ad writers have invested 'better' with a mysterious toniness that even 'best' somehow now lacks." The copywriters also recast the word "shop" into a transitive verb and the public was no longer expected to shop "at" or "in" the stores. Shopping was now something one did to the store itself. Customers who were *au courant* shopped the better stores. "Those who live far from the madding admen can shop the mail-order catalogs," suggested Mr. Copperud.

The word "better" was given other unique services to perform. An ad for a cigarette holder, for instance, insisted that "nicotine and tars are better in this than in you," grammatically implying of course that nicotine and tars were good for people. It was entirely possible that some scrupulous users of the language after reading this ad may have taken to worrying whether they were getting enough nicotine and tars daily.

"Old" was a split-personality word applied only to consumer possessions but never to what the advertiser was selling. The consumer traded in an old car or old house or old furniture. But he bought an "older" or "earlier model" car, house, furniture, and so on. It was even a bit antisocial to speak of people as "old." Either the word was avoided by referring to them as "senior citizens" or infused with youth by crossbreeding it with "youngsters" to produce "oldsters."

Adverbs fell like chaff before the copywriters who advised the public to light up a cigarette and "Live Modern" or save the middleman's profit and "Buy Direct from the Maker" or go on a vacation and "Fly Direct to Europe." The word "real" was ever popular and everyone was urged to enjoy a wide range of real good products and services. The preposition "of" got short shrift in ads offering a "fine type cigar" or a "better type pen" or any other type of product.

Grammarians must have exacted some measure of malicious

joy from ads that proclaimed to the world that the products advertised did not actually exist. "There's nothing like a Coke" or "There's no gin like Gordon's" may have been lingual admissions that such products did not exist, but alas for the grammarians, the stores carried them nonetheless. Perhaps the prize exhibit in the grammatical chamber of horrors was the ad which stated: "There Is No Place in the World Like Bermuda—And No Place in Bermuda Like the Elbow Beach Club"—presumably selling a nonexistent hotel on a nonexistent island—but reports from travelers indicated the contrary was true.

In addition to fractured grammar the copywriters gave wide employment to hyphenated words, and their ads were chock-full of sun-drenched, flavor-rich, ocean-fresh, full-bodied, vacuum-packed, tree-ripe and other assorted product virtues. But in the end all these veins of lingual exploration gave out and the copywriters were forced into coining their own currency. Although they were fully aware that coined words and expressions carried with them the danger of being misunderstood, or worse still of being meaningless and going in one ear of the customer and out the other without doing anything to his mind in between, the compulsion to find new ways of selling the growing tonnage of goods and services made the step inevitable. No group in society ever flogged words and phrases harder than the copywriters to sell goods and no group ever left more words and phrases dead from overwork as a result.

Some of the coined words they came up with were relatively descriptive, such as "oven-ly" bread flavor, "flavor-ific" chewing gum, "flavor buds" for instant coffee, "smileage" for tires, and "secure-ance" for insurance. Others were more muted in communicative power, such as stratopower, halolight, cosmic eye, magic monitor, super cascode, turret tuner, optically-filtered, imagineered, mony, hydromatic, fordomatic, and ultramatic. Some took on meaning only by dint of heavy advertising, but most undoubtedly acted as blockages to understanding.

A brand new language was even invented by some copy-writers in their bid to capture attention from a word-battered public. For the United Fruit Company, for instance, they invented "banana talk," in which words were fused to form such items as havabanana, eatabanana, peelabanana, enjoyabanana, sliceabanana. For the Schlitz Company they created "Schlitz talk," and as new approaches to the public were opened for more companies Samm Sinclair Baker urged the copywriters in *Casebook of Successful Selling Ideas for Advertising and Selling* to put on their thinking caps, "crack open the dictionary, annawaywego!"

Despite all the wheezing and straining to find new entrances to the public mind, one thing remained stable in the ads, and that was their unrelieved cheerfulness. It could not be gainsaid even by the severest critic of advertising that it was anything but a highly cheerful world which presented to the public a happy set of people. Surely no model ever opened a refrigerator door without curling her lips into a smile, no cigarette was ever puffed at without a confirming nod and grin, no automobile ever glided over the ribbon highways without the driver's looking like a Cheshire cat. Indeed, compared to the grim columns of cold war, divorce, and robbery in the newspaper tabloids, and the soap operas, gunmen, and mayhem on the airways, the sunny world of advertising offered a welcome, if somewhat unnatural, relief. In the wonderful world of advertising the public found "peace and contentment," noted S. Watson Dunn in *Advertising Copy And Communication.*

Suggestive of the diligence with which copywriters and other admen worked at this was the ad agency which even tried to make the weather more sunny for the public, thus disproving the Mark Twain canard about everybody talking about the weather but nobody doing anything about it. Since inclement weather, or the reporting of it, had an adverse effect on the business of department stores, drive-in movies, bus lines, restaurants, car washes, and a host of other enterprises, the agency wrote to disk jockeys and weather forecasters asking their forebearance in giving the public such dismal news. It was hewing just as much to the truth, the agency argued, to forecast the weather as "partly sunny" instead of "partly cloudy," and think of the effect on people. The "positive attitude" should be applied to the state of the weather in the same way that it was applied to the condition of a drinking glass. "Generally you don't refer to it as partly empty. You say it is partly full." The agency concluded its letter with the enthusiastic reminder: "What a wonderful approach to a day can be generated by the positive approach of 'partly sunny.' " The letter aroused interest and followers among "quite a few radio and television outlets," a trade publication reported.

In the same way the American Institute of Laundering advised member laundrymen to stay clear of such words as "grime, soiled, mildew, germs, dirt and odor." To strike a happier note in their ads the laundrymen were supplied with a handbook which listed more than 300 friendlier words and phrases to use. Recommended were "abloom," "abundant," "youth," "zest," "help for the homemaker," "flower fresh," "silken loveliness," "longer wearing fabrics." And the ads could be brightened still more by a frequent sprinkling of colorful adjectives.

Indeed if anyone was unknowing of U.S. home life and gained a picture of it only from a careful study of the ads, he would probably arrive at something like this—

The man of the house rose that morning and brushed the rich, creamy lather into his stubble and got a perfect shave as usual. It left his face soothed and refreshed. On other mornings he used an electric razor which also delivered supreme shaving pleasure. Even when he began using it he shaved with it expertly. It was equipped with multiple-shaving heads, self-starting, high-speed, quiet-running motor that never needed oiling.

The aftershave lotion he splashed on had a distinctively masculine scent. The hair tonic, rubbed in vigorously in a 60-second workout, stimulated scalp circulation and encouraged the hair follicles. Then he brushed his hair in place where it would stay neatly groomed all day, and returned the brush to its accustomed place where it reassumed the role of a smart dressing table accessory.

He dressed carefully, selecting one of the smart pin-striped shirts he had picked up in that little shop so famous for workmanship, and tie to match. At breakfast he greeted his wife with a good-morning kiss as she handed him a glass of juice to help him fight fatigue, colds, and maintain his alkaline balance all day. There was wholesome goodness in every sip. It was never thin or watery.

He glanced over the newspaper headlines as the cereal, cooked in a jiffy, enriched with vitamins, was placed before him. Coffee brewed to perfection wafted its glorious bouquet around the kitchen. His wife handed him a cup that brimmed with flavor.

After breakfast he lit a real cigarette. His precision-engineered lighter worked every time. He glanced at his watch, famous for accuracy, and realized he would have to hurry to catch the 8:15. The new, improved dentifrice with which he brushed his teeth also neutralized his mouth acids, combatted his bad breath, stimulated his gums and brightened his smile. He slipped into his coat, checked his supple wallet, made of the finest leathers, for the commutation ticket.

Then his wife drove him to the suburban station, with the car giving unbelievably fine performance, flattening the hills, hugging the road, and giving more miles for less money. It had plenty of pick-up-and-go at green lights and sure-footed traction at red ones, and the tires were longer wearing because of special construction.

After a rushy morning he stopped off before lunch at the friendly bank to arrange for a personal loan in minutes at low sensible bank rates. After lunch, which was also a bit rushy, he slipped into his mouth a digestive aid to unblock his digestive tract and bring safe, gentle relief. He enjoyed a cigar made of the choicest tobaccos before heading back to the office for the afternoon's stress.

Meanwhile, back at the ranch-type house, his wife zipped through the breakfast clean-up thanks to the all-purpose cleanser that had twice the cleansing power. Glassware, pans, dishes sparkled after a few dabs. The kitchen, with its perfect working surfaces, superbly designed cabinets with deep storage space, sagproof and warp-proof doors, and countless other features, all exclusive, turned work into sheer fun.

When the fun was over, she went to shower, pausing long enough to look at her lovelier figure in the full-length mirror, a figure she had gained the pleasant, easy way, without violent exercises, without starvation diets, simply by swallowing a few pills and enjoying all the foods she liked. A palmful of shampoo formed rich, billowly lather instantly, gently floated away film and dandruff, rinsed out easily and restored the natural loveliness to her hair. She washed with an extra-mild, deep-cleaning, scent-laden toilet soap that left her skin more radiant.

After she dried, and thoroughly enjoyed the few minutes of relaxation under the hair drier, she touched up her hair which banished gray hair worries, dabbed herself with a deodorant to guard her daintiness, smoothed in a facial cream to supplement the natural skin oils and revive her skin beauty. She applied a wipe-on depilatory for new leg allure, nail polish in a provocative new shade, eye makeup for bewitching, sparkling eyes, face powder to gain that glowing look, hand lotion to smooth the knuckles, soften the cuticles and beautify her hands, and a spray of perfume finally to make her a worldly woman with a touch of mystery.

She pulled on a girdle that shaped her for compliments, a bra that flattered her bosom, a slip for that sculptured silhouette, hose to make her legs sleeker, shoes that gave her that barefoot look. The chic dress she chose minimized her hips, gave her a trim little waist, the kind sure to win admiring glances. Then came the necessary accessories—the belt to dramatize her waistline, the bag to complement her ensemble, the extravagant-looking brooch to add a touch of excitement, the adorable little hat—and she inspected herself in the mirror. She felt all woman.

Before leaving, she made out a shopping list and the fountain pen's perfect writing point made for effortless writing. She glanced at the clock on the mantel, a smart-looking clock that gave years of perfect time-keeping, no noisy hum, and never needed winding. It was 10:30 so she hurriedly closed the door and walked down the flagstones mindful of the fabulous masses of blooms that were the envy of all the neighbors and at the vegetable patch that was heavy with prize crops.

She was at the station in time to meet the 6:25 and on the way home she suggested that they dine graciously that evening in a little restaurant that was famous for old-world atmosphere, fine cocktails, vintage wines, and real French cuisine at reasonable prices. After a rough day at the office he preferred dinner at home, however. So while she disappeared into the kitchen he fed the dog a can of fortified dog food to keep the animal in peak condition with boundless energy, and mixed two highballs. She brought in some hors d'oeuvres—exquisite cheese aged in natural caves and crackers made from a cherished old recipe. They teased his appetite and he made a second round of highballs. The whiskey was mellowed to perfection and made a world of a difference.

The fried fish they had for dinner was marvelously tasty and he savored one tender flaky forkful after another. After dinner they enjoyed a brandy of rare bouquet. She put the dishes in the dishwasher where they did themselves and he turned on the hi-fi to listen to FM at its finest. He related the latest machinations at the office after which she suggested a weekend of relaxation at that hotel which attracted the smart young crowd, for it offered the best of country and cosmopolitan living. Soon they were talking of the luxury cocktail lounge, picturesque bar, moonlight hayrides, barbecues, private bathing beach, all land and water sports, and superb cuisine that awaited them on the weekend. . . .

Advertising's highly stylized language was known by heart by the public, for it was simple language, language stripped clean of its gray matter, and presented in stark black-and-white, good-and-bad terms. It pandered to the two-dimensional thinking that was so prevalent in the public, to the polar judgments that avoided the tiresome problem of thinking. In this it was like the entertainment world which depended for its popular appeal on the stripped-down conflict of good and evil. If the entertainment world had for stigmata the moustache and the swarthy appearance for its villain and the white horse for its clean-cut hero, so did advertising have its symbols for the Elysian world it presented. It simplified reality for consumers and thereby seemed to make life more manageable for them. To describe a product in terms short of sheer perfection was considered not only foolhardy but treasonable to the entire advertising world. The result was that the nation's advertising seemed in a sense to have been written by one person on one typewriter, and offered to the public a confusing array of product heroes, and not a solitary villain to reject in the marketplace.

The admen defended their extravagant copy on the ground, first, of poetic license and, second, that it was typically American anyway. "Exaggeration is an essential characteristic of American humor," argued *Advertising Agency Magazine*. "It is a product of the civilization of the West, and to expect that it can be routed completely from our advertising writing is to expect a great deal indeed." The magazine prophesied that it would be a sorry day if "the element of fantasy, of poetry, of showmanship" had to be eliminated from advertising.

Gray Advertising Agency similarly predicted in its house organ that if all advertisers stuck to the plain unvarnished truth for one month the people would put up a howl out of boredom. It argued that the public not only liked but expected ads to be spiced with exaggeration. The flights of fancy were "part and parcel of our national mores."

Advertising Age attacked the critics who felt that straightforward, factual copy would do an equally good selling job. "This is the pleasing thing to believe. But it is not necessarily true. Corn, clichés, and similar nonintellectual expressions are a part of everyday life, and a very effective part of it."

The only trouble with the unrelieved use of hyperbole was that it exhausted the meaning of words, and the problem Gillette faced when it introduced its Super Blue Blade symbolized the problem of advertising as a whole. The steady pounding of the public consciousness with hyperbole left each selling message with lessened impact. When the superlatives came thick and fast on the airways the public went to the refrigerator for a bit of refreshment, and when they came in print the public dismissed them with a flip of the magazine or newspaper page. With the cheapening of advertising's word currency, the superlatives moved more of the public to yawn than to buy, and advertisers increasingly found themselves depending on the sheer weight of multi-million-dollar ad campaigns to crash their sales messages into the public consciousness.

Fortune came to the conclusion that the American consumer had become "a connoisseur of advertising . . . he is in on the game. The language of advertising is no longer manipulating him. It's not deceiving him. It's not even making him mad. It's just boring the hell out of him."

The problem was a serious one. It moved Whitman Hobbs to tell the Advertising Federation of America, the Advertising Association of the West, and the American Association of Advertising Agencies, at a joint session, that the consumer was becoming "harder to satisfy. Harder to fool. Easier to bore." The consumer was building up "an immunity to advertising," learning how "to look at advertising and not see it . . . to hear commercials and yet not listen." Richard Crisp, after a four-year study of print ads, told the Association of National Advertisers that the average consumer had learned to skim ads "at truly astonishing speed. Most ads get less than a glance, because from the consumer's standpoint, that's all they're worth." Confronted by a "deafening and clamorous advertising barrage," consumers had "reacted to protect their sanity" by developing a defense mechanism—the "Shutter Mind."

What particularly distressed admen was the heavy discounting of claims by consumers. Wendell D. Moore told the Advertising Club of Washington of a nationwide study involving 5,000 consumers which uncovered a high order of such disbelief. Cigarette claims were disbelieved by 56 percent, toothpaste claims by 52 percent, headache remedy claims by 49 percent, soap and detergent claims by 48 percent, automotive claims by 28 percent. "They can't swallow the obvious exaggeration. . . . People resent it, and resentful people make lousy customers." It simply meant that more advertising dollars had to be spent to compensate. "At today's prices, this is a greased track to bankruptcy," he added.

But nobody in the audience—indeed, nobody in all of advertising, knew how to get out of the common fix.

14 The Engineering of Consent

The growth of public relations was spectacular in the postwar period, for many advertisers found in it a kind of secret weapon with which to turn the tide of battle in their favor in the great commercial Armageddon.

One commonly cited index of its growth was the number of public relations practitioners listed in the Manhattan classified telephone directory. Whereas in 1940 there was one column, by 1961 there were eight columns of such counselors. Another favorite index was the multiplication of public relations courses in college and university curricula, indicating the alteration of the educational structure to meet the needs of commerce. Several hundred colleges and universities offered such courses in 1961, whereas a generation ago a public relations course was unknown in any institution of higher learning. Indeed so numerous were public relations courses in some such institutions that they offered the discipline as an undergraduate major, and Schools of Public

Relations took on equal status with other schools of specialized learning.

According to the Public Relations Society of America, about 100,000 people were employed full time in different phases of public relations work in 1960, a figure that was four times the number so occupied in the late forties. Considering the lusty rate of growth, PR circles prophesied 250,000 practitioners by the end of the sixties.

Most of the 100,000 were employed by corporations either as part of corporate PR staffs or as outside counsel. Many of the blue-chip corporations worked both sides of the street on the assumption that an outside PR consulting firm would be less subject to internal corporate pressures and would be more likely to bring an objective standpoint to top policy discussions. A *Business Week* survey in the late fifties found among the nation's top 300 corporations, three out of four operating full-fledged PR departments—a far cry from the mid thirties when one company in 50 dabbled in the art—and led the magazine to the conclusion that PR had "become firmly ensconced in the superstructure of U.S. business." The new business handmaiden had in fact outmushroomed all other management service groups; in personnel and in budget (about $2 billion a year) it had grown even faster than advertising.

How deeply ensconced it was in the estimated 5,000 corporations using its services was suggested by the number of vice-presidencies bestowed on the corporate PR directors. By the mid-fifties F. Waltman reported in the *Public Relations Journal* that a poll of 92 of his colleagues had turned up 16 as vice-presidents, whereas ten years previously only five had been so honored. It even became a stepping-stone to the corporate pinnacle. Eugene Miller told the Public Relations Society of America that in the Bell System six major Bell companies were headed by presidents who had spent at least ten years in public relations.

A survey of salaries paid by corporations to their PR directors showed them largely in the $25,000-$50,000 range, but a few hovered around the $100,000 mark, an attractive enough reason to pull in workers from newspaper, advertising, magazine, academic, personnel, and other less well paying vineyards. It made public relations a "largely unorganized and largely undisciplined" field, as Stephen E. Fitzgerald wrote in the *Public Relations Journal*. For the novitiates flocked into the field often ill-prepared for the duties that were given them; certainly most of them lacked anything in the way of academic training. They claimed fitness to operate in the field for such assorted reasons as being able to get along well with people, knowing something about the techniques of human persuasion, or simply because they were articulate. In many cases they landed the job, in the caustic words of one critic, only because they were able to "read and write better than the clients." More than one lone-wolfer hung out the public relations counselor shingle with nothing much more than a mimeograph machine and a closet for an office. Offering "glibness instead of analysis, jargon instead of ideas, cant instead of thinking," they effectively frustrated the frequent attempts by the public relations associations to "professionalize" the trade and to uplift some of the practices that were badly in need of uplifting.

Nonetheless the huge and growing army of practitioners not only wove themselves into the woof and warp of the nation's business life but they sprawled over into the political parties, labor unions, churches, and "cause" groups. Many of them devoted their talents to the promotion of national celebrities, although they were read out of the field by the more "professional" brethren as mere press agents. Press agentry was looked down on as circus barking was looked down on by the professional salesman. But it could not be gainsaid that they performed an astonishingly wide range of tasks, running from the grinding out of publicity releases to the managing of trade shows and exhibits, labor relations, proxy fights, lobbying, and the supervision of annual reports, personnel, and institutional advertising. Some were even put in charge of all company advertising or helped to pick the advertising agency.

Of the estimated 1,400 independent PR outfits operating in the country, most had only a handful of people, but a few like Hill & Knowlton and Carl Byoir & Associates grew to giant size with 200 or more employees. Most of the larger advertising agencies showed their respect for the growing power of public relations by adding a PR department, whose mere presence was helpful in the courting of new clients or the charming of old ones to stay in the fold. Some advertising agencies like McCann-Erickson and Benton & Bowles set up a public relations arm to handle not only their own clients but to service independent accounts. *Printers' Ink* reported that by 1961 the McCann-Erickson arm had grown to perhaps the fourth largest PR firm in the country.

First because it was so new, and second because it was given such multifarious duties to perform, public relations was viewed from many angles by the brass in many corporations. Some executives felt that a dose of PR medicine was just what was needed to boost sales over the competition. Others seemed to take to public relations less out of faith in it than because everybody else seemed to be getting into it, and they did not want to be left out if it should turn out to be good. Judging by their statements in the trade press, however, most executives felt that public relations was well worth the money spent on it, even if it produced few of the sales miracles prophesied by its most ardent admirers.

What lent an air of enticing mystery to public relations, and undoubtedly helped sell corporate management on its value, was the apparent inability of executives to define precisely what it was they were paying for. Nor were the practitioners themselves able to agree on a definition. Public relations seemed to be something of a Rorschach test, depending for its interpretation on what was in the eye of the beholder; and what the beholder saw depended on who practiced public relations and how. Much of the trouble resulted of course from what *Fortune* called the "considerable numbers of cheap-Jack publicists, promoters, greeters, lobbyists, and fixers who appropriate the label 'public relations man' as a cover for their manipulations." The trade press fulminated against them periodically, much as the advertising trade press fumed against its own adventurers, but little if anything was done by the associations to force the practitioners to live up to the high-toned codes of conduct promulgated for them.

Among the more enthusiastic definitions of public relations was the one which went: "Ours is a group superbly suited . . . to take the initiative in bringing about the integration of spiritual principles and material progress which, and which alone, can assure for us and our fellow man a maximum of happiness." Another saw public relations as "letting your light so shine before men that they may see your good works." Another saw it as a fruitful combination of "philosophy, sociology, economics, language, psychology, journalism, communication, and other knowledges into a system of human understanding." Another said it was no more than "understanding and being understood." Another said it was "living a good corporate life and making certain you get credit for it."

Less enthusiastic were the definitions of some of the critics of public relations. Robert Heilbroner called it in *Harper's* "the business of the Invisible Sell," for it operated not by overtly campaigning for the public's favor but by covertly creating "situations of reality," as the condition was euphemistically referred to by the PR boys, from which blossomed the "spontaneous" acceptance and approval of the public. To Mr. Heilbroner the real-life dramas staged by the PR practitioners contained "not a hidden moral, but a hidden commercial." To Alan Harrington the practitioners made "flower arrangements of the facts, placing them so that the wilted and less attractive petals are hidden by sturdy blooms," as he wrote in *Esquire*. He concluded that public relations was the "art, science, skill, dodge or trade of lying."

Almost unheard in PR circles was one of the earliest definitions advanced by Edward L. Bernays, a PR pioneer, that it was the "engineering of consent," and for good reason it was unheard, for it had the chill of Big Brother about it that was considered a PR blunder in itself.

It was not so considered in the thirties, when the business community was up to its neck in criticism for its then incapacity to produce jobs and a decent standard of living for people, and public relations got its real start. The few PR practitioners around in those days had been urging the business community for more than a decade to get rid of the "public-be-damned" attitude, but the Babbitts of the twenties had paid them no heed. In the thirties, public relations was hurriedly called in to put the business community in right again with the people. Businessmen needed the expert "third party" voice of public relations to get across to the citizenry that private business was in the public interest. The ugly mood of the times was such that it demanded "business leaders who recognized that private business is a public trust," as Edward L. Bernays wrote in *Public Relations*.

Big business in particular was jittery for it felt that of all segments of the business community it was the most unloved. So Bethlehem Steel moved in 1930 to open a public relations department, General Motors opened one in 1931, U.S. Steel in 1936, International Harvester in 1937, Pittsburgh Plate Glass Company and the New York Central in 1939. *Business Week* took a dim view of their frantic efforts when it said: "Business is up against an impossible job trying to make the masses think it is one hundred per cent good." But *Fortune* was sufficiently impressed with the public relations program of General Motors to spell it out in detail, probably the first time such a report ever appeared in a business publication.

When the economy got back on its feet after the war, and public relations was no longer a grim matter of life and death for U.S. corporations, public relations was solidly entrenched. Still mindful of the nightmarish thirties, the U.S. Chamber of Commerce issued a booklet titled "It's Good Business to Explain Your Business," which urged all companies, large and small, to set up "truth squads" with the mission of correcting the "existing misconceptions and untruths about the American business man and the free enterprise system." The Public Relations Society of America was told by Lammot du Pont Copeland that the toughest problem faced by business in the years ahead was the public attitude not only toward the nation's "business institutions, but our social institutions, and even our government, and the governments of others." The "clichés and fancy phrases" were no longer enough. The public henceforth would "demand to know not only what is done, but why it was done, how it was done, and what are the social and economic implications of it all."

William G. Werner termed public relations in *Credit and Financial Management* a dike to hold off the floodwaters of angry happenings, and Robert H. Davidson called it, in *Public Utilities Fortnightly*, corporate preventive medicine, somewhat along the lines practiced by the medical profession. Corporate PR men were urged to be on the alert for any danger signals that portended social trouble, which was "no job for an amateur."

A common theme that turned up in many an executive talk was that "the business corporation . . . exists at the sufferance of society to serve the broad interests of society," as Henry Ford II told the Minneapolis Junior Chamber of Commerce. But if the theme had a Salvation Army ring to it, the corporate executives and PR men recognized its serious under-purpose. While the shibboleth was public interest, as Irwin Ross noted in *The Image Merchants*, the real goal was "public acceptance of the *status quo* in our economic arrangements."

Public relations took on another task in the postwar economy, as a drayhorse harnessed to the nation's sales effort. It was particularly well fitted for this task for, unlike advertising, which operated out in the open and in the obvious self-interest of the seller, public relations operated for the most part subterraneanly and in the presumed self-interest of the buyer. A public which was "battered, bruised, bothered and buncoed," as Victor T. Raeburn wrote in *Editor & Publisher,* and whose resistance to ads mounted daily, could hardly erect a defense against sales efforts which it could not see.

Public relations hence became "a new means of sales-communication" and high testimony was paid to its effectiveness. *Business Week* made mention how at times "smart public relations can be more useful and cheaper than advertising in getting a product better known or halting a slide in a product's sales." Leonard J. Mordell wrote in *American Business* that "public relations . . . makes selling easier." William C. Payette wrote in *The Management Review* that it worked to "build a favorable climate for . . . advertising." Lee Schooler wrote in *Advertising Requirements* of the facility of public relations in bringing "companies, products and ideas before the public in such a way that they win public support." John W. Fearn wrote of advertising and public relations in *Western Advertising* as "two hands, working together," accomplishing "more than one hand working alone." Bernard K. Schram envisioned advertising and public relations before the St. Louis Advertising Club as "Siamese twins of communication. They should be joined at the side so they are both facing the same direction and coordinating their efforts to improve both sales and attitudes for the client."

Indeed public relations introduced a new dimension in the economic thinking of corporate executives, as Dilman M. K. Smith told the American Mutual Alliance, which concerned itself "not in producing and distributing but in talking about things." The talk could be most valuable, for astutely done it could convert stockholders into pressure groups against government regulatory measures and tax proposals. "It is possible now," concurred John W. Hill in *Corporate Public Relations*, to get "truly substantial waves of protest against anti-business measures and stifling taxes."

An ad manager, an ad agency PR director, a company PR executive, and the head of a PR firm, joined in adulation of public relations before the Association of National Advertisers. R. M. Gray, ad manager of Esso, urged advertising and public relations to work closely together "if our mutual goals are to be achieved." W. B. Stevenson, PR director of Benton & Bowles, told how PR laid down "a backdrop of understanding and acceptance" which fertilized the ground "in which advertising must take root." William G. Werner, PR director of Procter & Gamble, urged that advertising men and PR men cross-check their plans with each other. Bert C. Gross, president of Hill & Knowlton, advised how "the forces critical of business in general" could be countered by smart corporate public relations.

The public relations press frequently scolded those backward elements in management which viewed public relations as an exercise in verbal magic, or as a patch to cover up the blemish of management deficiencies. The press insisted that corporations could not sweet-talk their way into the hearts of people, that in Voltaire's words "The only way to compel men to speak good of you is to do good," and that corporations had to perform acts obviously, even exaggeratedly, in the public welfare.

Hence a remarkable movement began to sweep the nation in the fifties in which giant corporations found time to worry about the mundane affairs of little communities. In one such community a private utility built a swimming pool for the local moppets and equipped them with T-shirts with the utility's name on the back. Another utility installed a drinking fountain for thirsty tots who would "some day be the company's customers."

Moreover companies bought supplies locally whenever possible and took pains to conform the architecture of new plants to the prevailing architecture. The local townspeople were encouraged to visit the plants. "When did you last take a troop of schoolboys through your factory or your office?" asked *The Management Review* of busy executives, reminding them that such visits were always good for local newspaper publicity; and "when you stage them, don't forget the photographs." A brass band and appropriate ceremonies were always in order on the corporation's 10th, 25th, or 50th birthday, and the entire community was invited to join and to read about it later in the local newspaper, which generally showed a picture of the mayor or some other dignitary beaming over a handshake with a corporation executive.

It was the common practice of big corporations to encourage their upper-bracket executives to head community chest drives, Red Cross fund-raising, and to go around making speeches before civic groups. Even professional skills were occasionally lent to a community beset by such problems as air or stream pollution, slum clearance, traffic congestion, sewage disposal. The corporate coffers were opened enough to pay for special radio or TV programs, open house events, scholarships and fellowships for college students, and to sponsor 4-H Clubs, Future Farmers of America, Junior Achievement, and other local bodies. "The company considers the public relations effects of the things it does," Standard Oil preciously stated its credo, "and does many things deliberately for the public good."

When Jersey Standard picked up a $600,000 tab for a 13-week sponsorship of a high-brow New York TV program scheduled for demise for lack of sponsorship, it was a dramatic display of public relations at work. The program attracted a small audience, ordinarily unworthy of sponsor dollars, but the case was plastered in the public eye by drama critics who wailed in the nation's press about the sad plight of American culture, which permitted this program to go off the air while the soap and horse operas found ample sponsorship. The hosannas in thousands of letters and hundreds of newspaper editorials that greeted

Jersey Standard's move convinced the oil company of the wisdom of its sponsorship. The case was summed up by a PR practitioner: "A loose ball worth millions in good will was bouncing around and the question was who would be smart enough to pick it up first."

The act of erasing from the public mind the ingrained belief that corporations were creatures of the business world with eyes only for the profit and loss statement, took years. "The art of public relations," Edward L. Bernays wrote in *The Engineering of Consent*, "is often analogous to the act of a boy dropping stones into a half-full pail of water. At first nothing much happens. But gradually the water level rises, and finally the bucket overflows—provided, that is, the boy keeps dropping stones long enough."

The objective, as John J. Pike stated in *American Business*, was to bring corporations to "the same institutional level of acceptance as the public library or the local waterworks." In the uplifting process, as thousands of corporations engaged daily in countless Boy Scout deeds which received proper publicity in the mass media, the corporations emerged with something that bore an astonishing resemblance to a corporate conscience. William T. Gossett, Ford executive, told a fraternity meeting in Detroit that "for the corporation this is a period of new enlightenment." In his opinion, much of the restrictive legislation of the thirties "was the result of the lack of restraint and good judgment on the part of big business," and could have been avoided. Commenting on the period of new enlightenment, *Fortune* said that management seemed to have developed "an acute sense of social responsibility—perhaps, from the stockholders' viewpoint, a somewhat *over*developed sense of obligation."

Corporations found multitudinous ways in which to do their public apple polishing. Even though the annual and interim reports of company earnings, dividend actions, changes in management personnel, stockholder meetings, expansion of facilities, new products, new processes, acquisitions, and so on, were of interest only to a limited audience, the corporate PR department let out the tidings to the general public in a regular waterfall of press releases. Much of the time the PR staff was hard-pressed to find some nugget in the dross of everyday corporate events around which to build a news story, and most editors of most consumer publications failed to recognize the value of the story, which ended up its life ignominiously on the editor's spike. The editors of business publications, however, were more hospitable, and frequently the press release that won a scant paragraph or two in a consumer publication became a glorification story of the corporation in a business publication.

The introduction of new products particularly by the big corporations ordinarily received advance publicity via by-line articles by company executives, engineers and researchers in the trade press, papers read to the professional societies and printed in the technical journals, and news releases to editors of consumer publications. Most of this was the hidden but not unsung handiwork of the corporate PR department. As the National Industrial Conference Board acknowledged in a bulletin titled "New Product Development": "Sometimes these activities are more important than the paid advertising." Not infrequently press junkets were arranged as an extra goodwill inducer for editors who were finicky over the newsworthiness of a story. The corporation arranged and paid for the editors' travel and hotel accommodations, and no *quid pro quo* was openly asked for, but it was the unlikely editor who would bite the hand that fed him.

Some corporations sought biographical enshrinement in books, and the fifties saw an increasing number of "commercials," as they were called, in hard backs. They represented a convenient arrangement by publisher, author, and corporation. "Publishers like them because they provide a risk-proof profit; authors like them because they provide good, steady income; corporations like them because they do a prestige job impressively," wrote Philip

Lesly and Ken Jackson in the *Public Relations Journal.* Publication ordinarily was in one of three ways. The corporation might publish the testament itself as a "handout," or it might be published by a standard book publisher in exchange for a flat fee by the sponsoring corporation, or the corporation might pledge the purchase of a stipulated number of books at a fixed price. Among the business enterprises and executives that achieved perpetuity between book covers in recent years were Alcoa, Bank of America, Chicago & North Western Railroad, Conrad Hilton, Crane, Insurance Company of North America, the Lackawanna Railroad, Metropolitan Life Insurance Company, Minnesota Mining and Manufacturing, and Sir Thomas Lipton. Such a convenient and inexpensive way was it to carve a niche in the business hall of fame that, according to Lesly and Jackson, "almost every publishing house now brings out two or three subsidized books annually."

Nor were the air media ignored by the publicity-hunting corporations, for there were "hundreds of radio and television stations over the nation . . . all hungry for news items," as Jim Atkins wrote in *Advertising Requirements.* Radio stations were anxious for tape recordings, television wanted film, and corporations learned to service them "just as newspapers are serviced." A typical example was the business college which sought to drum up students for its modeling course, and produced a film pointing up the need by the modern secretary to have poise, be able to meet people, and do more than just take shorthand and work a typewriter. The film story followed a girl as she entered the portals of the college, to a typing class, to a modeling class, and on to a good job at the fadeout. Everyone was happy. The business college got its desired publicity, the station got a usable film at no cost, and the viewers got some ostensible information plus a look at a classroom of exceptionally pretty girls.

Donald G. Softness wrote in *Television Age* of the importance of building a personal relationship with TV and entertainment editors and making more likely their acceptance of PR material. "Take them to lunch occasionally. Invite them into the studios. Hold occasional press parties. Arrange for their children to participate in kiddie programs and meet the emcees. And, when you come across an editor in a restaurant, buy him a drink."

The air media indeed became such a wonderful host for product or service "plugs" that Philip A. Seitz noted in *Advertising Age* that "even the most 'aware' admen may not recognize them in all their forms." Although continuity editors, sponsors, and their ad agencies were admittedly tough to get by, those seeking to plant free publicity on somebody else's paid program were stimulated "to greater ingenuity than ever." The simplest plug was the straight product mention, thrown off in a single sentence, which the plug specialists sold for a straight fee, generally upwards of $250 plus the gift of the product itself. Whenever spotted, continuity editors pulled it out of the script, or cut it out of the film, but on "live" comedy or variety shows one such plug after another could be tossed off with impunity. No vigilance could stop or recall the "ad-libbed" plug.

Other plugs were the "travel arrangements by . . ." or "gowns by . . ." as part of the end-titles, or those injected by Hollywood, TV or night club personalities for their own pictures, programs or engagements. Most subtle of all were those which involved brand merchandise as props in shows (most auto makers, for instance, had arrangements for exclusive use of their cars on certain programs). So bountiful were the air media with silent commercials that they may even have outnumbered the more strident kind. As one PR man said, "You don't need brains, ideas, or skill, just money, to get on programs," which tied in with the trade scuttlebutt that almost everyone, from the producer down to the script girl and the property master, had a hand out for a payoff.

The print media, however, were the traditional target for the PR offerings, and although no one knew with any degree of certainty the percentage of handouts that worked their way into the nation's news columns, everyone agreed it was high. The St. Louis Advertising Club was told by a speaker that a survey of New York newspapers showed that 40 to 65 percent of their total contents were derived from the press release. Professor Ralph Ober of New York's New School for Social Research estimated that 80 percent of all stories in newspapers emanated from PR sources, according to *Business Week*. Clyde Mathews agreed with the latter estimate in a pamphlet titled "Public Relations in the Sixties." Newspapermen were reported as occasionally engaging in the pleasant pastime, between assignments, of marking stories in various editions whose parentage was public relations, and coming up invariably with high scores.

In *The Mass Communicators* Charles S. Steinberg quoted an editor who complained that across his desk flowed "enough news releases and feature stories, *in one day*, to fill the pages of an average novel!" (underscoring Steinberg's). Denny Griswold, publisher and editor of *Public Relations News*, reported that the editor of a Western newspaper said that his business and financial departments were deluged with about 400 publicity releases a day. *The Express*, a Pennsylvania newspaper, conducted a two-week study of "Operation Handout," which was described by Charles Seller in *Editor & Publisher*. In the two weeks *The Express* decided that nearly 780 typewritten pages containing more than 200,000 words of publicity were suitable for nothing else but the wastebasket.

Although most of the releases were bannered "News—For Immediate Release," the editors griped that they generally contained no more than the sweat of a PR man with nothing to say. What added insult to the proverbial injury was the scattering of follow-up phone calls from PR men asking if their material had been received or was going to be used. But what caused the editors to blow their collective stacks were the occasional handouts that were baited with polite notes that publication might be followed by an advertising contract.

Withal, publicity features were used by more than 13,000 editors in the U.S., according to an article in *Public Relations Journal*, and in some cases it was hard to see the connection between the magazine and the feature. In an editorial, *Madison Avenue* called the placement abilities of PR men "little short of miraculous," and supported its judgment by pointing to an airline story which landed in *Padre*, a Boston religious publication, sandwiched between "Blessed Are the Meek" and "Count Your Blessings"; a story on how to pack a suitcase that wormed its way into *Extension*, another religious publication; a story on vanilla that managed to get into *The Retail Clerks' Advocate*; a five-page airline story that appeared in *The Carpenter Magazine*; and a story on "Breakfast Around the World" that somehow captured the interest of the *Railway Carmen's Journal*. PR men modestly claimed that these feats were matched elsewhere.

So highly organized were the publicity machines that anyone with pretensions to magazine editorship could have put out a well illustrated, well written magazine at no editorial cost at all, simply by availing himself of some of the wealth of free material that was around. Two magazines, *Précis* and *Feature*, even offered editors a steady supply of canned features on food, fashion, science, industry, home, each running from 150 to 1,500 words and illustrated with from one to eight glossy prints. To order, editors needed but to mark "the code number of the stories" wanted and they arrived by return mail "without fee or obligation of any kind." In most cases the sell was cleverly woven into the story material and it would take an alert reader indeed to catch the corporation's sotto voce commercial in the enchanting story he was reading.

Scores of mat-service companies got into the business of converting the advertiser's commercial into news pellets for the nation's newspapers. Derus Media Service, for instance, claimed that it serviced newspapers with a combined circulation of nearly 25 million. Special Correspondents claimed that 4,500 newspapers "have sent us a written request for our material." It was a tricky art to work sell into a mat release, one best left to the experts; the unskilled might "kill the goose which is laying the golden egg." The experts knew that the newspaper editor often decided whether to use the mat release after reading the opening paragraph, and avoided the planting of the commercial "in the first few sentences." Cost of such expert service was about $200 for each one-column release sent to 1,000 newspapers, and $300 for each two-column release.

Scores of clipping bureaus sprang up, whose hundreds of employees worked all day culling publicity mentions from the nation's media. The bureaus charged about $20 per month to reap the clippings that the PR machines had sown, plus 15 cents per clipping. Almost all the big corporations, trade associations, and ad agencies subscribed to one or more of the clipping bureaus, which sometimes were also hired to snip publicity mentions of competitors to see how each was faring in the free-space grab.

By and large, newspaper editors had a deep-seated and historic antipathy toward the "flacks," as the PR men were derisively referred to, who arrived hat in one hand and news release in the other. Back in the twenties, when PR lacked the respectability it later gained, the newspaper editors conducted open warfare against the space grabbers, typified by a 1929 article in *Editor & Publisher* summarily headlined "500 Grafters." The article concerned itself with a list, compiled by the American Newspaper Publishers Association, of 500 brand articles that were being press-agented in "grafted" newspaper space. By the fifties, the warfare had simmered down to sultry suspicion and the list of proscribed items that formerly was issued by ANPA almost regularly, appeared less frequently. Occasionally, however, *Editor & Publisher* still rose editorially to flay the PR set. For instance, when The Can Manufacturers Institute sent around to newspapers a hefty package of public relations material containing stories, speeches, and other promotional tidbits, *Editor & Publisher* was miffed that some of the stuff would turn up as news items in weeklies and dailies. "It reminds us of the old saying about publicity in general. Why should they buy it [advertising space] when you give it away?"

The suspicion embroidered with contempt came out in any number of surveys of editors' opinions. G. R. Johnston wrote in *Advertising Requirements* that most of the press releases were held by the editors to be "99.44% pure—pure tripe." Lee Schooler noted in the same publication that a survey of 300 editors turned up "an eagerness to express their feelings" on PR; among other things, they considered more than half of all press conferences self-serving and "downright unnecessary." Don Baines argued in *Retailing Daily* that "a free people need a free press, uncluttered by PR men and their handouts." A Connecticut newspaper editor railed in *Editor & Publisher* at the "twin disorders known as adjectivitis and throw-the-bullitis."

An opinion survey of 1,700 newspaper editors cast the PR men in quite a different light from that held by the PR men of themselves, according to Lee Feldman in *Editor & Publisher*. The same questions asked of the editors were also asked of 117 members of the Public Relations Society of America, and the editors provided the less charitable answers on the practice of PR. One question asked whether PR men did not "too frequently insist on promoting products, services or other activities which do not legitimately deserve promotion." Some 75 percent of the editors said yes, but 76 percent of the PR men thought this expressed the behavior of only a negligible few of their brethren. Another question asked whether PR men did not "too often try to deceive the press by attaching too much importance to a trivial, uneventful happening." Some 62 percent of the editors agreed, but 68 percent of the PR men denied that this was so. What grievously hurt the PR men was that more than half the editors insisted that publicity was nothing more than free advertising, a concept that the PR men had hoped had been laid permanently at rest. "Most of the publicity releases . . . are straight advertising or thinly disguised advertising," as one of the editors said.

Even the lavish wining and dining of editors by the PR fraternity came in for an occasional brickbat. One editor reported in the *Journal of Commerce* that at a sumptuous luncheon "the wine was poured so freely that the editors could not have done justice to that story that afternoon even if they had wanted to." Gay Pauley, Women's Editor of United Press, urged the American Public Relations Association: "Quit wooing us with loot and luncheons." Robert J. McAndrews described in *Printers' Ink* the gala evening at a plush hotel where 200 radio, TV, and newspaper gentry were plied with cocktails, a steak dinner, and a handsome gift to help them remember the evening. "Nobody said so in so many words, of course, but obviously it would be nice if we paid for our evening with some kind of publicity for the product," which Mr. McAndrews was sure would be forthcoming "to salve a conscience for accepting the free loading."

Nonetheless, despite the griping by editors and the demeaning of the mass media reporters, a variety of pressures including mounting labor and material costs forced the media to live and work with the vast army of publicity seekers. "Without them," as *Business Week* commented, "only a handful of newspapers and radio and TV stations would have the staff or resources to cover business activities." There was growing hazard of course in making PR men the unofficial reporters of the nation, more so for the unsuspecting public which read and believed what the PR men wanted it to believe than for the hapless editors who knowingly, if grudgingly, ran their plants. "Editors and public relations men lead a symbiotic existence," as *Advertising Requirements* said. "Neither one can live completely without the other, but neither likes to have his dependence on the other rubbed in."

A considerable battle of vast proportions, in which cotton fought wool, steel fought aluminum, glass fought tin, trade association fought trade association, groups fought for or against legislation, and other groups fought to safeguard or destroy each other's economic stakes, went on silently every day in the news columns of the mass media. The objective was to capture the sympathy of the public mind by planting in that mind ideas that the public would blithely call its own and take action upon.

Public relations was considered the panacea for sudden ills. For instance, when the TV industry was mauled by Congressional committees, federal agencies, and the press in the wake of the rigged quiz and payola scandals in 1959, it hired PR talent to calm down the growing public storm. When the drug industry was hit by a Senate probe of high drug prices, it turned to PR for quick help. When the tobacco industry was shaken by the lung-cancer-cigarette scare in the early fifties, its PR men worked frantically to nullify the impact in the news columns. When Madison Avenue decided it had to do something to allay growing public criticism of advertising, it produced a PR program to impress the thought leaders of the nation that advertising was really a responsible industry.

Public relations also came to the aid of long-ailing industries. The millinery industry, which had lagged for years in sales, gained some succor from PR efforts to make hats synonymous with fashion in the public mind; in the process free hats were supplied to fashion models, fashion editors, movie stars, TV performers, society girls, and pictures of national celebrities (in hats of course) turned up with increasing frequency in mass magazines. The fur industry moved to popularize the cheaper furs of rabbit, muskrat, beaver, fox, and thereby widen the fur market, by PR efforts which produced a Young Fur Department in stores, a Miss Fur Coed on college campuses, and a campaign to convince American women that mink was not the only fashionable fur. Baseball, which became less of a national pastime as it dropped in attendance from 40 million in 1952 to 3 million in 1956, gained all sorts of PR ideas on how to lure more people into ball parks, including a primer on baseball and a light-hearted movie aimed at inducing the little woman to go with her husband through the turnstiles.

Private utilities learned how to gain rate increases without arousing too much public resentment. In accomplishing this, PR task forces went to work even before the rate-increase application was filed with the public service commission, by getting the utilities' viewpoint across to newspaper editors, business executives and important civic groups.

The American Iron and Steel Institute ran a PR ad campaign in more than 400 newspapers to relieve the public of the idea that steel prices were high and an inflationary force in the national economy. A variety of pleasant pen-and-ink drawings made the same point: "What can you buy today for eight cents a pound?—besides steel, that is."

The American Petroleum Institute had a tougher PR problem, for studies showed that the material contributions of the oil industry to American well-being were taken for granted; what made people look cross-eyed at the oil industry was the memory of its rapacious past. The Institute hoped that a campaign stressing the oil industry's current good citizenship and sense of fair play would live down that memory.

Sometimes the PR men worked the newspaper, magazine, radio, and TV éclat into something of a national celebration for a company event, such as the Motorama for General Motors, the National Bake-Off for Pillsbury Mills, and the Miss Rheingold contest for Rheingold beer. Sometimes they garnered publicity by a stunt, such as Pfizer's turning the Waldorf-Astoria into a barnyard of animals to point up the advances made in agricultural science. Sometimes they showed up in the pulpit, such as Bon Ami's giving cash contributions to hundreds of New York churches in return for the collection of Bon Ami labels from congregations.

They tried to dream up promotions that obviously coincided with the public interest, for these opened the broadest avenues to civic group cooperation and publicity. The Keebler Biscuit

Company, for instance, hit upon a back-to-school, safe-driving campaign that was enthusiastically endorsed by municipal governments and a long list of civic organizations. The campaign sold safe driving to motorists, implanted Keebler as a firm interested in the welfare of schoolchildren, and inevitably added to the brisk sales of Keebler's cookies and crackers. Similarly, the Parker Pen Company promoted teachers into starting letter exchanges between pupils in different parts of the country. The promotion served the needs of education by teaching the importance of good handwriting, and the sales needs of Parker by instilling brand identification at an early age. And the New York Life Insurance Company's career-choosing ads ("Should Your Child Be a Doctor?" "Should Your Child Be an Architect?" and so on), which drew requests for 20 million reprints in six years, considerable editorial comment, and a sackful of letters of praise from people in high places, also not unexpectedly was a valuable sales aid for company agents.

Other promotions were more openly commercial, such as the Operation Home Improvement which encouraged homeowners to improve their homes and the lumber dealers sponsoring it to fatten their sales; and the Mrs. Homemaker Forum which urged housewives to find new uses for the company's products and incorporated the best of them in a 250-page *Encyclopedia of Household Hints* which further brightened the company's sales.

Still others were more subtle, such as the promotion of bourbon as a cooking ingredient via recipes, special bourbon glasses for women, and the promotion of bourbon as a fashion color. Food columnists and radio women commentators were plied with PR material in the hope that eventually the housewife would reach for the liquor cabinet instead of the spice shelf for food flavoring. The cognac PR promoters were also busy, giving it away to food editors, to Santa Clauses shivering on the street in the pre-Christmas cold, to TV cooking programs, and wherever else it could garner publicity. They scored a great triumph when a keg of 67-year-old cognac was presented to President Eisenhower on his sixty-seventh birthday, and pictures of the event flashed in the nation's mass media.

Thanks in part to public relations, American wool took its place alongside British woolens, Scottish woolens and Italian woolens, as a result of ads and publicity that picked up about 11 million lines of copy in consumer publications in 1959–1960 compared to 850,000 lines the previous year, according to the PR firm handling the push. Among the events that helped capture this publicity was the designation of September as American Wool Month by the President and 42 governors, the presentation of a wool map of the U.S. to the Vice-President, and the raising of a wool flag over Fort McHenry, subsequently enshrined in Federal Hall, all the events being accompanied by appropriate news coverage. A Miss Wool of America did her bit for wool by displaying her pulchritude in a fanfare tour of major cities.

Royal Jelly became a first-class miracle ingredient in beauty preparations as a result of skillful publicity that found its way into nationally syndicated newspaper columns and built up into feature stories in magazines, such as the four-page illustrated spread in *Look*. Scoffed at by health authorities, the mysterious food given by worker bees to the queen bee nonetheless was snatched off cosmetic counters by American women who wished to stay the hand of Father Time. The advance publicity had so presold the women that no claims were needed in the ads.

Public relations helped the American Trucking Association to transform the image of the truck driver from a toughy who threw his truck weight around to a courteous, helpful, pleasant chap. When Emily Post acknowledged in *Motor Manners* that she was fond of truck drivers because they were "truly the gentlemen of the highway," the PR promotion scored a signal success. It was particularly welcome to the American Trucking Association which counted on public sympathy as a help in its battle for the transportation business with the longer entrenched railroads.

The Union Pacific Railroad aroused interest in the West by sending photos showing the glories of Western scenery, history, agriculture, and industry to picture editors. Aeronaves de Mexico displayed its own brand of Pan-American friendship by featuring well known travel editors in newspaper ads. The American Bakers Association drummed up business by sending around to newspapers a four-page photographic splash depicting the summer joys of outdoor eating. The Book-of-the-Month Club sent a complimentary book to the newspaper editor who ran an 800–900 word piece on "The Story Behind the Book" in his news columns. The Society of American Florists put steady pressure on newspaper editors not to run "Please Omit Flowers" in obituaries, offering as reasons that friends of the bereaved should not be deprived of this form of remembrance and that it constituted a discriminatory act against florists. The New York Stock Exchange pushed an ad and PR campaign on the theme "own your own share of American business" to widen the public's holdings of corporate stock.

In their exuberance PR men at times overstepped the bounds of ethics and morality, which was perhaps inevitable in a field of action almost entirely hidden from the public view. No one was willing to hazard how frequently, but the periodic instances of bribery, chicanery, and subornation of officials that erupted in print made it likely that the practice was far more widespread than the PR societies knew of or were willing to admit. There were borderline practices, like the free transatlantic flights offered by airlines to pliant writers in return for story plugs, the watches bestowed on TV critics and newspaper columnists for "private" advice on a TV spectacular, the liberal expenses paid to writers researching stories of special interest to PR men, the hiring of key communications personnel to carry out nonexistent assignments, the handsome payment to writers and magazines for reprints of articles in which favorable mention was made of something or other. Indeed in the year-round atmosphere of lavish parties and loot that ranged from cases of Scotch to Tiffany trinkets and reached a showering climax at Christmas, it was hard to distinguish between the proper and the improper. Even the sturdiest integrity, like the mountains themselves, eroded under the steady rain of manna.

Other practices were clearly on the shadier side for they included the placing of reporters on private payroll and the use of dirty PR tactics. Not infrequently writers on boxing, wrestling, and racing were placed on a promoter's payroll. Irwin Ross recalled in *The Image Merchants* that the Providence *Journal-Bulletin* had disclosed that 26 newspapermen, employed by nine newspapers and two wire services, were on the New England racing tracks' payrolls for $30,000 in one year; one track showed $12,000 going to 11 sports writers.

Of the 78 managing editors who responded to a query for the reasons for slanted or suppressed sports news, many listed the side "payments to sports reporters for services as official scorers or statisticians" and "gifts or payoffs from sports management," according to *Editor & Publisher*. The managing editor of a Kentucky newspaper told the University of Minnesota Conference for News Executives that bribery, which he branded the "shame of journalism," operated in newspaper reporting of sports, entertainment, women's news, and politics. Ezra Goodman in *The Fifty-Year Decline and Fall of Hollywood* pilloried movie industry reporting as containing "more nonsense . . . than about the Abominable Snowman and the Loch Ness Monster combined." He charged that "press and press agents go together, like the two sides of a counterfeit coin, like Romulus and Remus suckling from the same fiendish teat."

The stock market became a fertile field for PR activity. Paul Windels, Jr., regional administrator of the Securities and Exchange Commission, expressed that agency's concern in an *Editor & Publisher* interview with the avalanche of "press agent types of releases designed to influence the market." He charged that these "deceptive and untrue releases" caused trading in stocks "not warranted by the facts." One PR firm was summoned for an SEC hearing when a stock on the New York Stock Exchange shot up from 8⅝ to 24½ in one week in the wake of a press release. It was common knowledge that PR firms often got stock options on the stock it was touting. The situation that seemed to be developing was sharply reminiscent of the late twenties, when the ebullient stock market was succored by phony news tips that came to light only in the Congressional hearings on Stock Exchange Practices in 1932. The knotty problem faced by the Securities and Exchange Commission was to find some way to avoid the suppression of news and yet weed out the dissembling press release that set the public to scrambling to buy up a stock in anticipation of a "killing" that never came off.

The classic postwar case of unsavory PR at work was in the struggle between the railroads and the truckers. The Eastern Railroad Presidents Conference hired Carl Byoir & Associates to do what it could to chop down the growing trucker competition. An immediate goal was to get the Pennsylvania governor to veto a bill increasing the weight allowance of trucks operating on that state's highways. Carl Byoir & Associates, using the traditional "third party" technique, aroused what appeared to be a popular hue and cry against the bill by getting front organizations like the Pennsylvania Grange and the Association of Township Supervisors to oppose it vociferously. The governor bowed to popular will and vetoed the bill. The Pennsylvania Trucking Association promptly slapped an antitrust suit against the railroads and Byoir. The defendants were found guilty by a U.S. District Court judge who castigated the PR technique as "one long known to political experts under the term 'the big lie.'" The judge condemned as illegal the use of third parties "as fronts to carry out a conspiracy to destroy a competitor." Byoir appealed the decision to the U.S. Circuit Court of Appeals on the ground that "basic American freedoms are the fundamental issue in this case." But the Court of Appeals affirmed the decision, although a dissenting judge found "no difference in substance between the methods employed by Byoir for the railroads and those by Allied for the truckers, except that Byoir was more vigorous, more vocal, and more effective." The judge added: "The methods employed might well cause justifiable fear to those concerned with the viability of our representative form of government." On appeal the Supreme Court reversed the lower court's decision on the ground that, reprehensible as the conduct might be, it was protected by the First Amendment.

Although the PR societies publicly condemned the "third party" practice, no Byoir, Allied, or any other practitioner was expelled for engaging in it. The PR societies worked up new codes of conduct which included the banning of payola in broadcast, the subornation of editors, writers, and reporters, and the "third party" practice. But it was extremely doubtful in view of the Supreme Court decision, which amounted in effect to an unrestricted hunting license, that the PR societies' codes or anything else would cause all the practitioners voluntarily to restrict the weapons at their command. Some would, for some were troubled by the awesome power of molding the public mind without any inhibiting social responsibility. It was not a wholesome situation for the admen to have laws to keep them in line, reporters to have libel to watch for, and PR men to account only to their own consciences. For in a business whose nature at its core was the distortion of truth and which operated out of public view, small store could be placed on its practitioners' consciences. Those with a conscience would continue to work out uneasy compromises between the client's wants and the public good and those unweighted with it would continue to try to persuade the public to act like lemmings and rush over the cliff into the sea.

The Research Techniques 15

The psychologists, sociologists, economists, anthropologists, and social psychologists, much of whose ivory-tower work in the colleges and universities had hitherto been looked upon with more than a touch of scorn, were called on hurriedly and increasingly by the advertisers in the postwar era to lend a needed hand in stepping up public consumption of goods and services. With the physical scientists producing their astonishing advances in the technology of production, it was now up to the social scientists to find ways of getting everything consumed, otherwise the economy was threatened with engulfment in its own produce.

The prewar history of merchandising had been marked by few formal attempts to get at a rationale of consumer behavior. There were the first field studies to learn something about consumer response to print ads—their format, size, illustration, color, headline, typography—which were undertaken by George Gallup, a Drake University professor, and Daniel Starch, a Harvard professor, in the late twenties. But prior to that, research in general had been remarkably circumscribed by the laboratory and given over to a priori rationalizations about the nature of human behavior. Much of the intellectualization about human conduct was stimulated by the "behaviorism" work of John B. Watson at Johns Hopkins. So far as consumers specifically were concerned, and their response to advertising stimuli, Walter Dill Scott's *Psychology of Advertising* still stood as the major landmark from the year it was published in 1908.

In the thirties, with the growth of fascism abroad and depression at home, many social scientists were stimulated to make their first serious attempts to take readings of the public pulse. But the methods they employed in public opinion polls were often quite crude and their results were unreliable, particularly in the tricky field of politics where the citizenry were wont to keep their own counsel or apt to change their minds. Indeed the demise of the *Literary Digest* after the 1936 election was attributable in part to their cockeyed sampling methods which induced the *Digest* to predict the wrong four-year tenant of the White House.

Even after the war their handicapping methods left much to be desired, for their political polls were unanimous in prophesying Dewey an easy victor over Truman in the 1948 election. Six months later at a meeting of the American Association for Public Opinion Research they still expressed mystification over the upset, plus a proper degree of mortification. Archibald Crossley acknowledged to the assemblage that "as seers of what the American pulse would do, we stack up as also-rans in a race of gypsy tea-leaf readers." Elmo Roper said he did not know what happened and George Gallup added, "I don't know more than Elmo Roper doesn't know."

In the 1952 election the pollsters warily avoided picking the winner though they did wind up their surveys by giving Eisenhower the edge in popular vote. This, at least, kept the public opinion polls technically in the win column and forestalled the cries for complete reevaluation of research methods that followed the 1948 boner. The trade press, however, demanded more than a technical win. As Robert A. Baker wrote in *Printers' Ink*, why did the pollsters fail to foresee a spread between the candidates of about 13 percent? Why did they call dead-even a race that ended up in a landslide? Were these typical of the methods used by the social researchers? If so, it left the uncomfortable suspicion that advertisers investing in market research might be wasting time, effort, and money.

In explanation, the pollsters assured advertisers that special problems were indigenous to election forecasting. First, public sentiment kept changing in the days or weeks before election and, second, figuring how the "undecided" voters would jump was an elusive problem. George Gallup characterized polling efforts as "normal performance, but obviously not good enough." Archibald Crossley acknowledged that "lots of people think we could have come closer, but we just can't do it"; he hoped that advertisers using market research would "not lose faith in it."

Aside from politics, market research had special problems too. Before the war the class structure had been relatively stable, for few families had possessed the income by which to filter up in the social classes. Much of the working class had been unemployed and need and price had domineered the family purchases. What little market research was around was simple, and advertisers had aimed their wares either at the "class" or the "mass" market.

After the war, however, the dimensions and rapacity for goods of the middle class startled advertisers as much as it delighted them. With wives abandoning kitchens for office and factory jobs, and husbands moving into jobs at good pay, nearly a million families every year shouldered their way into the lower-middle class. They won the admiration of economists as they led the national push of the Gross National Product to annual new peaks. They made obsolete the class structure charts of sociologists almost as soon as the charts were prepared. And they churned up class relationships into a potpourri of working-class and lower-middle-class conflicts, frustrations, aspirations, attitudes, and customs.

Advertisers loved them for becoming one huge sales target. But advertisers were confessedly at a loss to know how to reach this burgeoning, mixed-up market. The Winston Churchill characterization of Russian society as "a riddle wrapped in a mystery inside an enigma," so far as the advertisers were concerned, applied equally to the lower-middle class. Disoriented to working-class values, not yet adjusted to lower-middle-class values, with income outpacing needs, price was replaced for the lower-middle class by obscure, noneconomic reasons for buying. And advertisers were desperately in need of market research to explain what made the new consumer act the consumer. With ad budgets doubling and trebling, they needed the predictive judgments of market research on which they could gamble multimillion-dollar campaigns. Suspicious of market research, nonetheless they had to rely on it increasingly. For they lacked even such basic knowledge as what breed of consumer tried new products, at what point a luxury crossed the line into a necessity, what media to use for what products, what TV programs were best suitable for what products.

So for answers they turned to the economists, psychologists, sociologists, anthropologists, and to splinters of the social disciplines. They gave the economists the task of charting the buying power of consumer groupings; from probably less than 100 in prewar days, the number of economists on corporate payrolls climbed to the thousands in the fifties. They told the psychologists to study the broodings of the new consumer mind and come up with the right kind of push-button ad appeals, and to suggest the most tempting package and product designs. Such were the hordes of psychologists who became consultants to business that the American Psychological Association founded a Consumer Psychology Division in 1961 to account for them. At an Association convention, one speaker referred to the psychologists as "the missing communications link between producer and consumer" and another enthused over the "tremendous opportunity" available to psychologists to light the way for business. The last ones through the business portals were the sociologists and anthropologists, and they were given the job of studying the consumer as a social and cultural animal. Figures on the number of sociologists hired by advertisers were lacking, but the American Sociological Society was certain it had jumped substantially from the 5 percent in 1950.

Advertisers were so eager for answers that "thousands of people, trained and untrained, part-time and full-time," entered the research business, as *Printers' Ink* said. Some set up shop in their homes, others broke away from the research outfits to set up their own independent groups. Soon no large-sized U.S. city was lacking in several competing organizations. The ad agencies opened up or expanded their research departments and retained outside research organizations as consultants; and articles on the "marketing concept" became fashionable in the trade press. Colleges and universities were sucked into the marketing field and conducted surveys paid for by advertisers' grants. The probes of consumer attitudes conducted by the Survey Research Center at the University of Michigan were studied intensely by advertisers seeking clues to the buying intentions of consumers. Indicative of the influx of researchers was the membership of the American Marketing Association which grew from 1,500 in 1945 to 6,400 by 1957. Even Western Union got into the act, offering to conduct marketing surveys.

So disorderly was the research field that the Advertising Research Foundation, a nonprofit organization of advertisers, ad agencies, and media, was formed to examine the research methodologies and to prune the fast-growing foliage of the inept and the unorthodox. Most pressing, in the opinion of the ARF, were appraisals of print and broadcast rating methods, media studies, and motivation research, each of which kept the advertising world in a constant tizzy with their claims and counterclaims. Life was not easy, for as unofficial arbiter the ARF was pummeled by the research outfits whose methods it criticized, and the air was occasionally blue from the most unscientific sounding language of some of the behavioral scientists.

One of the ARF troubles was in clearing the underbrush of the special terminology that many research outfits bestowed on their techniques. Such was the competition, that a nicely turned word or phrase served to appropriate a procedure and simultaneously label others who used it as cheap imitators. Sometimes the adaption of a clinical procedure that had been in use for years was enough for a self-styled Columbus to hail his discovery in the trade press. Another of the ARF troubles was in explaining to wary advertisers the growing marketing jargon that lent to market research the aura of an occult science. Terms like "image profile," "respondent," "humanization," "in-depth expansion of market," "problem area," "stimulation device," "geographical spread," "margin-dollar concept," added spice, if not always lucidity, to market reports.

If size of research budgets was any indication, advertisers welcomed the swarming researchers with something less than rousing cheers. In a 1945–1946 study, for instance, the American Marketing Association found 62 percent of the 4,786 firms surveyed not doing any market research. A repeat AMA study in 1952, which was narrowed to several hundred firms "likely to be advanced in their use of this management tool," found advertisers still unfired with enthusiasm for the research oracles. The highest reported figure allocated to research was 1 percent of sales; the lowest was $\frac{3}{10,000}$; and the median was $\frac{1}{10}$ of 1 percent of sales, or 10 cents for each $100 in sales. Similarly, a survey by the Association of National Advertisers in 1958 showed less than 1 percent of advertising budgets allocated to research; dampening executive ardor, according to ANA, was lack of understanding of research techniques, distrust of research, lack of research-goal clarity, and misuse of research.

Still, pressure built up steadily for research, if for no better reason than making a stab at safeguarding the astronomical sums wagered on a product's success. As one company executive warned: "The high cost of bum-guessing and hunch-playing can break our economic backs." Advertisers simply had to know how many advertising dollars were being wasted, what would happen if advertising were doubled, or cut in half. They chafed at their inability to get at exact measurements of advertising effectiveness with anything like the ease with which they calculated production costs. They found progress toward the measurement of advertising effectiveness, as Robert F. Elder wrote in *The Marketing Job*, frustratingly "slow and halting. Yet this is the key measurement."

As for the admen, they looked on market research with mingled feelings. A few felt it stifled their personal creativity, some that it handed them a convenient scapegoat in case a campaign went sour, but most probably cordially welcomed research for the clues it gave them into the multiple and often contradictory motivations of the lower-middle class. If nothing else, research helped the upper-middle class admen better understand the denizens of the lower-middle class.

The backbone of most research was probably the direct questioning of a consumer sample in the hope of gaining insight into what consumers in general wanted. Interviewers were sent out by the research outfits to buttonhole strangers on the streets and ask them for their likes and dislikes. Interviewers were sent into the supermarkets to take secretive notes of shoppers' behavior and ask shoppers to explain their purchases. The housewife who answered her doorbell might also be confronted by interviewers asking her opinions. Indeed the solicitation of consumer opinion became a thriving business plus something of a nuisance to harried shoppers, a few of whom complained to the Better Business Bureau about being pestered by interviewers with clipboards full of questions. Not helping matters any, a wave of door-to-door salesmen, posing as "researchers," proceeded to sell unwary housewives considerable quantities of high-priced merchandise. The National Better Business Bureau found it necessary to distribute nearly two million circulars warning housewives that the genuine interviewer would "never ask you to pay any money, and never ask you to sign an agreement to buy anything."

Admen conducted their own vicarious research into the consumer mind. Although denied by some of the trade press, and treated as a joke by the rest, admen did nose around for consumer opinion on ad themes, new products, or whatever else required a promotional decision. A *Tide* survey, for instance, found three out of four ad executives confessing that they did conduct informal polls among their wives, friends, neighbors, or whoever else was handy. Wives turned out to be the overwhelming favorites as consultants, but one vice-president admitted he asked his maid. Although the validity of this private research was doubted, most executives acknowledged it affected their thinking.

Admen also went in for what was called "brainstorming," which was in effect a group assault on a marketing problem. It became quite fashionable in the mid-fifties among some of the larger agencies. The assumption behind brainstorming was that under proper conditions groupthink would be much more productive than lonethink. Three rules operated in brainstorming sessions. First of all, criticism of the off-the-top-of-the-head suggestions was unwelcome, for it tended to inhibit the panel and dry up the free flow of ideas. Second, wild suggestions were encouraged; in fact the wilder the suggestion the better, for it was considered easier to tone down an idea than to think one up. Third, the goal was sheer quantity, on the ground that with more ideas there was greater likelihood some good ones would result.

One of the pioneers in the brainstorming movement, Alex Osborn, of Batten, Barton, Durstine & Osborn, told the Creative Problem Solving Institute that 53 groups at his agency produced in one year more than 15,000 ideas. Surplus ideas that were considered usable were deposited in a "bank" to be drawn when needed.

Scoffers of the group approach to creative thinking were not lacking. One speaker, reminding the New York Art Directors Club that the dictionary meaning of "brainstorm" was "confusion of mind," crisply added, "I sometimes suspect this may not be far from the truth." Another denounced the "false standards" of the brainstorm sessions which rewarded talkers over thinkers, fast thinking over clear thinking, and quantity over quality. Another demanded: "Could *Hamlet* have been written by a committee? Or the Mona Lisa painted by a club?" The scoffers were urged by still another speaker to join "Brainstormers Anonymous," a fictitious organization dedicated to fight the "pernicious panacea" of "shallow-root ideas." When a test conducted at Yale University turned up a number of individuals who, working alone, produced in the aggregate more and better ideas than the same number of individuals operating as a group, the scoffers were jubilant. The brainstorm adherents pointed out, however, that the Yale experiment was conducted under conditions somewhat different from those on Madison Avenue.

The motivation researchers kicked up an even bigger storm. Although they often hotly disagreed with each other's methodology and interpretation, they were generally agreed that consumer motivations could not be unearthed by direct questioning of consumers. Nor could tabulations of consumer income, education, age, sex, occupation, and so on, explain consumer behavior. "After you dissect the frog—after you memorize the Latin names of all its organs, muscles, nerves, and how they relate to one another—you still know nothing about the 'frogginess' of frogs," as one of the motivation researchers told the American Marketing Association. All these dissections of consumer externals did not reveal the inner consumer. What was needed were psychological probes deep into the consumer mind.

In an age of abundance, the motivation researchers argued, the noneconomic reasons why people bought were also mostly nonrational. There were three levels of consumer motivation. At the first level, the consumer was aware, able and willing to explain motivation; at the second level, the consumer was aware, able, but unwilling to betray motivation; and at the third level, the consumer was unaware and hence incapable of explaining motivation. If pressed for reasons, the consumer would offer surface reasons which served to protect the consumer's view of himself as a rational human being. Only skillful psychological probing could get at buying motivations that lay entombed in the subconscious.

The motivation researchers produced an elaborate system of principles, techniques, and theorems to guide their research. They offered what one of them told an advertising group at Ohio State University was "a new science which we call psycho-economics." To buying and selling, production and consumption, supply and demand, and other traditionally economic concepts, they added psychological appurtenances. And they issued warnings to advertisers to "accept the reality of psycho-economic behavior" or face the risk of being driven to the wall.

Advertiser interest in motivation research perked up markedly after a study of coffee buyers of instant and regular coffee appeared in the *Journal of Marketing*. In that study, which became the darling of the motivation researchers, two shopping lists had been prepared, identical except that one list had included Nescafé and the other Maxwell House coffee. Housewives had been told to look over the two shopping lists and try to characterize the woman who prepared each. The study had uncovered unmistakable bias against the woman whose shopping list included the instant coffee. She had been described by 48 percent as lazy, whereas only 4 percent so described the Maxwell House buyer. She had been taxed by 48 percent with improper planning of household purchases, whereas only 12 percent had this to say about the Maxwell House buyer. She had been visualized by 4 percent as a spendthrift, but nobody so visualized the Maxwell House buyer. When directly questioned, however, housewives had said they did not buy Nescafé only because they did not like the taste of instant coffee.

Other studies hammered home the same point, that psychological factors did do strange things to consumer shopping behavior. Often the consumer bought the box not the contents, the appearance not the performance, the illusion not the reality. Shopping choice seemed to emerge from the interplay of the product personality and the consumer personality.

For instance, when a test panel was asked to taste a biscuit in a red wrapper and another in a brown wrapper, one-third of the panel chose one over the other. Among the reasons given for the preference was that one biscuit was sweeter than the other, or creamier, or more nutritious, or more digestible. Yet the two biscuits were in fact the same. Somehow, by psychological transfiguration, the wrapper difference became a product difference. Similar goings-on were reported when other consumer products were tested.

The motivation researchers scored again when a panel was shown the titles of eight magazine articles plus a synopsis of each to aid recall and asked: "How many articles did you notice? How many did you read?" Although only six of the eight articles had actually appeared in a magazine, and the other two were "dummies," one of the "dummies" achieved the distinction of being the second-best "read" article of all. In fact 91 percent of the panel "recalled" or claimed to have "read" either one or both of the "dummies" that had never been in print. The reason for the monkeyshines, the psychologists said, was that the two "dummies" were attributed to prestige magazines and the other six were not, and the panel members were unwilling to confess they read the trashier rather than the classier magazines.

To break down consumer defenses the motivation researchers borrowed many of the techniques of clinical psychology. They subjected consumers to tests ranging from word-association and sentence-completion to role-playing and situational. The Rorschach and Thematic Apperception tests were widely used as was the so-called depth interview which, because of the play it got in books, magazines, and the press, bestowed on the motivation researchers a socially evil role. They were accused of poking about in the consumer mind to learn things that advertisers could later turn against consumers.

The depth interview was a sort of quickie psychoanalysis, with the subject talking for an hour or so until wrung dry of certain emotional memories. The interviewer asked no direct questions, only the open-end kind designed to prod the subject whose meanderings down memory lane showed signs of halting. About fifty depth interviews, each consisting of 20 to 30 typewritten pages, ordinarily were enough for the motivation researchers to spot the threads of common motivation running through them. The motivation researchers claimed that the larger samples required of traditional "nose-counting" research were unneeded by them, both a claim and a descriptive phrase that did not endear the motivation psychologists to partisans of other research methodologies.

Advertisers who gave the motivation researchers the job of hunting down the symbolic meaning of goods to consumers were not always happy with the reports. Sometimes the reports fascinated advertisers with their psychological insights, but often the going was heavy because of their larding with unfamiliar psychological lingo. Although the id, ego, superego, Oedipus complex and libido were sparingly used, there was an unmistakable Freudian flavor in many reports that hard-bitten advertisers found distressing. *Printers' Ink* suspected that "so much mumbo jumbo" in the reports was part of the drive by the motivation researchers "to become the high priests" in research, which made many marketing men "suspicious of the whole field."

With the superimposition of the Freudian ethos on the marketplace, many of the motivation researchers urged on advertisers the bolder use of sex in ads. The Institute for Motivation Research, for instance, found that the trouble with most ads was they did not have enough sex and the little they had was of the wrong kind. In a study of 100 TV commercials and 200 print ads the Institute had come across not a solitary one that was "sexy," psychologically speaking. In fact advertising had become so prudish in the U.S., the Institute lamented in its house organ, that "whenever an actress appears on the scene—a Jane Russell or a Gina Lollobrigida, whom nature has endowed with a greater abundance—a sudden shudder runs from coast to coast, partly in amazement and partly in indignation, that there is such a thing as a feminine bosom." Equally distressing to the Institute was the way sex had been preempted in advertising by scary ads for beauty products, deodorants, and body care. This played havoc with the healthy, libidinal relationship because themes of bad breath, body odor, dandruff, and so on served to fix in impressionable minds that "the road to love is fraught with unpleasant physical hazards." The Institute told advertisers to get rid of their parlor-room ads and "put the libido back into advertising."

What the Institute sought to do for the libido, it also sought to do for the American image overseas. Dr. Ernest Dichter, president of the Institute, urged the U.S. State Department in *The Strategy of Desire* to apply the teachings of motivation research to erase the negative aspects of the U.S. image abroad and thus call a halt to anti-Americanism.

The mounting anguish with which market researchers regarded each other's methods burst into open warfare by the mid-fifties. Before an American Public Relations Association assemblage, Alfred Politz, head of Alfred Politz Research, let fly at motivation research as "pseudoscience," "pseudoresearch," and nothing more than the "unearthing of hunches and hypotheses." He denounced the gratuitous dismissal of statistical research as mere "nose-counting," mocked the idea that the techniques whose validity were still open questions in clinical psychology could provide reliable answers for marketing problems. He flatly denied that consumer motivations hid somewhere in the back alleys of the consumer mind where only the motivation psychologists could find them. Such was not the case at all: "Consumers really don't know what they want. The job of the marketer is to make them want what he wants them to want." Madison Avenue was being taken in, he said, by the psychology boys who offered sweeping explanations for consumer behavior from small samples, and did not bother to verify their hunches by traditional quantifying methods. He attributed their popularity to the simplicity of their answers and to the sarcastic appraisal that "Madison Avenue doesn't like anything heavy or complicated."

He conceded that advertisers were turning to the depth psychologists because of the "emptiness" of many statistical studies, but insisted that advertisers were getting a lot of theatrical entertainment from the psychologists. He cited as an example a study for Bristol-Myers which unearthed greater hostility toward life on the part of Bufferin users than on the part of Anacin users. It was a fascinating psychological finding, he said, "but how will it help to sell more Bufferin?"

Other attacks were heaped on motivation research, and in equally bitter language, many from psychologists peddling their own brand of research. For instance, Albert J. Wood took a page ad in the *Wall Street Journal* to warn advertisers to stay far away from the Freudian explanation of marketing. He said he was an old hand at motivation research. "We started using this tool when most of the present practitioners were still having their professional marketing pants held up by safety pins, and developing those infantile inhibitions which they now seek to uncover in others." Mr. Wood was convinced that "psyche is not behind *all* purchases. In fact, millions of people aren't buying your brand simply because it is faulty in comparison to other brands, and not because it reminds them of the time their mother beat the old man over the head with a frying pan."

George K. Bennett, president of The Psychological Corporation, predicted "the present fad will go the way of its predecessors."

Cornelius Du Bois told the American Marketing Association: "If you took some of the motivation researchers literally, you would conclude that a person's attitude toward a brand of coffee or bath soap could be traced to an inferiority complex derived from adolescent pimples, or to a feeling of guilt and inadequacy caused progressively by the can opener, the instant mix, and the frozen TV dinner, and perhaps most of all, to sibling jealousy, early toilet training, and a yearning to return to the security and warmth of the womb."

The marketing director of Campbell Soup Company commented: "Surely there are better ways of finding out why consumers do or do not like canned soup than by getting their interpretation of an ink spot or of a picture."

The marketing director of Pabst Brewing Company told the Premium Industry Club that motivation researchers invented "ridiculous" reasons why people buy merchandise. "They are attempting to prove that sales are controlled by the libido or that people buy merchandise because subconsciously they hate their fathers." He marveled that "the ordinarily hard-headed businessman" was intrigued with "their light-headed fancy."

S. I. Hayakawa, editor of the semanticist journal *ETC*, assailed the motivation researchers as "harlot social scientists who, in impressive psychoanalytic and/or sociological jargon, tell their clients . . . that *appeals to irrationality are likely to be far more profitable than appeals to rationality*" (underscoring Hayakawa's). Such doctrine had understandable appeal to advertisers because it implied that "if you hold the key to people's irrationality, you can exploit and diddle them to your heart's content and be loved for it." He reminded advertisers that only mentally ill persons act out their irrationalities and compensatory fantasies, that everybody else was in closer touch with reality.

Few issues ever kicked up more of a fuss in the ad agencies and in the trade press than motivation research. It was hailed as a savior by some for supplying insights into the buying behavior of consumers, denounced by others for seeing motivations in the consumer mind that existed largely in the minds of the psychologists. Much of the rancor stemmed from the insistence by a segment of the motivation researchers that the consumer lie down on the Procrustean bed of Freudian theory, a segment that Harry Henry in *Motivation Research* called a "lunatic" fringe.

Typical of the fusillades that ordinarily judicious marketing men fired at each other was the article by Robert J. Williams in the *Journal of Marketing*, titled "Is It True What They Say about Motivation Research?" It was rebutted in a subsequent issue of the *Journal* by G. D. Wiebe, whose article was titled "Is It True What Williams Says about Motivation Research?" Mr. Wiebe raked the statistical researchers with "suffering from tired decimal points" and at times measuring "the obvious, the ambiguous and the trivial with elegant precision" which left the client "wondering what to do with this 'bag of beans.' "

Advertising Age expressed the belief that the research experts were "too inclined to shoot off their faces." It had some faith in motivation research even though it suspected that "a great deal of pure, unadulterated balderdash has been passed off on gullible marketers as scientific gospel" and the motivation reports sounded at times like "an out-loud reading of the Rosetta stone in the original hieroglyphics." *Printers' Ink* cautioned advertisers to be wary of the "expert who claims too much" and saw market research as "on a threshold of a threshold."

In 1957, in the midst of the motivation research brouhaha,

Madison Avenue's attention was wrenched away by a new arrival
—subliminal advertising. The trade press reported an experiment
at a Fort Lee, New Jersey, movie theater in which two messages,
projected every five seconds on the screen at a speed of $\frac{1}{3,000}$
of a second, urged the audience to eat popcorn and drink Coca-
Cola. The company conducting the test reported that the invisible
messages had increased popcorn sales by 57.5 percent and Coca-
Cola by 18.1 percent. Subliminal stimulation was not new, but
this was its first application to advertising.

The Orwellian possibility of projecting stimuli that were sub
(below) the limen (threshold) of consciousness and exercising an
influence on consumer behavior probably made some admen light-
headed. But it also added to the Svengali image of the admen in
the public mind and caused a tremor in the networks, the federal
agencies, and in the legislative halls of Congress. If a movie audience was persuaded to buy popcorn and drink Coca-Cola, a whole
nation might be persuaded to take to drink, to dope, or to become
Zombie users of advertising brands. In devilish political hands,
subliminal stimuli might even get the electorate to vote into the
White House a man on horseback. The experimenters protested
that subliminal advertising projected only the mildest message
which, like hypnosis, could never induce a consumer to do or buy
anything he ordinarily would not do or buy. But their protestations were not heard in the hue and cry.

About a score of Congressmen called on the Federal Communications Commission to protect the public from the secret
pitch. A bill was introduced in the House which called for penal-
ties up to $5,000 and 30 days in jail for each use of subliminal
advertising by a broadcaster. In the New York State Senate a bill
was introduced which banned subliminal advertising for any
"commercial purposes." The Television Code Review Board of
the National Association of Broadcasters declared against any use
of the subliminal method on television. The networks issued policy
statements which denied the airways to subliminal advertising

until the whole matter could be further studied. Such was the public uproar that the trade press recoiled in editorial unison at the "immoral and unethical" implications of the invisible sell.

A Chicago radio station tried a variation of subliminal advertising by whispering "Fresh up with Seven-Up" and "Oklahoma gas is best" during soft music passages. The experiment drew about 300 quick phone calls, about 75 percent of which favored the tactic either for its novelty or because it was a welcome relief from the customary ear-shattering commercials. The other 25 percent condemned the ads as sneaky, unethical, and so on.

A subliminal experiment was tried in Canada, with the consent of the Canadian Broadcasting Corporation, during which a message was projected 352 times during a 30-minute TV show. Viewers had been alerted in advance, told of the popcorn and Coca-Cola experiment in the Fort Lee theater, and asked to write in immediately after the telecast to relate what they thought they saw or felt. Almost 500 letters poured into CBC offices, not one with the right answer. Almost half the letter-writers said they responded to an impulse to eat or drink something, indicating more the potency of parallel suggestion than subliminal persuasion. One writer reported: "I felt like a beer, my wife had an urge for some cheese, and the dog wanted to go outside in the middle of the program." The CBC subliminal message actually projected was "Telephone now," but activity on the CBC switchboard stayed quiet and a later check of telephone companies across Canada showed no upsurge in telephoning.

Several experiments with admen as guinea pigs similarly came to naught. For instance, not one of the 300 delegates to the Western Radio and Television Conference felt a desire for a long, cool drink of Coca-Cola despite such subliminal urging which was flashed on the screen during a 30-minute film. Among the assorted desires the viewers later said they felt, an inexplicable sex urge was reported by seven, which led the presiding psychologist to the conclusion that the experiment proved "nothing much." In another experiment, the staff of a large ad agency was subjected subliminally to a popular trademark during the showing of a film. At the end of the film the viewers were shown five trademarks and asked to pick the one they thought they had been exposed to. Only 12 percent chose the correct trademark, a hapless achievement that probably could have been bettered by random selection. Some challenged the test as "unfair," others were sure this proved subliminal advertising was "humbug."

Many psychologists, however, were not so sure. Marvin Zuckerman reported some tests in the *Journal of Abnormal and Social Psychology* which indicated that "subliminal suggestion may produce some effect." Richard L. Cutler told an Advertising Conference at the University of Michigan that subliminal advertising might have some effect on the consumer, even though it had yet to be proved scientifically. Elton B. McNeil confided at the same conference that psychologists and admen had such a burning desire to find ways of influencing people that both tended to marry new devices "after a shockingly short courtship. Then we abandon them when we find out about [their] limitations and follow in hot pursuit the next device that passes and catches our fancy."

Three psychologists reminded their professional brethren in *American Psychologist* that their first responsibility was to society. In the hoopla over subliminal advertising the psychologists had been cast in the public mind as "invaders of personal privacy and enemies of society." The psychologists were reminded that the code of ethics of the American Psychological Association subordinated their personal and professional welfare to "the welfare of the people." Each psychologist was asked to be the "watchdog over his own actions as well as the actions of those to whom he lends his professional support."

Although subliminal advertising was outlawed for human persuasion, the trade press noted a commercial in the making that planned to try it on dogs. The pitch would go something like this: "Do you know why your dog is running around the room and barking at this moment? He wants (Blank) dog food." It was hoped that the burst of barking in the commercial, audible to the canine ear but not to the human ear, would stimulate Rover into noises and action. Results were not disclosed, if indeed the experiment took place.

Another first-rate hassle was produced by the growing number of researchers who got into the business of counting the house. Advertisers had to know how many people read their print ads and listened to or watched their commercials. Moreover, they had to get some idea of the degree of message penetration into the skulls of consumers.

Out of the many methods, three main ones emerged to measure print readership. There was, first, the "aided recall" technique which determined readers by their ability to describe an ad in some magazine whose cover alone was shown to them. The readers were then shown a cue card which contained the brand and advertiser's name. They were asked to "play back" what they remembered of the ad. There was, second, the "recognition" method which put the label of readers on those who, when shown a magazine cover, claimed they saw or read any part of the issue. If they were doubtful, they could look inside. Then they were taken through the entire issue and asked to point out all the ads they remembered. The impact of each ad was measured on a three-step scale: "noted," "seen-associated," and "read-most," with the last representation meaning that more than 50 percent of the ad was read. There was, third, the "reader interest" method which was worked entirely by mail, and which asked some magazine subscribers to mark those ads they had "read with interest."

A study of these three main rating systems by the Advertising Research Foundation turned up wide disagreements in their reader estimates. This came as no great surprise to admen, who had learned to pull high readership scores by "shocker" ads, designed to grip the reader. Since advertisers, for want of other standards, assumed high readership scores meant effective use of their advertising dollars, admen commonly sacrificed the sales value in ads to the shock value. Hence advertising's inability to measure its effectiveness served oddly to increase its ineffectiveness.

Advertisers were dismayed to learn that the estimated audience for their ads, and the degree of impact, varied according to the research method used in the sample testing. In the ARF study, all three testing methods were applied to one issue of *Life*. And whereas, for instance, the "recognition" method estimated 18,785,000 adult readers of the issue, the "aided recall" method toted up only 12,241,000. There were similarly wide discrepancies between the methods in their age, sex, education, income level, and so on, estimates of the readers.

Citing chapter and verse, the ARF study pointed out that for a Cashmere Bouquet ad "aided recall" found 1 percent readership, "recognition" produced a "noted" score of 30 percent and a "read most" of 5 percent, and "reader interest" turned in a 15 percent score. For a pineapple juice ad "aided recall" checked in with a 1 percent readership, "recognition" with a 27 percent "noted" and 4 percent "read most," and "reader interest" with 19 percent. For a Camel ad "aided recall" found 5 percent readership, "recognition" tallied 33 percent "noted" and 3 percent "read most," and "reader interest" racked up 20 percent. For a Schlitz ad "aided recall" produced a 3 percent readership, "recognition" a 17 percent "noted" and 1 percent "read most," and "reader interest" 10 percent. The methods also turned in different results on the male and female readership of some ads. An Old Taylor ad was found to have mainly male readership by the "recognition" and "reader interest" methods and mainly female by the "aided recall" method. A Kleenex ad was found to attract more men than women according to "aided recall," but the other methods found the opposite to be true. *Advertising Age* judged the study might become known in the future as "a researcher's nightmare."

An ARF speaker told the Association of National Advertisers

that the research organizations' methods did not measure up to modern advertising needs. The "recognition" method he judged to be "overstimulating," inasmuch as the "exposure to the advertisement is frequently longer and more intense than it was during normal readership of the magazine." The "aided recall" method, on the other hand, was held to be "understimulating," since the cue card aid to recall was so weak that an "advertising impression has to be almost overpowering before it can be recalled at all."

On behalf of the ARF, the speaker unveiled before the assembled national advertisers a new contraption, the Communiscope, which he averred would tend to correct the weaknesses in the rating methods. It was a portable slide projector which was so hooked to a light-timing device that it flashed ads for $6/10$ of a second. Following the flash, readers would be asked for a detailed playback of what they remembered of the ads, tape-recorded for further study.

Not entirely unexpectedly the Communiscope was hooted down by the research outfits whose methods were criticized. Not only did they hotly defend themselves in the trade press but they mounted a counterattack against what they saw were "inadequacies" in the ARF procedures in the *Life* study. Also not unexpectedly, the ripple of interest aroused in the Communiscope in the advertising world soon subsided and, like so many other innovations in this gimmick-ridden world, within a year or so it scarcely received a line of mention in the trade press.

In the measurement of radio and TV audiences, methods also were varied and tempers equally frayed. In general, three main methods were used to estimate the size of the audience tuned in at any one time to any one station. First, there was the diary method, which required the jotting down of information by household members about the programs they were watching. Second, there was the interview method, by telephone or in person, the telephoning done while the program was on the air and the home interviewing within 24 hours. Third, there was the mechanical method, involving an electronic device attached to the receiving set which automatically recorded either in a central office or in the home when the set was on and the station tuned to.

Complicated by differences in sampling procedures, time periods covered, geographic location, and even in definition, the different methods produced disagreeably different estimates of audience size. Not knowing what to make of the situation, perplexed advertisers and harried admen made the most of it by manipulating the audience ratings for their own ends. In defense of the rating services, and attempting to bring some order to them, the Television Bureau of Advertising pointed out in "Summary: Research Services" that no one service could be considered "right," that each covered different aspects of the audience and its size.

Competing for advertisers' dollars, the rating services seemed less inclined to explain their differences than to fight over them. Particularly in the early years they were "at each other's throats nearly every hour on the hour," as *Printers' Ink* said. The trade press assumed a prize-ring atmosphere as Trendex, Inc., gave low ratings to TV spectaculars and A. C. Nielsen Company handed them top ratings, one service came up consistently with higher ratings for daytime shows than the other services, Hooperatings were at variance with The Pulse, Inc., and the trade press was filled with charges and countercharges. Typically, when A. C. Nielsen Company added the diary method to its electronic recorder for certain programs, its head, Arthur C. Nielsen, was assailed by The Pulse, Inc., for using the diary after having once condemned it. In a bright yellow mailing piece "Arthur" was condemned for having once said "thumbs down on diaries. Now, attempting to sell them, Arthur says diaries are dandy." In his public reply, which smelled strongly of acid, "Arthur" pointed out that his diary not only was "an entirely different animal" from Pulse's but was going to be put to different uses.

Following a trade ad headlined "Two Umpires Behind the Plate Isn't Any Good in Broadcasting Either," the Advertising

Research Foundation moved into the middle of the free-for-all. The ARF was worried that improper measuring rods by the rating services would lead to "unreliable estimates—and wrong decisions." It set up 22 standards for what it considered proper audience measurement, which not one of the rating services met, some less so than others.

That did it. Hooper promptly labeled the ARF report a "promotion piece" for the Nielsen method and charged it with being "one of the most unenlightened and potentially misleading pieces of work to be released by any responsible advertising group in the past 20 years." He suggested that "all copies, save one, be destroyed. One should be retained as an example of what not to do." The Pulse, Inc., attacked the "double-talk" in the report and the "monotheistic worship of the machine." It only succeeded in giving "sound rating service objectives a black eye. Which in turn gives other research a black eye." Trendex concluded its criticism with the demand that the ARF "reconsider its decision."

The individual stations and networks had meanwhile learned how to live in the rating jungle, and some had even learned how to live well. Many subscribed to several rating services and at the strategic moment hauled out the rating service that gave *their* programs the highest scores. A *Television Age* study, for instance, showed that the average station contracted with two or more competing services and paid an average of $5,761 annually for them. It also showed that, by and large, station executives disliked the rating frenzy. They held major reservations about the accuracy of the ratings: only 27 percent of the station executives polled thought them adequate, and then "in varying degrees."

Many stations learned they could hypo their ratings by the judicious insertion of one "blockbuster" program during rating-week time. Nobody knew how common this practice was, or at least was willing to say, but steady references in the trade press to the sly practice made it appear that it was far from isolated to a few stations. "You don't have to look at the calendar to know when the local TV shows are being rated," WTVJ-Miami sounded off on the practice in an ad in *Sponsor*. "It's the week the movie telecasts stop playing reruns of Charlie Chan and begin featuring Clark Gable and Gary Cooper—and schedule large-space newspaper ads to alert readers." WTVJ-Miami charged that the practice was a disservice to the public, which got a one-week entertainment feast followed by a three-week famine, a disservice to the rating services whose ratings were fouled up, and to advertisers who unwittingly spent ad dollars for less of an audience than they thought they were getting.

Rating time was also particularly hard on the nerves of the admen. Trendex figures were the first ones to be released. Admen with shows on CBS breathed easier, while those with shows on the still unrated networks got a bad case of jitters. Next came American Research Bureau estimates, and those who had bet on ABC shows began to smile again, and those who had backed NBC shows also felt a bit more cheerful. Finally Nielsen figures came out and those heavy with NBC shows had their turn to be jubilant. The smiles froze only when the ratings were mediocre and unlikely to please the advertisers.

Since the ratings had such a stranglehold on programming— shows lived and died by them—the ratings became a public issue of prime importance. Many critics of TV programming held them accountable for the poverty of program fare. Several Congressmen expressed the belief that "the networks, stations, Madison Avenue—all are victims of the rating systems." LeRoy Collins, president of the National Association of Broadcasters, charged that broadcasting had allowed "an outsider to become master of its own house." At his confirmation hearing, Newton N. Minow, later FCC chairman, expressed the opinion that ratings were a proper "concern" of the FCC.

Although acknowledging that the rating systems were not entirely adequate, the trade press in general belittled the public shooting-up of them. *Advertising Age* reassured the would-be executioners that advertisers and broadcasters did not conspire to downgrade the viewing habits of the American people. If there were more Westerns on the air "than warblers of operatic arias, and more ghastly trash than Greek comedies," it was because the public tuned in to them in great numbers. Advertisers, for one, had no interest whatsoever in program fare other than to give the public more of what it liked. As for their fascination with high ratings, "it's an American characteristic, and probably a human characteristic, to like big numbers better than small ones, no matter how much or how little meaning there is to the numbers," *Advertising Age* philosophized. Other sections of the trade press warned against governmental tampering with the ratings systems as infringing on Constitutional freedoms.

In summation, then, it can be said that no area of advertising research was unmarked by internal squabbles among the researchers and a distrust yet growing need of them by advertisers. There was also a Greek chorus of doomsters who generally stood on the sidelines and scoffed and scorned at the labors of the researchers. E. B. Weiss, for instance, put at least one annual pox on the researchers in *Advertising Age,* charging that any competent scientist could take about 90 percent of their studies and rip them into statistical shreds. "We have too many amateurs, too many totally untrained people, playing with statistical fire." He likened their fussing over their charts and graphs to the soothsayers who once performed their rituals over steaming cauldrons.

Market research in particular came in for heavy criticism. John E. Jeuck, dean of the University of Chicago's school of business, scorned it as "vastly overrated." Too often, he said, it was a hodgepodge of cookbook statistics and hopelessly poor interviewing which produced results that were as definite as they were irrelevant. Although offered as "a panacea for marketing aches and pains" it carefully avoided the "money-back guarantee of patent medicine copy." Dr. Jay W. Forrester, a professor of industrial management at Massachusetts Institute of Technology, stunned an Advertising Research Foundation conference by his summary dismissal of research: "First, by definitions accepted in the scientific fields, most of advertising research is not research. Second, the amount of true research is woefully inadequate. Third, much of the so-called advertising research is itself merely advertising."

Benedict Gimbel, Jr., told the Philadelphia Merchandising Associates: "I don't think marketing research is worth a damn." He said that marketing was "a sense of what will sell, a sense of when to sell it."

A. R. Graustein, market research director of Lever Brothers, told the American Marketing Association that at first he had toyed with the idea of entitling his speech, "Alchemy, Astrology and Marketing Research," but had refrained from fear of giving offense. He held aloft a sheaf of papers: "Here in my hand are 23 pages which summarize 194 different research findings" for one Lever product. "Now, here's the shocker: virtually none of the surveys from which these data were taken . . . could pass the standards . . . now set for experimental research. Most wouldn't even come close."

Ben D. Mills, head of the Lincoln-Mercury division of Ford, told the Adcraft Club of Detroit that the researchers utterly failed to prophesy consumer acceptance of compact cars. They had "no tools sensitive enough" to catch early public opposition to big cars. "The antennae of economists, market researchers, motivation researchers and executives old and young alike were all too short and inadequate." They could only engage in *ex post facto* soul-searching. "We will give the brass ring to anyone who can tell us what kind of automobile Mr. and Mrs. America will be buying in 1965. We would like very much," he added, "to be selling that automobile."

Few held the iconoclastic view reputed to the late Albert D. Lasker that "Research is something that tells you that a jackass has two ears," but even the most passionate devotee of market

research stumbled over an explanation as to how an army of researchers with the purse of Croesus to spend presifting the public
feeling over the Edsel could have been so wrong. What disturbed
many was the growing reliance by management brass on research
before making a move. Jack Baxter was appalled in *Printers' Ink*
by the conversion of advertisers into "listening posts instead of
leaders." David Ogilvy told the American Association of Advertising Agencies of the growing timidity of executives to use their
own judgment. "There is a tendency to rely far too much on
research, and to use it as a drunk man uses a lamppost—for support
rather than illumination."

Some urged the restoration of intuition in the marketing
process from which it had largely been ousted by the IBM machines and surveys of the researchers.

The new consumer, who was the target of all these ministrations of the advertising brotherhood, clearly was a tough microbe
to trap. But the brotherhood was determined to trap him and,
given continued prosperity, would increasingly allocate ever more
millions to do so.

The Mass Media 16

Nothing like the immense outpouring of advertisers' dollars—from $2.9 billion in 1945 to $11.9 billion in 1961—was ever seen in this country, and nothing like the bitter struggle that ensued for these advertising dollars by the mass media. About 60 million daily newspapers, 200 million magazines, 3,500 radio stations, and 530 TV stations, poured the heaviest volume of entertainment, news, and advertising in history into U.S. homes in the course of this struggle. Almost the entire nation was wired for radio and television, the postman stuffed magazines into the mailboxes in the remotest hamlets, and newspapers made daily entry in almost every household.

The struggle had begun in the late nineteenth century when the U.S. made the transition from agrarian to industrial economy and newspapers and magazines, then the only mass communication media around, became part of the U.S. marketing system with the job of inducing mass consumption for what was being mass produced. Indicative of the germinal forces at work, Congress had recognized the commercial needs of the time by granting the print media low-cost mailing privileges in 1879, newspapers were widely available at one and two cents, magazines dropped to ten and five cents per copy, and if the cost of putting them into the hands of the reader exceeded their cover price, advertising more than made up the difference. In 1879, for instance, newspaper revenue came in about equal amounts from purchasers and advertisers, but by 1909 advertisers provided nearly two-thirds of the revenue, according to Edwin Emery in *History of the American Newspaper Publishers Association* (formed in 1887, and dedicated to the expansion of newspaper advertising as its "most constant and important single activity").

Magazine circulations showed lusty rises. Whereas before the turn of the twentieth century magazine circulations of 100,000 to 200,000 were distinctly unusual, by 1914 the *Ladies' Home Journal, Collier's, Cosmopolitan, McCall's, Saturday Evening Post*, each could boast of a circulation over one million. Typical of their rise was the *Saturday Evening Post* which in 1897 muddled along with 2,231 in circulation and $6,933 in advertising revenue, but by 1922 had swollen to more than two million in circulation and counted more than $28 million in advertising revenue, as noted by Theodore Peterson in *Magazines in the Twentieth Century*.

Although newspapers then had the lion's share of advertising, the rise of national brand advertisers who sought a national market put the magazines in a better strategic position to contend for their advertising dollars than the newspapers, which were local media. Somewhat alarmed, the American Newspaper Publishers Association ran a series of ads in 1911 immodestly explaining why "newspaper advertising is the best advertising there is on earth." Although recognizing the advertiser's desire for a national market, newspapers insisted (as they do to this day) that all sales are local. Between 1909 and 1921 advertising revenue for both newspapers and magazines more than tripled, with newspapers holding about even in the contest for national advertising.

A new contender arrived on the scene in 1920, radio, even if few then recognized it as such. It was first fondly believed that radio's chief purpose was to stimulate the sales of radio receivers, a belief enhanced by the evidence that the first radio stations were owned by Stromberg-Carlson, RCA, American Telephone & Telegraph, and Westinghouse. If radio competed with anything, it was with the phonograph. It was the generally expressed belief of government and radio industry officials alike that radio was ill-suited for commercialism, that there was something indecorous and improper about allowing advertising to roam the airways owned by the people. In fact, at the first annual conference of commercial broadcasters held in 1922, it was firmly resolved that direct advertising should be absolutely prohibited and indirect advertising should be limited to announcement of the call letters of the station and the name of the company responsible for the matter broadcasted, as Robert Horton wrote in *The Reporter*. Herbert Hoover, then Secretary of Commerce, had expressed the government view: "It is inconceivable that we should allow so great a possibility for service, for news, for entertainment, for education, and for vital commercial purposes to be drowned in advertising chatter." This view of radio found itself embodied in the original Communications Act of 1927, and in the succeeding 1934 Act, and suggested that radio, invested with a public interest, was somewhat in the same class as a public utility. Even so strong a partisan of business interests as Calvin Coolidge held this public-utility view.

From its first year, however, radio steered a collision course with newspapers by commencing the broadcasting of special news events. WWJ and KDKA, for instance, aired the 1920 presidential election return, World Series baseball scores, speeches by several national celebrities, and a prize fight. That year too the Detroit *News* deciphered the handwriting on the wall and became the first newspaper to own a radio station. Two years later, in 1922, the American Newspaper Publishers Association discovered in a survey that more than 100 newspaper publishers owned radio stations that were broadcasting to the more than 600,000 radio sets in U.S. homes.

The organization of radio networks, the National Broadcasting System in 1926 and Columbia Broadcasting System in 1927, established radio as a dangerous contender for national advertising. In the 1928 presidential election the two major political parties spent an estimated million dollars to make electronic promises to eight million radio homes, dollars that the newspapers writhed at losing.

In 1929 the national advertising was divvied up 47 percent to newspapers, 37 percent to magazines, and 3.4 percent to radio, and the newspaper publishers moved to slow down the growth of radio. In 1931, at an ANPA convention, the publishers decided that radio logs would be published in their newspapers, if at all, only as paid advertising. They questioned the legal right of radio, which operated under government license and used the public ether, to compete with private media for advertising. The following year a survey of ANPA membership showed that 66 newspapers published radio logs as paid advertising, 320 published sharply abbreviated listings, and only 24 published the listings in full. Further hampering the growth of radio, an Associated Press convention in 1933 voted to withhold news from the radio networks and to put an outside limit on the broadcasting of news by AP members owning radio stations to 30-word bulletins that were not sponsored commercially. The other news-gathering agencies, the United Press and International News Service, soon joined with similar restrictions. But the infant industry could not be held down, for denied ready access to these news sources, the radio networks undertook the job for themselves.

In 1939, with 45 million radio-equipped homes in the U.S., the newspaper share of national advertising shrank to 34.4 percent, the magazine share to 32.2 percent, and radio gobbled up 25.4 percent. In 1942 newspapers were ousted from first place in national advertising by magazines and found radio pressing hard for second place.

What effectively undermined newspaper opposition to radio was not only radio's visible ability to capture the public fancy (which compelled newspapers to print radio logs as news, or risk losing readers), but the growing corps of newspaper publishers owning radio stations (which watered down ANPA's and other Fourth Estate opposition to the electronic competition). So many publishers owned radio stations indeed that in 1941 when 27 of the first 94 applications for FM licenses arrived from newspaper publishers the FCC expressed alarm at the possible monopoly of opinion at odds in a democracy where conflicting opinions were desired.

The commercial take-over of radio was a personally disheartening development to the late Dr. Lee De Forest, the "father of radio," who, according to one of his letters published in *Sponsor,* "lost no opportunity to cry out in earnest against the crass commercialism . . . of the vulgar hucksters, agencies, advertisers, station owners—all who . . . continue to enslave and sell for quick cash the grandest medium which has yet been given to man to help upward his struggling spirit."

Television was the most fortunate child in the communications family for it benefited from the general acceptance of radio as a commercial vehicle, after which it patterned itself, and it arrived in the U.S. coincidental with the period of greatest national prosperity. It was also the most gifted, for it combined sight, sound, motion (and later color), something no other member of the communications family could match. With the number of TV-equipped households climbing from 5 million in 1950 to nearly 48 million in 1961—nine out of ten households—and TV-watching becoming the favorite pastime of millions, the new medium rapidly won the affections of national advertisers. Of

the top 100 advertisers, 98 were soon heavily budgeted in TV—
the two exceptions being liquor companies barred from the
medium.

Television had vast and almost cataclysmic impact on the
other media. It virtually knocked radio out as a national commercial medium, accomplishing in a few years what newspapers
and magazines had failed to do in decades. Radio found a new life
for itself as a local medium, and the number of radio stations in
the U.S. rose from about 900 in 1945 to 3,500 in 1961, as radio
began to specialize in broadcasts to small shopping areas, to the
rock 'n' roll set, to ethnic and foreign language groups. Radio
chronicled local community events as parochial as traffic accidents,
PTA meetings, high school games, and as a local medium it became a more formidable competitor to newspapers for the advertising of local merchants.

Although newspapers pointed to the record number of daily
newspapers sold in the U.S. as a prime index of health, the fact
remained that the number of newspapers dwindled over the decades as the nation urbanized itself. More significant, the number
of newspapers brought into the average household was steadily
dropping. A Gallup study conducted for the newspaper industry
showed that from 1.32 per household in 1932 (the peak), the
number slipped to 1.18 in 1940 and to 1.10 in 1960. The nearly
60 million newspapers sold daily in the U.S. was hence made possible only by the expanding U.S. population.

The population migration to the suburbs after the war provided newspapers with a new set of problems, moreover, for the
big metropolitan dailies not only had the editorial problem of
retaining the interest of readers who became less interested in the
goings-on in the cities they vacated, but the cost problem of bringing the city dailies to the suburbanites and exurbanites, which
became serious. The newspapers had to follow the readers to
the outlying districts, however, both to maintain circulation and
because higher income and greater buying needs made the mi-

grating readers of special interest to national advertisers. As it was the national advertisers squawked about the disadvantageous national-local rate differential, which made them pay more for advertising space than was paid by the local advertisers. The differential in 1958 was 59.6 percent in daily papers and even steeper in Sunday papers, according to a study by the American Association of National Advertisers. But for newspapers to lose these suburbanites and exurbanites as readers would undoubtedly drive more national advertisers to television, an event the newspapers could ill afford, for despite loss of national advertising it still accounted for about one-quarter of all newspaper advertising revenue.

The growth of television intensified the troubles of newspapers, for it struck at the innermost citadel of the newspaper function, picking up the onslaught where radio had left off. The printed word was no match for the speed of light, and as news events were telecast as they were happening, and news commentary became a daily staple on television on which ever more millions relied, it was bruited about in communications circles that "a man no longer needs to read a daily newspaper in order to be well-informed," as Carl E. Lindstrom wrote in *The Fading American Newspaper*.

The magazine industry found itself caught in a squeeze between loss of national advertising revenue and rising costs. Over a ten-year period the industry absorbed a 50 percent increase in the price of paper, 35 percent in printing, 15 percent in freight, and 30 percent in second-class postage, according to *Printers' Ink*. The same ten-year period witnessed the demise of 48 general magazines, several with circulations in the millions. It was clear that unless the industry could exorcize the TV hex many more magazines, whose names were household institutions, were destined for early interment in the magazine graveyard.

The cold war between the media for national advertising dollars erupted into hot war in the late fifties, following the TV quiz show scandals which the broadcast industry accused the print media of playing up for partisan advantage. Many of the broadcasters detected in a *Fortune* article titled "TV: The Light That Failed" the signal for an all-out war of ruin against TV. Lawrence H. Rogers II, board chairman of the Television Bureau, labeled the article "a nifty piece of Goebbels propaganda." *Sponsor* charged it with being "by far the most prejudiced of the recent attacks made on TV in the print media." *Television Age* said many of the broadcasters were "aghast at the wholesale, brutal manhandling and sweeping condemnation" and were convinced that such mass desecration of a rival medium had as its only purpose the cold-blooded destruction of TV as a commercial medium.

The *Fortune* article had characterized TV programming by and large as "bathos from Boot Hill, counterfeit cerebration via quiz shows, barbarism from the police blotter, inanity from outer space, monstriphilia from Hollywood's celluloid cemeteries." It had advanced the thesis that, now that TV had nearly saturated U.S. homes, TV's programming mediocrity acted to reduce the audience, the reduced audience in turn weakened the medium's economics, and weakened economics in turn acted to compel more mediocrity. Moreover, there was gathering evidence that television was something less than the magic genie it first seemed to be to advertisers, capable of selling every kind of consumer goods to entranced millions of viewers. Indeed, the television industry was headed for inevitable trouble unless it could find some way out of the self-destructive cycle in which it was caught.

The broadcast press, refusing to suffer the slings and arrows of outrageous *Fortune,* as someone put it, struck back with a fusillade of intemperate and ill-tempered rebuttals. But the broadcasters were anguished by the growing inventory of articles written in acid that were piling up in the print media, ranging from the quiz scandals to the overcommercialism of TV to programming and other inadequacies. Singled out for special broadcast anger were the *Saturday Evening Post*'s series on "Television:

Wasteland or Wonderland?" *Look*'s article on "The Crisis, Conflict and Change in TV News," and the spate of articles in *Show Business Illustrated* titled, for instance, "Paradise Mislaid," "The Parr Phenomenon," and "The Sacred Cows of TV." Some of the women's magazines were accused of running egg-on-your-tie portraits of TV personalities to tarnish the good name of TV. Some of the broadcasters were even suspicious that cartoons in the print media about TV constituted some kind of subtle flanking movement against the medium. As exhibits they pointed to the *New Yorker* cartoon, showing a mordant housewife asking her harried spouse, "Well, if you don't want to sing along with Mitch, what *do* you want to do?" and to the *Saturday Evening Post* cartoon captioned, "We will resume our commercials after a brief pause for entertainment."

A *Life* article titled "Fireworks Ahead on TV rating systems" was interpreted by *Sponsor* as a blast at "ratings, networks, agencies and advertisers with all the fine moral fervor of fanatics whose pocketbooks have been hit." It was called a "hodge-podge of emotional editorializing" and although *Sponsor*'s editors could watch unmoved at the copious weeping of "some mammoth crocodile tears" by the Luce publication over certain TV practices, they found "sad and somewhat frightening" the effect the article might have on its millions of readers.

An article in *McCall's* deploring TV programming as "shoddy, corny, stupid, vulgar, obscene," and suggesting that network TV was becoming "an instrument for the wholesale debasement of the public taste and moral fibre," drew denunciation for its writer, Mrs. Clare Luce, in the broadcast press as "a sizzling Cassandra" for her "hysterical" outburst. Similarly, when *Esquire* ran "A Last Look at Television," the magazine was counterattacked as "struggling to shed its girl-and-kooky image" and the article as lacking in "intellectual honesty and fairness." And when *The New York Times* concluded that television had sunk into "a malodorous quagmire," for permitting its programs to be swamped with commercials, for permitting its star performers to get up on the soapbox for patent medicines, and for accepting advertisements "that most self-respecting publications would reject out of hand," the judgment was lambasted as "hysterical, exaggerated, unreasonable and irresponsible."

Time was accused of a bad case of myopia for failure to see anything but "stupendous mediocrity" in the season's TV offerings, for saying that the TV'ers were "importing packaged pap from Hollywood by the case," and for the conclusion: "There is only one reason for anyone to turn on his TV set this fall: because it's there." *Reader's Digest* was charged with a gratuitous slap at a rival medium for failure to take kindly to "bathroom" commercials in the living room.

The broadcasters were also resentful at the guffaws drawn by one speaker before the National Newspaper Promotion Association who referred to TV as "the garbage pail of the entertainment world," and by another who advised the American Association of Newspaper Editors of two great advantages of newspapers over television: "They can be used as barriers against wives. Also, you can't line a garbage pail with a television set: it's usually the other way around." *Sponsor* charged that the remark attributed to RCA's David Sarnoff, and delighted in by the print media, was taken out of context: "We're in the same position as a plumber laying a pipe. We're not responsible for what goes through the pipe." *Sponsor* demanded that the print critics "stand and deliver like men" instead of acting like "frantic and frightened old women."

At one point the warfare between the media hove into public view when *Look, Saturday Evening Post,* and *Newsweek* addressed full-page ads to "people who watch TV—but love *doing* things more." The ads counseled TV viewers who asked themselves, "Why did we sit through all that?" that inherent in the question was more criticism of themselves than of television. What they were saying in effect was, "*doing beats viewing,*" and the magazines suggested that a great way of *doing* was "reading one of America's great magazines."

The broadcast press roundly condemned the nation's newspapers and magazines for "having a Roman holiday at the expense of a competitive medium." *Variety* warned the publishers that the broadcasters were preparing to meet "every newspaper-mag onslaught with retaliatory exposés of the phoniness and malpractices within the publishing fraternity." And a columnist in the broadcasting press suggested that if TV did not fight back harder it was because "some segments of the printed press can be pretty vindictive when they are attacked; and who wants to start a fight with anyone who is vindictive and also owns a printing press?"

Editor & Publisher, however, expressed its editorial outrage at the way it said certain TV news commentators converted the suspension of two Los Angeles newspapers early in 1962 into a commentary on the "weaknesses" of the newspaper business compared to the "strengths" of TV: "It wasn't even fair comment —it was dirty pool." The organ of the Fourth Estate also detected as the malevolent motivation in the program "WCBS-TV Views the Press" the desire to "retaliate against newspapers that have given wide play to stories of TV quiz scandals and . . . the inadequacies of TV programming." It charged that the program did "a real hatchet job on the New York press," holding up as a reprehensible commentary: "An awful lot of what passes for news in a newspaper looks like news, tastes like news, but it doesn't tell you anything." It also attempted to club to death the persistent "one-party press" charge against the newspaper industry, at least on the airwaves, by countercharging that more than 200 TV stations—almost 40 percent of the total—were in one-TV-towns.

Although in the media warfare the general battle lines were drawn between the print and the air media, the intense competition for advertising dollars allowed at best uneasy alliances, and the print allies in particular were not above taking swipes at each other. Almost every magazine article appraising the nation's newspapers referred to the growing "one-party press." As one critic stated the danger: "A city with one newspaper, or with a morning and evening paper under one ownership, is like a man with one eye, and often the eye is glass." Others charged the press with being "nothing but glorified conglomerations of public relations handouts, stories cribbed from other papers, and wire services to plug up holes." If TV was guilty of payola, it was said, so were newspapers for disguising advertising as news and running hand-outs as editorials.

In *Time*'s appraisal of New York's newspaper situation, two of its morning papers "and all three of its evening papers are fight-ing for their lives." This drew the retort in *Editor & Publisher* from several newspaper publishers that *Time* "take a look at the mote in its own eyes." One publisher said that the *Time* appraisal might lead readers to the mistaken notion that the newspaper business was as sick as the magazine business. Another said that in the very same issue of *Time* which looked down its editorial nose at the "décolleté pictures" and "trivia" in New York's evening papers, one alluring female was depicted as a "cannibalistic sex kitten" and another as taking "umbrage behind a beach blanket."

When a *Holiday* article called newspaper presentation of news "sound, moderate, lucid," it drew hosannas from *Editor & Publisher*, which found it a refreshing change from the run-of-the-mill magazine articles which went out of their way to lambast the press "for assorted and imagined shortcomings." *Editor & Publisher* confessed editorially: "We never expected to see the day when anything favorable about newspapers would appear in a national magazine."

Occasionally the media strife became *opéra bouffe* as, for instance, when the head of the American Newspaper Association's Bureau of Advertising, Charles Lipscomb, Jr., climbed into a simu-lated boxing ring set up on the ballroom stage of the Waldorf-Astoria and, taking figurative blows at radio and TV, declared to the assembled newspaper publishers: "We want everybody to know that we are right in the middle of the ring, punching as hard as we can with competitive, combative hard selling." And again, when Kevin B. Sweeney, president of the Radio Advertising Bureau, in the full regalia of a Confederate general, rallied a radio executive audience in the Conrad Hilton's grand ballroom with the cry: "The civil war continues." He identified the enemies of radio as newspapers, magazines, TV.

It was characteristic of the media strife that it proceeded unabated in a barrage of statistical claims and counterclaims designed to establish each medium's clear superiority over the competition in the ability to sell the advertiser's wares. Each medium turned out an impressive array of studies to prove that its audience was the best "buy" for the advertiser. Oddly, the $12-billion-a-year advertising business knew precious little about the core problem of which medium's audience would be most responsive to the advertiser's ads, which would give him the best return on his advertising expenditure. The Advertising Research Foundation, after laboring over the problem for several years, came to the conclusion that valid intermedia comparisons just could not be made. Since the advertising dollars had to be spent, however, the media departments of the ad agencies worked out at times convenient rationales to bridge the unbridgeable, to compare the incomparable, which, if nothing else, served to convince suspicious advertisers that their money was well spent. In the absence of scientific data, the thinking of the entire advertising industry tended to be dominated by the vastness of the audience, by the concept of the cost-per-thousand in reaching this audience. This thinking was reinforced by the practical consideration that it was simpler—and more profitable—for the ad agencies to spend the allotted advertising dollars on a few ads reaching larger audiences than on many ads reaching smaller audiences.

Television, of course, ordinarily won this size of contest hands down. No other medium could reach 1.3 million homes per minute betwen 6 A.M. and 8 A.M., with the number climbing during the day to reach a peak of 31.1 million homes per minute between 8 P.M. and 10 P.M., the prime viewing hours. Nor did any other medium bewitch the average U.S. household for about six hours daily.

Newspapers derided the boxcar figures of TV, insisting that the real payoff for the advertisers was not the vastness of a bored TV audience, which paid nothing for entertainment and frequently barely listened to commercials, but in the alert citizenry who plunked down their nickels and dimes to get newspaper information and were more susceptible to advertising. Newspaper readers included the higher-income, better educated, more influential people, more professionals, larger families, and the age range that did the heaviest buying. The newspaper had an intimate relationship with them, was their main channel for news, and a surprising number of them said they looked over newspaper ads even when they were not planning to buy. Whereas TV figured in the public mind as interesting, entertaining, and glamorous, the newspaper was associated with such solid traits of character as courage, morality, reliability, credibility, providing a good psychological climate for advertising persuasion. Also striking in many newspaper studies was an incapacity to find either the multitudes watching TV or much recall of the commercials, implying a squandering of the advertiser's money on a darkened TV screen or on a partly somnolent audience.

The magazine industry tried to carry water on both shoulders. Like the newspapers, the magazines produced studies proving that theirs was a higher caliber audience than TV. Magazine readers were found concentrated in the higher-income, better educated, best age range, and were the heaviest spenders. And the magazine ad outlived the newspaper ad, which died with yesterday's paper, and the fleeting TV commercial which, once delivered, was gone. The magazines also slugged it out with TV in the matter of audience size. They had discovered their pass-along circulation back in the thirties in time to combat radio's millions, a discovery that automatically tripled or quadrupled the number of claimed readers, and in the fifties they invented the concept of "exposure" to combat TV's escalation into the tens of millions. For instance, one study showed that a single full-page ad in *Reader's Digest, Saturday Evening Post,* and *Look* achieved an "exposure" of 152,620,000 times to 67,802,000 people (ten years and older), reaching a bigger—and richer—audience than TV. Similarly a *Redbook* study calculated that a $139,000 advertising investment would garner 35,720,000 impressions in *Good Housekeeping,* 37,950,000 impressions in *Woman's Day,* 32,625,000 impressions in *American Home,* but a total of 41,400,000 impressions in *Redbook.*

Radio delivered commercials to people in places where the other media were generally absent, in the bedroom, in the kitchen, in the utility room, in the car; and the arrival of the transistorized radio enabled people to take their programs—and commercials— with them everywhere. Radio listening rose with the tide of commuter automobile traffic to and from the city, and in the summer months when many of the 42 million radio-equipped cars took to the highways. Radio was also intimate and timely. It brought a shaving-cream commercial to a man while he was shaving, sold a gasoline brand to a motorist while he was driving, told the housewife about a special sale of canned fruits 10 minutes before she left for the supermarket. Radio studies also found that instead of a dial-twister the housewife developed strong loyalties both to radio stations and personalities. She picked one station as her favorite and another as second best, did most of her listening in the morning (when radio outpulled TV), and totaled about four and one-half hours daily (compared to less than half an hour with her newspaper).

Much of the media research of newspapers, magazines, radio, and TV exhibited an enormous passion for the fragmented fact, as each medium proved by statistical gymnastics that it had more of, or was better than, the competition in something or other.

Indeed media research was one of the few fields of human endeavor in which everybody came out a winner. Media studies proved by questionnaires and motivational research and personality portraits and sociological tomes that such-and-such audience was steadfastly loyal to brands, dying to buy new products, turned fads into staples, luxuries into necessities, and was composed of Joneses whom other people kept up with. So full of numbers were the media studies that one adman said he expected at any time to hear someone shout "Bingo." And so full of dimensions, variables, and recondite correlations were they that a speaker told the Advertising Research Foundation: "We are like the Sorcerer's Apprentice. Having started the magic flow of media figures, we cannot stop it, or slow it, and we are all in imminent danger of drowning in it."

So boastful were the media studies, so certainly did they prove that practically every newspaper, magazine, radio, or TV program was going to hell except the one for which the study was being made, that media departments in ad agencies had small use for most of them. The general feeling was summed up by one media director who, when asked, "What is useful media research?" replied, "I don't know. It hasn't been done yet."

In a page ad in *Sponsor*, a radio station spoofed the bravura statistic that masqueraded as media research. "WMT radio gets up 13% earlier than 47% of the stations of the U.S.A. and plays 23% louder (in barns) than 38% of the victrolas in the attics of 89% of the ramblers built before 1929." WMT research also discovered that three-quarters of the dogs in its listening area "can't turn on a radio."

Similarly an unpublished *New Yorker* ad (reproduced in *Advertising Age*) claimed that in one year it ran "more dog food advertising than the *Wall Street Journal*, more men's wear advertising than *Progressive Grocer*, *Vogue*, and the *Saturday Review* combined. More bicycle advertising than magazine *A* or magazine *B* . . . and almost as much as magazine *C*. And virtually no peanut butter at all. And editorially . . . more cartoons than *Forbes*, more fiction than *Gourmet*, more poetry than *Cue* and a lot of other stuff. But that's not all. With a circulation of literally thousands of people, the *New Yorker* last year sold more copies than *Life*—sells in two whole weeks." The ad was signed: "*The New Yorker*—America's Tallest Midget."

The frenetic competition for the advertisers' dollars led the consumer media to offer the kind of merchandising help that used to be almost the exclusive province of the business media, which performed a variety of sales chores for their advertisers. A *Printers' Ink* survey in the late fifties showed that seven out of ten consumer magazines offered merchandising services to their advertisers, that the bigger the magazine the more likely it was to offer them. Such services ranged from a generous supply of reprints of articles, "as advertised in" stickers, cover folders, and copies of the magazine for special advertiser mailings, to letters to the trade calling attention to the ads and the installation of in-store displays for the advertisers.

In radio and television, especially radio, merchandising also became widespread. A *Sponsor* survey found six out of ten radio stations offering some kind of merchandising aid, discovered that most ad agencies took merchandising into consideration when setting up schedules and some were even "using spot radio contracts as a club." It was generally agreed that the advertiser who hollered the loudest got the most help out of the stations and the advertiser with the biggest advertising bankroll automatically possessed the most decibels. The merchandising help included calls on trade, mailings to trade, billboard and poster tie-ins, store checks, newspaper tune-in ads, lobby displays, car cards, and the setting up of in-store displays. There was also on-the-air support in the form of giveaway prizes, product mentions, tune-in announcements, and advertiser participation on special programs. In return for merchandising support many stations set up minimum advertising schedules.

A speaker told the Radio and Television Executives Society that ad agencies demanded ever more merchandising from radio and TV stations "and are getting it." *Television Age* observed that the advertisers were pressing TV station representatives "literally to move goods off the shelves. And stations and packagers, almost without exception, have cheerfully agreed to do just that."

Not too many eyebrows were raised when the Watchmakers of Switzerland through its ad agency, for instance, asked for free merchandising in return for a 13-week schedule of twenty 30-second announcements per week. The stations were asked to furnish gratis a weekly contest, gift certificates for Swiss watches, newspaper ads, billboard announcements, streamers, countercards, entry blanks at jewelry and department stores, and grand prizes for the campaign's fadeout week. The stations were advised they would have to stipulate how much of this ballyhoo they would give before the ad agency went to work on compiling the station list.

Newspapers also extended a helping hand with the auto industry a special beneficiary. The National Automobile Show, for instance, received saturation coverage in the nation's newspapers, with scores of newspapers turning out special auto sections during the show run. As the public relations director of the Automobile Manufacturers Association was quoted in *Editor & Publisher*, "Anyone not deaf, dumb and blind will know about the show."

During the 1958 recession the nation's newspapers promoted the slogan "You Auto Buy Now" with the fervor of a revival meeting to stimulate lagging auto sales. The following year a group from the American Association of Newspaper Representatives pilgrimaged to Detroit to promise the auto manufacturers that the nation's press would enthuse its readers with the "irreplaceability of the American automobile" and "help restore the sense of pride . . . the feeling of excitement that once came with buying a new car," according to an account by George W. Parker in *Editor & Publisher*.

Sometimes the big advertisers coordinated the efforts of several of the media, as Du Pont did annually through its agency, Batten, Barton, Durstine & Osborn, on behalf of the Du Pont anti-freezes Zerex and Zerone. In 1959, for instance, letters went out to 340 newspapers asking their "best possible merchandising assistance," accompanied by a questionnaire on which the newspapers were asked to indicate just what merchandising assistance would be forthcoming. The Bureau of Advertising of the American Newspaper Publishers Association put its official sanction on the program by sending a follow-up letter urging the newspapers to return the questionnaire promptly. Cooperating newspapers were supplied with window display material, posters for circulation trucks, suggested copy for promotional letters and cards, and photographs of Miss Anti-Freeze. It was suggested that newspaper classified ad takers close each telephone call with the reminder, "Now is the time to buy anti-freeze and make sure it's Zerex or Zerone."

The newspapers reported they made about 1,000 personal calls on the trade, mailed 36,842 reminder announcements to dealers, and included spots about Zerex and Zerone on their radio-TV shows. Participating radio stations reported mailings to more than 25,000 retail accounts; outdoor plants reported wide distribution of maps pinpointing the location of Zerex and Zerone posters, and sending miniature Zerex billboards to distributors as desk reminders of the campaign. It was calculated by Batten, Barton, Durstine & Osborn that the coordinated merchandising effort had produced more than 65,000 measurable pieces of advertising. The agency sent all the participating media a "Thank you" note.

From time to time the trade press carried stories of advertiser attempts to foray into the editorial matter of the media, as did the railroads on the "featherbedding" issue, a Hollywood executive for bigger and better movie reviews, a food company executive for a working marriage between food editors and advertisers, implying the tricky position of the media in maintaining editorial independence in the face of growing financial reliance on advertisers. Like an iceberg nine-tenths submerged under water, the implied weight of the advertising dollars on editorial opinion, however, was for the most part unseen.

What happened in the magazine industry perhaps most poignantly illustrated the strife for the advertiser's growing largess in the postwar period and the effects on the industry. The collapse of *Collier's* in 1956 followed by *American Home* and *Woman's Home Companion* brought the grim realization that television's ability to attract advertisers would bring the angel of death quickly to more magazines. In 1961 *Coronet* expired at the peak of its circulation because enough advertising was not forthcoming to match its rising production and distribution costs.

In a ferment, the magazine industry tried in a variety of ways to entice advertising dollars. Some magazine publishers quietly bought into broadcasting, book publishing, and other pursuits more profitable than their own, in a hedge against possible magazine losses. Many offered new conveniences to advertisers, such as the split-run, regional editions, ingenious space units, more color. The split-run enabled the advertiser to gauge the pulling power of two ads, each of which appeared in half the magazines printed. The regional edition served a variety of advertiser purposes, permitting the promotion of a regional brand or a seasonal product, the market-by-market expansion of a new brand, the testing of a new product or a new copy appeal, the exertion of pressure in certain markets where sales were weak, the exploitation in markets where sales were strong, the check-mating of local competition with special promotions. There were metropolitan editions, suburban editions, regional editions, sectional editions, as magazines tailored their distribution for the convenience of advertisers to fit major market areas. *Life* offered advertisers a "Regional" plan, *Look* a "Magazone" plan, the *Saturday Evening Post* a "Select-A-Market" plan, *Good Housekeeping* a "Match-A-Market" plan, and other magazines had their own nomenclature. By 1961 the Magazine Advertising Bureau announced that 142 magazines offered split-runs, regional editions, or both. And for those advertisers who had to reach narrow-interest audiences the publishers turned out an increasing number of specialty magazines.

They also gave advertisers an extraordinary number of cleverly contrived new advertising space units: gatefolds, accordians, Dutch doors, French doors, Venetian doors, and even inserted samples of products between pages of the magazine. Some of the makeup ingenuity veered to the bizarre so that one adman commented to a group of magazine publishers that "many a magazine today looks like a convention issue of *Gadget & Gimmick News.*"

They enticed advertisers with a rainbow of riotous colors. By the early sixties the Magazine Advertising Bureau announced that one in every three pages of magazine advertising was a four-color page, and nearly half were in at least two colors. *Media/ Scope* found that in two years color ads in leading consumer magazines had jumped 158 percent and constituted about half the advertising linage.

They shook up editorial formats, experimented with design, story presentation, type faces, photography. In the women's magazines huge color photographs of salads, meat casseroles and hairdos bled off the pages, leaving many admen wondering what the editors would do next. Typifying the editorial revolution that overtook magazines was the *Saturday Evening Post*, whose advertising had declined about 37 percent in ten years during which circulation climbed from 4 to well over 6 million. Attempting to get out of the deadly vise of climbing circulation and dwindling advertising, the *Post* came up with a drastic new look with the hope of revitalizing advertiser interest. The new *Post* said it would "make reading an adventure" again by offering "a forum for the odd-ball who won't play ball. For the loner who won't run with the pack." It called on national celebrities with a beef "to swing wildly. And wickedly." It touched on the heart of the magazine problem when it said it would leave the announcing of headline news "to the smooth-voiced gentlemen of the 15-minute programs, who can do it much faster."

Competition with TV led the magazines into a feverish drive for extra millions in circulation, a drive which tended to homogenize the magazines. The picture magazines began to use more text, the text magazines more picture stories, the women's magazines lured the whole family, and the general magazines went after more women readers. The dangers in leveling and trading down editorial content troubled Ben Hibbs, former editor of the *Saturday Evening Post*, who told the Public Relations Society of America: "Every editor worth his salt knows there are ways to reach further down the scale of human intelligence and emotions and pile in the readers."

The drive to broaden circulation, raise advertising rates, and thereby retain solvency, led the magazines to live dangerously by what the admen called the "numbers game." Each magazine announcement of a higher circulation guarantee to advertisers led competing magazines to intensify their own circulation efforts. The dynamics of competition impelled some magazines to predict their higher circulations in advance for the psychological effect on advertisers, and to issue frantic calls to the circulation department to achieve the circulation at any cost. Failure to meet circulation guarantees meant not only a proportionate dollar rebate to advertisers but, in the quixotic magazine industry, an indelible stamp of failure that might send advertisers scurrying to the competition.

The growth of the "numbers game" troubled many in the advertising community, for although it provided advertisers with ever huger markets, it was also viewed as achieving circulation without readership, as an uneconomical extension of magazine circulation. It was bound to result in the end in higher advertising rates for lower-quality circulation. It also brought on economic problems unnecessarily on the magazines.

In the circulation war the magazines increasingly took to the U.S. mails in the drive for readers, abandoning the single-copy newsstand sales that were considered a prime index of value to advertisers in the prewar era. A study by the Association of National Advertisers showed that whereas in 1946 subscriptions accounted for 48.6 percent of magazine circulation, by 1960 the figure stood at 82.6 percent. Whereas in 1946 movie and romance periodicals obtained only 8.6 percent of their circulation by subscription, by 1960 more than 40 percent came via subscription; in the same period mechanics and science magazine subscriptions went from 25.1 to 67.8 percent. Considering the rate at which magazines came to consumers by mail rather than from newsstands led some observers to predict that in another decade the familiar U.S. newsstand would fade into Americana.

Readers were deluged with the same kind of cut-price offers that the big soap companies customarily used when launching a new product. The nation's mailboxes were stuffed with 50-percent-off offers, and gimmicky Savings Certificates and Special Stamps whose big values were made available to any obliging reader who scribbled his name on a reply card. No money was ever asked for, credit was generously allowed to everyone on a we'll-gladly-bill-you-later basis. Once a reader assented, he was subjected to a series of increasingly favorable last-chance offers as his subscription approached expiration. The patient reader simply had to wait for the rock-bottom terms.

The number of subscriptions sold between 1946 and 1960 at less than basic price rose from 41.5 percent to 59.3 percent. How many were faithful readers, and how many could not resist receiving the magazines at a fraction of their cost, was an unknown quantity. One adman called many of the new readers merely conscripts in the circulation war. And the war was prosecuted with mounting vigor by the magazines seemingly in the hope that competing magazines would be driven to the wall.

In the drive for readers the magazines also increasingly depended on field-selling crews, whose no-holds-barred approach often got them into trouble with the Better Business Bureau. These high-pressure salesmen often used "crips" (short for cripples) and "gimps" (phony cripples) to generate a sympathy appeal. Among the standard equipment of the "gimps" were crutches, braces, slings; sometimes they faked being mute, carrying a pad and pencil to make the sale. Sometimes the crews used a "bird-dog" technique, sending a teenager to make a cold canvass of a town or neighborhood. The teenager was trained to get a foot in the door and turn on an anguish story. Where the approach worked, the home was visited later in the day or evening by the crew manager who closed the sale. In 1958 a Gallagher Report (a management service for advertising and publishing executives) charged that "shifty, shoddy magazine subscription practices" were "worse than ever," that the phonies were peddling subscriptions to the major magazines in huge numbers. The Report charged that "outlaw" crews were in full operation. "They say publishers know all about their activities and freely give permission to list and sell subscriptions." "Outlaw" crews were unaccredited, and were not able to send subscription orders directly to the publishers, but they "cleared" the orders through registered agencies which simply rewrote the orders on their own subscription blanks.

The mad race for numerical leadership was at feverish pitch among the women's service periodicals—*McCall's, Good Housekeeping, Ladies' Home Journal*. In 1961 when *McCall's* announced a planned circulation jump from seven to eight million its two competitors promptly denounced the move. The *Ladies' Home Journal* told the advertising community in an ad: "It has seemed to us that sooner or later some publisher would reduce the 'numbers game' to an absurdity." The *Journal* expressed the opinion that no magazine could pile an extra million circulation on top of a brand-new 7-million peak without resorting to "forcing" methods. The *Journal* refused to be drawn into "a senseless race for numbers of doubtful value" and saw no virtue in "winning a race to the poorhouse."

In the mad thrust-and-parry that went on practically daily on the back page of *The New York Times,* the common warring ground of the magazines, *McCall's* charged the *Ladies' Home Journal* with adding to its circulation by buying the rights to use the defunct *Coronet's* subscription list, to which the *Journal* retorted that *McCall's* was not exactly a blueblood either, having absorbed subscriptions earlier from the defunct *Woman's Home Companion.* The *Journal* hastened to add that there was nothing wrong with this kind of circulation but "in making hoity-toity remarks about defunct magazines, methinks the lady protests her virtue over-much."

Good Housekeeping jousted at *McCall's* by denying that box-car figures were a necessary criterion of quality and pointing out that "modern circulation promotion methods permit a publication to add circulation almost at will, *provided it is prepared to pay the price.*" The price was made clear in a fable addressed to "advertising men who are businessmen." The fable related the sad end of a toad which burst into pieces after puffing itself up out of envy of an ox. The moral: "When a toad puffs to impress, she pays the penalty. When a magazine puffs to impress, it's the advertiser who pays." With that, *Good Housekeeping* took itself out of the fracas by raising its price to 50 cents and declaring itself a premium-priced noncombatant.

When *McCall's* won its promised 8-million circulation it emblazoned the digits in bold black type and announced: "*McCall's* wears its numbers proudly." It claimed more circulation than "any other magazine in the world, except that other phenomenon of publishing, the *Reader's Digest.*"

Advertising Age found it "a little saddening to see the three women's magazines trading verbal blows. . . . As the system operates presently, broadcasting is almost entirely a numbers game: nothing much counts except the rating and the cost of the show. In newspaper and other media it is pretty much the same thing; the only thing that really seems to count in most instances is the cost per thousand." Similar expressions came from other sections of the advertising trade press.

But alternatives were not easy to come by. The public got its free radio and TV entertainment and bought newspapers and magazines at a fraction of their cost, but at a price. To deliver the mass audiences required by advertisers the editorial content of the mass media by and large sought little more than to attract public attention and to hold it long enough for the advertiser to have his say. There were in the U.S. "more television sets and more consumption of newsprint than all the rest of the world together," as Dan Lacy wrote in *Freedom and Communications,* but there was for many an underlying sense of dissatisfaction with the "banality" and "conformity" of the mass media. But this was inevitable in mass media whose survival depended on advertisers and which largely served as clotheslines on which to hang their wares.

The Golden Fleece

The odd thing about all the criticism of advertising is that nobody has suggested doing away with it. At least not since the depressed thirties has anyone seriously suggested it. Instead, in the postwar period, advertising has been accorded wide recognition by critics as a handmaiden of abundance. They point out that advertising is not specially needed in economic depression, when lack of money makes consumers automatically immune to advertising's persuasion. But when consumers have the money and willingness to buy, advertising then serves a vital purpose by manufacturing consumption to match the manufacture of production. Advertising is the one force relied on to dispose of the mountains of goods that a remarkably prolific economy is capable of turning out.

Needless to say, however, the critics do not view advertising as an unmixed blessing.

First, they are doubtful that advertising actually fulfills the

classic economic function claimed by its evangelists—expanding
the market, thereby lowering costs of production, leading to lower
consumer prices. By and large it works that way with useful
consumer goods that do not have wide distribution, but with
scores of advertisers today selling almost identical products in markets approaching saturation, advertising's clamorous persuasion
tends more to get consumers to switch brands. Expanding an
almost saturated market is, to say the least, more difficult and
costly.

Moreover in such basic industries as auto, steel, petroleum,
pharmaceuticals, prices are no longer set by the forces of supply
and demand but by administrative decision. The "administered
price" is the reality in many sectors of the economy. A U.S.
Senate subcommittee, after hearings on the workings of the administered price in the auto industry, concluded that whereas
advertising expanded the market in the early days of the auto
industry this might not be true today, with the auto so endemic
in U.S. life. The subcommittee estimated that advertising accounts
for more than $100 of the retail price of the average car, and ob-
served: "This is not an insignificant cost which the buyer must
assume for the dubious privilege of having the merits of the different makes thrust upon him." The subcommittee also estimated
that the $100 on a $2,000 car would "tend to reduce annual sales
by several hundred thousand cars," raising the startling possibility
thereby that in certain sectors of the economy advertising may
have come full circle and might in reality be acting more as a
brake than a spur to consumption. It would be of major illumination, if not in the national interest, for some nonpartisan group
to study the many-faceted impact of advertising on today's national economy.

Second, the critics decry as needless and wasteful the manner in which the full force of advertising creates artificial wants
and aggrandizes their satisfactions while so many of the real
needs of the people remain unfulfilled. They object, as artifice and

diversion, to the way advertising prods consumers relentlessly to pile up personal material possessions in the face of "large ready-made needs for schools, hospitals, slum clearance, sanitation, parks, playgrounds," as John K. Galbraith suggested in *The Affluent Society*. The critics see as a pressing need the redressing of the growing imbalance between our affluent private lives and our impoverished public lives.

Third, the critics are particularly anguished by the *modus operandi* of advertising which selects, from the enormous range of human impulses of which man is capable, primarily the discreditable ones, because they have been found to be the most profitable. Fear, jealousy, envy, ambition, snobbery, greed, lust, and other appeals antithetical to society, are incessantly played up in popular ads to the disfigurement of human values. Such concepts as love, manliness, femininity, friendship are portrayed as though the very real human values they represent are attainable through the purchase of a new shaving lotion, a new deodorant, a new car. Man is conditioned by the ads to regulate his conduct in large measure by external considerations. As Henry Steele Commager wrote in *The American Mind*, "He read books to make conversation, listened to music to establish his social position, chose his clothes for the impression they would make on business associates, entertained his friends in order to get ahead, held the respect of his children and the affection of his wife by continuous bribery." According to the portrayal of Americans in ads, they are decadent, yet few truly believe this. And statesmen who know the American character "appealed to higher motivations, and not in vain. The problem remained a fascinating one, for if it was clear that advertisers libeled the American character, it was equally clear that Americans tolerated and even rewarded those who libeled them." This condition results from advertising's steady devaluation of the quality of man's experience and the stereotyping of his capacity for social response.

These, in brief, are the three main areas of criticism of advertising as it operates today, without diminishing any recognition of it as the historic vehicle of abundance. Yet, oddly, so thin-skinned is the advertising community that any criticism is quickly interpreted as a full-fledged attack on the institution of advertising itself. This is remote from the truth. The critics are concerned because advertising wields such enormous influence in the shaping of popular standards and yet has no social goals. Unlike the school and the church, with which advertising has been compared in magnitude of social power, advertising has no "social responsibilities for what it does with its influence," as David M. Potter wrote in *People of Plenty*. Whereas the school and the church are self-conscious about their roles as guardians of the social values, seeking to improve man by teaching qualities of social usefulness, advertising lacks such social values "unless conformity to material values may be so characterized." Whereas the school and the church exert their influence in the direction of beliefs and attitudes held to be of social value, advertising turns its energies to the stimulation and exploitation of emulative anxieties and material accumulations, imposing them as standards of social value.

The advertising community is not unmindful of lack of social purpose to balance social power, and even those of its practitioners unfreighted by a social conscience recognize the patent danger in too freebooting an operation which would only serve to add to the ranks of influential critics and raise the level of popular criticism. The advertising trade press is distinguished by recurring articles and editorial pleas for a greater show of public responsibility. At trade meetings the same plea is heard. As Donald S. Frost, newly elected chairman of the Association of National Advertisers, told that group, the industry had to set its house in order, "If we don't, someone else is going to do it for us."

Most of the industry's efforts are bent toward the elimination of the obvious friction areas with the public. Advertisers are asked to exercise self-control in their ads. Patently only one automobile can provide more gasoline mileage than the rest, only one cigarette can filter best, only one soap can produce the whitest wash. Advertisers are asked to steer clear of the raw depiction of pain, suffering, sex, fear, and other human emotions; to refrain from pounding commercials, screaming jingles, and inopportune blackouts of the TV screen at dramatic moments. To reinforce these strictures the industry abounds in instruments of self-regulation so that the proliferating organizations of advertisers, ad agencies, and media all bristle with high-sounding codes of conduct. The broadcast codes, for instance, effectively outlaw ads for fortune-telling, occultism, spiritualism, astrology, phrenology, mind reading, tip sheets, character reading, few of which, of course, are thriving businesses today. They keep hard liquor ads off the air, out of deference to the strongly organized "dry" sentiment in the country, permit beer and wine ads only when modestly presented (nobody is ever shown drinking beer or wine on the TV screen). They require products of a "personal" nature —laxatives, deodorants, toilet tissue, corn removers, headache and cold remedies, and intimate garments—to be treated with special concern for the sensibilities of the public.

But the ineffectual nature of the codes is apparent to any TV viewer who is treated seven nights a week to elementary courses in physiology, replete with hammered brains, animated intestines, mist-filled lungs, burbling stomach juices, choked sinus cavities and nasal passages. The codes are no more than framed wall decorations in the executive offices of advertisers, agencies, and networks when it comes to big business. As *Advertising Age* observed: "Codes of practice and ethics are all too often just pleasant mouthings of pious committees, without real effect in their industries." There is even disagreement in the advertising community as to who bears the final responsibility for good conduct, the advertiser, the agency, or the media. Some say the advertiser who O.K.'s and pays for the ads, some say the agencies whose persuasive skills are often so overzealously employed on his behalf, and some say the media which should act as the final backstop of good conduct for the industry. Each of the participants admits to a share in the responsibility but none wants to take on the whole job. In this piecemeal approach to responsibility each tends to say, "Let George do it," but by that no one means any of the government regulatory agencies. The government, as one adman put it, represents an "outside interfering hand."

It would be visionary, of course, to expect to sell sweetness and light to the advertising community unless it could be established at the same time that sweetness and light sell goods. The advertising community says its job is to sell the world, not to save it; the saving it leaves to education and religion. And the selling job is so important to the continuation of the nation's prosperity that it invests the advertising community with a special license to indulge in small and medium-sized built-in selling deceptions. Regrettable as it is to have to proceed by these somewhat shabby methods, it is considered a small price indeed for the citizenry to pay for their material well-being.

It is doubtful, however, that certain changes in the law for the greater protection of the citizenry will place their well-being in jeopardy. The James M. Landis report to the President in 1960, for instance, recommended more regulatory power for the Federal Trade Commission and the Food and Drug Administration so that they could operate more effectively and more commensurately with today's marketing realities. The report noted that "inordinate delay characterizes the disposition of adjudicatory proceedings before substantially all of our regulatory agencies." So far as the FTC is concerned, since the burden of proof rests on it to disprove advertising claims, which it often lacks the manpower, the laboratory facilities, and the funds to do, the inevitable result is to bog the FTC down in lengthy hearings. To cite an extreme example, it took 16 years and nearly 12,000 pages of testimony before the FTC could pin a cease and desist order on Carter's Little Pills which required the toning down of product claims. Customarily cases drag on for years before the successive administrative remedies open to advertisers are exhausted. Even to disprove the claim that "four out of five doctors" recommend a product imposes on the FTC the burden to amass considerable evidence. This burden "significantly emasculates the Commission's power to deal with the spate of deceptive advertising that floods our newspapers, our periodicals and our air waves." The report recommends a sanction more effective than those presently possessed by FTC: "The interlocutory cease and desist order appealable to a court would be a first step."

It is true, of course, that under the Wheeler-Lea Act the FTC is empowered to obtain temporary court injunctions when it can establish that the advertising of foods, drugs, cosmetics, or devices threatens to inflict irreparable injury on the public. But in actual practice the FTC has found that the courts demand such extensive proof before they will issue temporary injunctions that the court hearings on the injunctions are no less burdensome than full FTC trials of the cases.

The upshot is that, since an ad runs until conclusively proved false, all too many advertisers promote deceptive campaigns and rely on administrative remedies to block FTC action until the campaigns have run their course. Frequently, before the FTC gets to the point where it issues a cease and desist order, the campaign is over and the advertiser is off on a new one. The chase then begins anew. Given the power to issue an interlocutory cease and desist order on the basis of a prima facie showing, however, the FTC could freeze the campaign indefinitely while the cumbersome process of taking evidence and reaching a decision unfolds. The public would gain the full measure of benefit.

The Food and Drug Administration also needs additional regulatory power. This was expressed dramatically by Abraham Ribicoff, former Secretary of Health, Education and Welfare, who told a Congressional hearing that "the time has come in the U.S. to give American men, women and children the same protection we have been giving hogs, sheep and cattle since 1913." He argued that "until we are allowed to require that a drug be proven effective before it is marketed, we must say to the American people: a hog is protected against worthless drugs, but you are not." He referred to the Virus-Serum-Toxin Act of 1913 which forbids worthless biologicals for the treatment of domestic animals but which, until 1962, had no counterpart with respect to drugs for human consumption. According to the law prior to 1962 the FDA was required to approve a new drug if it was safe even if it was totally or partially ineffective for the claims made for it. Only when placed on the market could FDA attack it, and then only by contending that it was improperly labeled. It was a matter of common practice, however, for advertisers to skirt FDA jurisdiction by using an innocuous label on the drug and making strong advertising claims for it in the mass media. As President John F. Kennedy observed in his special message to Congress on the need for more consumer protection: "There is no way of measuring the needless suffering, the money innocently squandered, and the protraction of illness resulting from the use of such ineffective drugs."

As a result of the unfortunate use of thalidomide, which caused countless deformities in babies, however, the law was amended in 1962 by an aroused Congress to require new drugs to be proved effective and safe before FDA approved their distribution. Nonetheless, since the overwhelming majority of drugs on the market are not new drugs, and require no FDA approval, the situation is only slightly improved. The needless suffering, the money innocently squandered, and the protraction of illness goes on apace.

Another law that requires retailoring to modern marketing realities is the packaging law. Hearings before a special Congressional subcommittee have demonstrated what many consumers already know, that food labels and packages are often far less trustworthy than they appear. Here again, in matters of safety, the FDA has swift legal recourse. But its authority over "economic cheats" is another matter. The quarter-century-old labeling law, which has never given more than a soupçon of protection to consumers, needs revision to give FDA specific power to crack down on cheats who "slack fill" containers, and who so obscure the facts about size, weight, and contents of packages as to make informed consumer selection difficult if not impossible.

The Landis report reserved its strongest language for the Federal Communications Commission, charging that it has "drifted, vacillated and stalled in almost every major area." The available evidence also indicates that the FCC, "more than any other agency, has been susceptible to ex parte presentations, and that it has been subservient, far too subservient, to the subcommittees on communications of the Congress and their members. A strong suspicion also exists that far too great an influence is exercised over the Commission by the networks."

Central to the problem is the manner in which the FCC grants radio and TV station licenses based on proposed programming in the public interest, which bears little or no resemblance to the actual programming after the station is licensed. "The Commission knows this but ignores these differentiations at the time when renewal of licenses of the station is before them. Nevertheless, it continues with its Alice-in-Wonderland procedures."

Hence in return for a promise to broadcast in the public interest, the licensee has handed over to him at no charge a public air channel for his private profit. Failure to live up to his promise means nothing, since the FCC has never revoked the license of a single station for this reason. At license renewal time, every three years, the FCC rubber-stamps renewals, only very occasionally applying what has become known in the broadcast trade as the "raised eyebrow" technique to improve programming. Although the broadcaster, as a matter of law, owns nothing but a revocable license, as a matter of practice, as James L. Fly, a former FCC commissioner, remarked at a Fund for the Republic discussion, he "has just as much permanence as a fee simple deed to the Empire State Building."

In 1961 the National Association of Broadcasters was reminded by newly elected FCC chairman Newton N. Minow that it was not enough to cater to the public's whims: "You must also serve the nation's needs. . . . Your obligations are not satisfied if you look only to popularity as a test of what to broadcast." The public interest was not merely what interested the public. He invited each broadcaster to "sit down in front of your television set when your station goes on the air and stay there without a book, magazine, newspaper, profit and loss sheet or rating book to distract you—and keep your eyes glued to that set until the station signs off. I can assure you that you will observe a vast wasteland."

It consisted of "a procession of game shows, violence, audience participation shows, formula comedies about totally unbelievable families, blood and thunder, mayhem, violence, sadism, murder, western badmen, western good men, private eyes, gangsters, more violence, and cartoons. And, endlessly, commercials—many screaming, cajoling and offending. And most of all, boredom. True, you will see a few things you will enjoy. But they will be very, very few. And if you think I exaggerate, try it." He said, in closing: "Gentlemen, your trust accounting with your beneficiaries is overdue."

The speech shocked the broadcasters. "No one has talked to them like that," observed *Advertising Age*, "since the dear dead days when the then FCC chairman, James Lawrence Fly, stirred the breezes in the ballroom of the Jefferson Hotel in St. Louis with his charge that the National Association of Broadcasters, whose convention he was at the moment addressing, was like mackerel in the moonlight—'it both shines and stinks.' "

The FCC implemented its warning to the broadcasters by granting short-term renewals in 1961 to 20 radio stations which allegedly failed to match performance with promise. As the "wasteland" speech made press headlines around the nation many stations discovered that considerable numbers of their listeners and viewers had become pen pals of the FCC.

The FCC might also take into account at the time of license renewal deliberations the deceptive advertising carried by stations in disregard of official notification of FTC findings in this regard. Is this not also in the public interest?

Congress might amend the broadcast law so that the networks are regulated. As the law now stands, the networks are not a fact of life and FCC exercises control over them only through control over the stations.

Lastly the task of the stations to meet their public service responsibility will be made easier if the control that advertisers have over program content is ended. There is no compelling reason, other than the commercial, for advertisers to control both commercials and programming. The principle that applies in the print media, that the advertiser controls the advertisement and the newspaper or magazine controls the editorial matter needs extension to the broadcast media. In an editorial urging advertisers to "get out of show business," *Advertising Age* said, "As long as the end-aim of all programming is to achieve a high rating, and as long as advertisers can associate their commercial messages with high-rated programs and refuse to associate them with lower-rated programs, stations and networks can attain truly balanced programming in the public interest only at great economic risk."

Admittedly these suggestions are only starters, and the road back to more rational national values is a long one, but to the extent that the grip of the advertisers is relaxed on the nation's media and citizens the nation can begin to look elsewhere for its lost national purpose. "With the supermarket as our temple and the singing commercial as our litany," as Adlai Stevenson wrote in his chapter on *The National Purpose*, "are we likely to fire the world with an irresistible vision of American's exalted purposes and inspiring way of life?" It may not be easy to restore a national purpose, but it is always helpful to know where not to look.

Index

293